Battleg...

# Krithia

## *Battleground series:*

*Previous page:* **The faces of a coalition campaign.**

**Battleground**

# Krithia

## Gallipoli

Stephen Chambers

*Series Editor*
Nigel Cave

Pen & Sword
**MILITARY**

First published in Great Britain in 2021 by
Pen & Sword Military
An imprint of
Pen & Sword Books Ltd
Yorkshire – Philadelphia

ISBN 978 1 47387 547 0

A CIP catalogue record for this book is
available from the British Library.

Typeset by Mac Style
Printed and bound in the UK by CPI Group (UK) Ltd,
Croydon, CR0 4YY.

Pen & Sword Books Limited incorporates the imprints of Atlas,
Archaeology, Aviation, Discovery, Family History, Fiction, History,
Maritime, Military, Military Classics, Politics, Select, Transport,
True Crime, Air World, Frontline Publishing, Leo Cooper,
Remember When, Seaforth Publishing, The Praetorian Press,
Wharncliffe Local History, Wharncliffe Transport, Wharncliffe
True Crime and White Owl.

For a complete list of Pen & Sword titles please contact

PEN & SWORD BOOKS LIMITED
47 Church Street, Barnsley, South Yorkshire, S70 2AS, England
E-mail: enquiries@pen-and-sword.co.uk
Website: www.pen-and-sword.co.uk

Or

PEN AND SWORD BOOKS
1950 Lawrence Rd, Havertown, PA 19083, USA
E-mail: Uspen-and-sword@casematepublishers.com
Website: www.penandswordbooks.com

# Contents

# Acknowledgements

Without the help of many individuals and organisations this walking guide would not have been possible. The Gallipoli campaign can only be truly understood by treading the ground that the men, from both sides of the trenches, fought, bled and died. Thanks, therefore, go to: Clive Harris, Rory Stephens, Peter Hart, Thomas Iredale, Mike Crane, Michael D Robson and Peter Biles, who have walked Gallipoli with me, inspiring me in different ways better to understand this campaign; in Turkey, my thanks to İsmail Kaşdemir Bey, the Chairman of Çanakkale Savaşlari Gelibolu Tarihi Alan Başkanliği (ÇATAB) [The Gallipoli Historic Site Directorate] and his dedicated team. Also to those who have a similar passion as I do for the study of Gallipoli: Haluk Oral, Kenan Çelik, Şahin Aldoğan, Mustafa Onur Yurdal and Bill Sellars, and some of the best battlefield guides on the Peninsula – Adem Biçer, Bulent Yılmaz Korkmaz and Erdem Keseli to name but a few; of course, and by no means least, to Nigel Cave, Series Editor, whose guidance along the way has kept me on the straight and narrow.

From individuals to organisations, museums, libraries, websites and the like, the list of those who have helped seems almost endless. I am very grateful to: the staff at The National Archives, the Imperial War Museum, the Australian War Memorial and a great list of friends from The Gallipoli Association and Great War Forum, both rich hives of valuable campaign information. I cannot fail to mention the unrelenting work of the Commonwealth War Graves Commission, caring for the British and Dominion war dead from Gallipoli, as well as their French and Turkish counterparts.

Sadly, the veterans have long since faded away; but they are not forgotten. Their stories continue to be told and are used here to illustrate the human aspects of war. Contemporary material in the form of war diaries, divisional and regimental histories have been referenced. The published diary of General Sir Ian Hamilton and Aspinall-Oglander's Official History are both a 'must' read, although both stand in the shadow of the Australian official historian, Charles Bean, whose detailed account of Anzac is second to none, even if some of his judgements and criticisms have been tempered by the years. I have made use, as appropriate, of some personal accounts in the form of letters and diaries as well as a large assortment of maps and photographs. I acknowledge the authors of all of these sources, for without this material there would be no story to tell. With historical documents it is always difficult to trace all the copyright holders, so for any who have not been contacted, please accept my apologies, and feel free to contact me if you feel it necessary. To all these people and others I have forgotten to mention, please accept both my sincere apologies and my thanks.

No research and writing would have been made possible without the support and love of my family, so by no means last thanks are certainly due to Joanne, Lewis and Jessica for their patience and understanding.

Stephen Chambers
*England and Gallipoli, 2021*

# The Series Editor's Introduction

The genesis of the series of *Battleground Europe* books on the 1915 Gallipoli campaign goes back to 2000, when I went out on a minibus tour to the Peninsula courtesy of my father, who asked me if I would like to accompany him on it; just short of eighty years old at the time and with a heart condition, it would not (fortunately for me!) really have been practicable for him to go without me. This excellent fly-minibus trip was organised by Len Sellers (the Royal Naval Division expert) and Kieran Hegarty and utterly memorable it was too. Hitherto I had a vague interest in Gallipoli but my interest was muted as I never foresaw the possibility that I would ever get out there and get a 'feel' for the terrain. Amongst the select few on the trip was Stephen Chambers.

As things worked out, and with me now well and truly hooked, we were both very keen to get back out there as soon as we reasonably could and so right at the beginning of September 2001 we flew to Izmir, collected a decent sized (and, most importantly, air conditioned!) car and made the drive up to the base where we had stayed in 2000, Pansiyon Helles Panorama, run by Erol Bacyan (whose family have a long relationship with the CWGC), situated on high ground on the edge of Seddülbahir. From the beautifully maintained gardens we had views of the Helles Memorial and, in the opposite direction, over the Straits and across to the Asiatic shore; whilst through the hedge boundary was the isolated grave of Doughty-Wylie VC. As I remember it, we were the only people staying and it proved to be an ideal place from which to launch our excursions and to which to retreat at the end of the day or when the heat became too much; the fact that we had a fortnight, more or less, meant that we were not forced to cram visits in or have to spend overlong days on the ground.

It was during this second tour that we explored the possibility of a series of *Battleground Europe* books on the events of 1915. Strangely enough, my notes tell me that we came up with six possible headings for the study of the battlefield that would fit with the series format. We ended up with the six titles, though the contents of each diverged slightly from the original scheme. At the time I had already arranged for Nigel Steel to write a revised edition of his *The Battlefields of Gallipoli*

(Leo Cooper, 1990) in the series style and which came out in 2003; and for Huw and Jill Rodge to write *Gallipoli: Helles Landing* (also 2003). When Nigel wrote his book, back in 1990, parts of the Peninsula still had considerable military zone restrictions that affected access to key areas that could be visited, notably some of the beaches: how times change.

And so to *Krithia*, the subject of what has turned out to be Steve's last book in his Gallipoli series. Although things may well have changed somewhat from the sleepy Peninsula of twenty years ago that I recall, a rural idyll seemingly locked in a time warp and largely untroubled by the outside world (though we were treated to a display of fire power and the sight of the Izmir squadron of the Turkish navy on manoeuvres on one memorable day when we were exploring Suvla), it cannot have been by so much that today a visitor will still have to exercise tremendous powers of imagination to transform the scene to what it must have been like through the spring, summer, autumn and early winter months of 1915.

For most visitors it is likely that time spent in this area will be focussed on the V Beach landings, the very start of the Gallipoli 'adventure'. It will, doubtless, extend to the imposing Helles Memorial, standing prominent as a lighthouse on the European shore of the western end of the Dardanelles. It is most likely that much more time will be spent at Anzac, whilst Suvla is probably the least visited of the three main beach heads. This is a shame, because not only did fierce fighting in the 'Helles Zone' extend over the next four months (and from then on in a more desultory fashion until it was the scene of the final stage of the extraordinarily successful evacuation) but it was also where the significantly sized French contingent fought. The French are the most 'forgotten' of all those who fought here in 1915 and this book does much to ensure that their contribution is properly acknowledged.

*Krithia* will lead the visitor to the later, post landing, battles at Helles; the actions at Gully Ravine are described (but are covered in more detail in *Gully Ravine* in this series) but perhaps most notable is the coverage of the battles that history regards as focussed on Krithia (First to Third Krithia were fought in the period from late April to early June) and the elusive heights of Achi Baba, an objective on the first day of the landings. There were several battles, usually ill-organised, poorly conceived, suffering from poor communications and shortages of guns and shells, and which continued through to the end of August. Things were not that much better on the Turkish side, assisted by a tiny, but very effective – far beyond their numerical value, German team of commanders and advisors. Whilst today most Australians and New Zealanders tend to confine their pilgrimage to Anzac, they miss the brave but hopelessly doomed contribution made by Australian and New Zealand battalions at Helles, most notably in the area of the Vineyard in August, a diversion (or, perhaps optimistically, part of a series of major attacks from Helles to Suvla) for the Suvla Landings to the north.

For all students of military campaigns and their associated battles and actions, time spent on the ground adds a crucial dimension to an appreciation of military actions. The landscape of the Gallipoli Peninsula is no exception to this rule. Whilst the conduct of the landing and subsequent events has rightly been the subject of scathing criticism, it should perhaps be underlined that 1915 – on all fronts – was a period when manpower was expended with what appears to the observer as great profligacy, making up for the then significant shortages in *materiel* and in a period of the war when the very considerable technological innovations that characterised the last year of the conflict were beyond most people's dreams.

Gallipoli 1915 was a relatively small campaign, what has on occasion been dismissed as a 'side show'. It was an imaginative endeavour that in principle had strategic potential, though how great in fact that was provoked profound disagreement, not least at the highest political and military levels; the fierce debate has shown little sign of diminishing ever since. It is also a campaign that for many has about it an enduring sense of unforced tragedy, in a war that was full of tragedy and disaster. Whatever the objective historical analysis might be, it was fought over one of the most fascinating, beautiful and evocative landscapes; and it is replete with tales of individual and unit heroism on both sides and on a scale that matches the Trojan Wars, the scene of which lies nearby. This book, and the other five that Steve has written, make a pilgrimage here so much more worthwhile, a pilgrimage that fully deserves a week and more to fully benefit from it: armed with the information and the great array of tours in this and his other books, there is not much more that a visitor could ask to have.

Nigel Cave
*Ratcliffe College, June 2021*

# List of Maps

# Introduction

## Gallipoli today

Gallipoli is an exquisitely beautiful and tranquil place, with its turquoise waters, stretches of sandy beaches, wild flower covered meadows and pine forested hills, such a contrast to what it looked like over a hundred years ago. Those visiting this battlefield often comment on its eerie atmosphere of sorrow and solitude, something that has certainly been experienced by me. In 1956 Alan Moorehead wrote in his book *Gallipoli* that:

> 'The cemeteries at Gallipoli are unlike those of any other battlefield in Europe … In winter moss and grass cover the ground, and in summer a thick carpet of pine needles deadens the footfall. There is no sound except for the wind in the trees and the calls of the migrating birds who have found these places the safest sanctuary on the peninsula … Often for months at a time nothing of any consequence happens, lizards scuttle about the tombstones in the sunshine and time goes by in an endless dream.'

The biggest change at Gallipoli since the time Moorehead wrote this has been the massive increase in visitors. Its history and the landscape's outstanding beauty make it a popular location for battlefield visitors from all over the world, not only Australians, New Zealanders, French and British, but also for the Turks. In Turkey, the Gallipoli (Çanakkale) battlefield is one of the most visited places in the country because of its association with Atatürk, the conception of modern day Turkey and because it was the greatest Ottoman victory of the Great War.

Annually over two million Turks make their pilgrimage to the ground where it is considered that modern Turkey was born. There are two major dates when the Peninsula becomes busy: 18 March and 25 April. In March the Turks visit in large numbers, as this date in 1915 was when their forces were victorious over the Anglo-French fleet in their attempt to force the Dardanelles. Anzac Day is on 25 April, a significant national holiday in Australia and New Zealand, whose citizens descend on the area in large numbers (though often neglect the Helles battlefield). However, away from these periods, at the weekends or if you venture away from the main tourist areas, you will see very few visitors and little to disturb the serene and beautiful landscape of this land.

Outside of the major commemorative dates, the best times to visit Gallipoli are in late spring or early autumn. In late spring (May) the weather is moderate and the days are long. You can experience the unique natural spring environment on the peninsula, with magnificent wild flowers, mild and fresh temperatures, local life and smaller crowds, and competitively priced hotels and services. In early autumn (September), after the stifling hot summer, the weather becomes milder again, but the days are shorter. The battlefield in autumn is no longer lush with greenery but would have turned a scorched sandy-brown colour

Fall In, a popular recruiting poster at the time.

after the long hot summer, reminiscent of the 1915 campaign photographs. A further bonus is that most of the crops will have been harvested and the lie of the land can be better seen. Whilst the autumn is a good season to travel to Turkey because of the mild and comfortable temperatures, it is, however, the high season for Turkey's popular destinations, so book hotels early.

**Why Gallipoli?**

Within a few months of the opening of hostilities on the Western Front in August 1914 there was deadlock and no obvious way to break it. Casualties had been enormous – just over two million men by January 1915, unprecedented numbers; there were no longer any illusions about a speedy end to hostilities.

It was clear that this conflict was different; armies had not been able to alter their tactics in response to the industrial scale of this war which, at this stage, made the defensive significantly stronger than the offensive. Destruction was on a massive scale, both in human cost and with the increasing devastation of the war zone area. With political and popular pressure growing, the British looked for an alternative strategy for 1915, making use of naval superiority. Opening a new front was discussed, but where? An amphibious landing on German's Baltic coast, an offensive through the Balkans or maybe an attack against Germany's ally, Turkey? Attention turned to Turkey at the beginning of 1915; Russia was threatened by the Ottoman Army on the Caucasus Front and she appealed to her allies for support. The British, with French support, decided that this could best be achieved by mounting a naval expedition to the Dardanelles.

The objective of this strategic vision was, by capturing Constantinople (now Istanbul), to force German's ally Turkey and its vast empire (which included the territories of modern Turkey, Syria, Jordan, Israel/Palestine, Lebanon, Iraq, Iran, Kuwait, Yemen and the western coastline of Arabia) out of the war. This knockout blow would open a warm water supply route to Russia from the Aegean, through the Dardanelles and into the Black Sea. Russian troops on the Caucasus Front could be released to reinforce her forces facing Germany and Austria-Hungary. It was also hoped that by opening a new front it could influence the neutral Balkan states and Greece to enter the war on the Entente side. A combined effort would then assist the Entente powers in removing the Turks and its Ottoman Empire, for many decades seen as the 'sick man of Europe', as a threat. They were seen as an easy target, due to over a century of decline and weakened by political instability, military defeat and civil strife.

The campaign would be a risk with a far from certain outcome. If successful it was hoped to shorten the war; but if it failed, the consequences were beyond calculation. Would the war be lengthened by not concentrating efforts on the Western Front against the main enemy, Germany? Would the neutral states join the Central Powers? Would the Suez Canal and Mesopotamian oilfields fall to the Turks? Would a defeat weaken Britain's influence in the east, in particular India, threatening the jewel of the British Empire? Although a valid gamble in the minds of the War Council, the campaign's poor planning and execution shattered any glimmer of hope through a catalogue of mismanaged sea and land battles.

The Gallipoli campaign can be described in four stages: the initial efforts of the Anglo-French navy to force the Dardanelles; the landing of the Mediterranean Expeditionary Force (MEF) in April 1915; the land offensives between May and August; and the final evacuation of the MEF in January 1916.

The objective of *Gallipoli: Krithia* is to focus on the bloody battles at Helles, from the landings to the final evacuation. Helles was a killing ground greater than Anzac or Suvla and until August 1915 it was witness

**Sir Winston Churchill, First Lord of the Admiralty.**

**Field Marshal Horatio Herbert Kitchener, Secretary of State for War.**

to the Allies' major offensives in an effort to achieve victory. Writing this volume completes a journey I took almost twenty years ago when Nigel Cave encouraged me to write *Gully Ravine*. This book is the last volume in the series to cover *Battleground Gallipoli* and my hope is the series as a whole will not only contribute to a better understanding of the Gallipoli campaign but will also attract more visitors to this picturesque and tranquil battlefield.

*Beauty is mysterious as well as terrible. God and devil are fighting there, and the battlefield is the heart of man.*

Fyodor Dostoevsky

The Gallipoli Peninsula 1: 250,000 Scale.

# Chapter 1

# The Landings

The beaches at Helles were little more than narrow strips of sand that lay under the shadow of high coastal cliffs before open farmland gently sloped up to the village of Krithia and the height of Achi Baba. The responsibility for defending Helles fell to 26 Regiment (Ottoman 9th Division), commanded by Major Kadri, who had deployed a battalion in the Sedd-el-Bahr area, another at Kum Tepe to the north and a third in the middle, near Krithia. He was supported by an engineer company, which was working on beach defences. These defences comprised barbed wire, trenches, pom-pom guns and field artillery pieces. Trip wire was laid under the surf line, mines were buried on the beaches and any natural obstacle that could afford cover to the attack

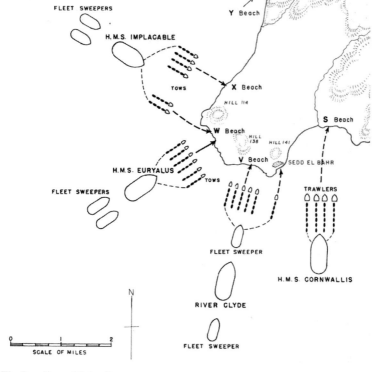

**The Landing – 25 April.**

was in the process of being removed. In the Sedd-el-Bahr area Major Mahmut Sabri's 3/26 Regiment, a single battalion of about 1,000 men, defended the whole tip of Cape Helles, including S, V, W and X beaches. Against this defence Hamilton pitched the bulk of the 29th Division, under the command of Major General Sir Aylmer Hunter-Weston, with the objective of taking the tip of the Peninsula and capturing the high ground of Achi Baba, standing 182 metres above sea level.

The amphibious assault that was launched on 25 April 1915 was worked in conjunction with the Royal Navy, which would provide the craft to land the army and provide fire support from their 12 and 15-inch guns. Unlike the Anzac landing, the Helles force was to come ashore during daylight, preceded by a dawn bombardment. Although this would alert the defenders to the pending landing, it was thought that the weight and accuracy of the naval bombardment would afford the best chance of success against the fortified positions.

The covering force's (86 Brigade) objective was to secure the main beachhead, between Sedd-el-Bahr and X Beach, providing a screen for the main force to disembark. On the flanking beaches of S, X and Y, 87 Brigade would land to protect the flanks before all forces would join up for the five-mile general advance to Achi Baba, the first day's main objective. 88 Brigade would provide the divisional reserve. Hamilton said of the landings at Helles that: *no finer feat of arms has ever been achieved by the British soldier, or any other soldier, than the storming of these trenches from open boats on the morning of April 25.*

**HMS *Cornwallis* bombarding the shore.**

# Y Beach

Y Beach is about four kilometres north of X Beach, just over a kilometre from Krithia and is nearest to the main objective, Achi Baba. The plan was to land a 2,000-man force behind the Turkish defenders and to hold this left flank position until it was joined by the main force from Cape Helles. Together, they would then assault Krithia and capture Achi Baba. In addition to the physical challenge of the sixty metres' steep, scrub-covered cliffs, the beach was little more than a narrow strip of sand, hardly recognisable from sea or shore.

This landing, at 5.30 a.m., was a *coup de main*, a total surprise to the Turks, who did not believe a landing would be attempted here. Because of this it was not defended. Two battalions: Plymouth Battalion, Royal Marine Light Infantry (RMLI) and 1st Battalion, King's Own Scottish Borderers (1/KOSB), supported by a company from the 2nd Battalion, South Wales Borderers (2/SWB), landed here unhindered. The landing was not the problem, the issue was that the force's objective lacked clarity, which was complicated by misunderstandings and disagreements between the two commanding officers.

The Y Beach operation was controlled by the 29th Division's headquarters on board HMS *Euryalus*, five kilometres south, offshore at W Beach. On the ground, there were two commanding officers, Lieutenant Colonel Archibald Koe (1/KOSB) and Lieutenant Colonel Godfrey Matthews (RMLI). Matthews attended the pre-landing conference and, as he was senior to Koe, GHQ put him in overall command. Koe was ill during this briefing so did not attend, but he believed himself to be in overall command. This did not bode well for the forthcoming operation, not made any better by the vague orders, such as, to take an example, to 'make contact' with X Beach. It was not clear if this was meant to be in physical contact or just visually. In the event neither was achieved. No contingency plans were made if the advance from the south did not materialise, which it did not, resulting in the force being left forgotten.

During the spring morning sunshine of 25 April all went well with the landing, the scouts walked to the outskirts of Krithia unmolested, and the few Turks found in the area of Gully Ravine were reported as showing 'no aggressive spirit'. The village housed the 26 Regiment's staff and nearby were the 2/26 Regiment, who were regimental reserve. The Turks remained unaware of the landing. Some distance south of Krithia the soldiers had clear views of Morto Bay and the battleships firing off Cape Helles, but apart from this the area was deserted.

'The scouts went on ahead and actually reached the outskirts of Krithia, a small village that we saw but never reached again

3

during the whole campaign. Our scouts came in contact with one or two Turkish scouts during their advance, two were shot dead and one brought in as a prisoner. He looked very depressed. His equipment consisted of a civilian overcoat, and from his size he wore plenty of underclothing, a soldier's head dress, and a white haversack full of loose ammunition and a rifle. His boots were in a very bad state, and rags took the place of puttees.'

Sergeant William Meatyard, Plymouth Battalion, RMLI.

For almost six hours the men at Y Beach were left unmolested. The commanders realised that opportunity was being thrown away and twice asked HQ for orders but received no reply. By 3.00 p.m. Matthews, realising that there was no movement from the south at Cape Helles, withdrew his patrols and dug a semi-circular defensive perimeter to cover Y Beach. It was barely an hour later that the Turks discovered this force and, realising its threat to their lines of communication, immediately sent their reserve 1/25 Regiment to attack. Fierce close-quarter fighting went on in the late afternoon and into the night, which made things increasingly difficult for the British. The war diary of the 1/KOSB described the situation:

'...several times the enemy approached within ten yards of our position... so close did the enemy reach to our lines that in one place a German officer walked up to our trench and said, "You English surrender, we are ten to one". He was thereupon hit on the head with a spade.'

**Y Beach and Gurkha Bluff.**

Lieutenant Colonel Koe was mortally wounded during the fighting, which at least settled the issue of who was in overall command; but with no reinforcements or any communication with HQ, and under almost constant enemy attack, ammunition was running low and casualties were mounting. As hostile fire increased, and the situation became more precarious, messages were sent back to HQ requesting reinforcements, all of which were ignored. By the morning there was much confusion and although no order was given by Matthews to re-embark, wounded were evacuated from the beach in large numbers, which gave the already beleaguered men holding the perimeter the illusion that a general evacuation was in progress. Without orders, men left their positions and returned to the waiting boats. By the time Matthews realised what had happened it was too late to stop the withdrawal. By 11.30 a.m. on the 26th the first evacuation of the campaign had been successful.

Hamilton, who was offshore at the time, witnessed this, believing that Major General Hunter-Weston must have ordered the withdrawal and so did not interfere. Ignored by Hunter-Weston, who never really approved of this landing in the first place, the 29th Division's HQ was focussed on the main events on W and V beaches, leaving Y to its own fate. The Turks, who had all but given up the fight at Y Beach, were amazed to see the evacuation, and wasted no time in securing this area and then moving the rest of the regiment south to engage the hard-pressed British trying to establish a beachhead. All the great opportunities that could have been exploited at Y Beach had been forfeited. The cost was 700 casualties, a third of Y force. It would take a hard month's fighting to reach this position once again.

## S Beach

Just over five kilometres away, on the other side of the peninsula, the remaining three companies of 2/SWB, under the command of Lieutenant Colonel Hugh Casson, were landed on S Beach with a detachment of engineers, medics and a few marines from HMS *Cornwallis*. The plan was to capture a Turkish observation post that was defended by a platoon from 3/26 Regiment. The post was sited in a redundant battery known as De Tott's (which dated from the Russo-Turkish War [1768–74], named after Baron Francois de Tott, a French artillery expert then advising the Ottoman Army) and was positioned on a seventy-two metres long promontory known as Eski Hissarlik.

Although the landing was supposed to take place simultaneously with those on V, W, X and Y, it suffered delays due to the landing trawlers struggling against the strong Dardanelles currents. Once the rowing boats were let loose from their tows, they did not ground ashore until 7.00 a.m., over ninety minutes late.

'I took up my position in the lower foretop of the *Vengeance*. Our orders were to shell De Tott's Ridge and, if possible, clear out hostile forces that might be in ambush. At 5 a.m., as if the very heavens had been rent asunder, every ship opened fire simultaneously on its allotted area. We simply hammered away for all we were worth. Trawlers and boats, which had been secured to the ship astern of us, now crowded with the South Wales Borderers, made for the end of the sandy patch just inside Morto Bay. They were met by a hail of bullets that killed a number of men, and therefore they withdrew for a short time, during which we increased our rate of fire. The trawlers then came round the south part of De Tott's; at 6.30 a.m., another attempt was made and, in spite of a heavy fire, the men landed and climbed up the side of the cliff. It was splendid to see them with their bayonets flashing in the sun, making the ascent – a sight never to be forgotten.'

Lieutenant Robert Seed RN, HMS *Vengeance*.

Supported by the guns of HMS *Cornwallis* and HMS *Vengeance*, De Tott's was taken within thirty minutes with very few casualties, 2/SWB losing two officers and twelve ORs killed, with three officers and forty ORs wounded. As for Y Beach, no consideration was given to reinforcing the success of these flanking positions or using them to support directly the stalled landing at V Beach, which was not going as well. The combined forces at Y and S beaches actually outnumbered the Turkish defenders south of Achi Baba, a known fact that was not exploited. The battalion maintained their position until two battalions of the French *175e R*égiment *d'infanterie (175 RI)* relieved them during the evening of 27 April. Casson and his battalion then marched over to X Beach, where they prepared for the First Battle of Krithia.

## X Beach

Similar to Y and S beaches, the landing at X was largely unopposed. X Beach is situated on the western side of the Peninsula and is little more than a shallow gouge in the coastline, about a mile north of Tekke Burnu. The beach is a narrow strip of sand 182 metres long, about seven metres deep and is at the foot of a steep escarpment some seventy metres high. The task of capturing X Beach was given to a battalion of the covering force, 2nd Battalion Royal Fusiliers (2/RF). The unit was supported by three platoons of D Company from the Anson Battalion, RND, which would act as a beach working party, and both the 1st Battalion, Border Regiment (1/Borders) and 1st Battalion, Royal Inniskilling Fusiliers (1/RIF). The objective of the landing was to secure the beach area and form a defensive flank to the northeast that was to offer protection for the main task, the capture of Hill 114 to the south. Once captured, 2/RF would then link up with 1/LF, who would be advancing towards them from W Beach. A link up to Y Beach would then occur.

The Official History notes: *The morning was absolutely still. The garrison of the peninsula gave no signs of life. A thick veil of mist hung*

**HMS *Implacable* landing the Royal Fusiliers.**

*motionless over the beaches. The sea was smooth as glass.* After HMS *Implacable* had dropped off one 1/LF company and Brigadier General Hare (86 Brigade) on W Beach, the battleship continued around Tekke Burnu towards X Beach with her four tows of 2/RF alongside. The cliff-top bombardment by HMS *Implacable* and subsequent covering fire was very effective. The Captain, Hughes Lockyer RN, managed to get to within 450 metres of the shore where, at point-blank range, its mighty 12-inch guns put paid to the section of twelve defenders from 3/26 Regiment. By 6.30 a.m. the Fusiliers had landed without loss.

> 'We got off very lightly while getting ashore; I can only put it down largely to the way our mother-ship plastered the beach for us at close range; however, we had our bad time later on. About 100 yards from the shore the launches cast us off and we rowed in for all we were worth, till the boats grounded, then jumped into the water, up to our chests in some places, waded ashore and swarmed up the cliff.'
>
> Lieutenant Colonel Henry Newenham, 2/RF.

When Brigadier General William Marshall, commanding 87 Brigade, came ashore at about 9.00 a.m. with his headquarters and the divisional reserve, 1/Borders and 1/RIF, his Brigade Major remarked:

> 'The landing differs from some others. I recollect a bright sunny morning, dead calm sea, not a shot fired. I had a bag in one hand, coat over my arm, and was assisted down a plank from the boat by an obliging sailor, so that I should not wet my boots. The only thing missing was the hotel.'
>
> Brigade Major Cuthbert Lucas.

The landing was a total success. Lieutenant Colonel Newenham, cheered on by the men of HMS *Implacable,* led just over a company towards the objective of Hill 114, where they made contact with 1/Lancashire Fusiliers, who had fought their way up from W Beach. To the north, the remaining Royal Fusiliers fanned out about 725 metres to set up a defensive perimeter. It did not take long before they came into contact with a reserve company from

**2/Royal Fusiliers entrenching above X Beach.**

2/26 Regiment, who subjected the British to almost ceaseless counter attacks. The northern flank soon collapsed and it needed 1/Borders and 1/RIF to re-establish the line. By the morning of 26 April the Turks had begun to withdraw, having successfully hampered the 29th Division's landing, stifling their advance. The ominous peak of Achi Baba lay in the distance, an objective that still lay largely undefended; an objective that would never be taken.

## W Beach

W Beach is on the south west promontory of the Peninsula by the headland named Tekke Burnu. It consists of an arc-shaped strip of deep, powdery sand, about 320 metres in length and approximately twenty-seven metres deep, with steep cliffs each side. The ground then rises up gently through sand dunes that then run up steeply to a low ridge. Trip wires had been placed in the surf line and mines planted on the beach. Behind this were two belts of barbed wire, surrounded by trenches that looked down onto the beach from the cliffs and low ridge. Despite some contemporary accounts, there were no machine guns covering W Beach, just a company of rifleman from 3/26 Regiment. Regardless, the defences were formidable.

The plan was for 1/LF, under the command of Lieutenant Colonel Harry Ormond, to effect a landing on W Beach and, when secured, to link up with the X and V beach landings, thus extending and then pushing forward the beach head, from where the covering force would provide the necessary protection to allow the rest of the 29th Division to land. To connect these beaches, two fortified hills needed capturing: Hill 114, assigned to 2/RF at X Beach; and Hill 138, the objective given to 1/LF.

To give the best chance of success a short but intensive thirty-minute bombardment by HMS *Euryalus* and HMS *Swiftsure* was to precede the landing, to lift some ten minutes before the boats hit the shore. Unfortunately, this lull in the bombardment was to give the Turkish defenders ten unmolested minutes to meet the landing. On board HMS *Euryalus* Hunter-Weston and staff observed the bombardment. He had earlier predicted the difficulties that the amphibious force would soon be facing, warning: *No loss would be too heavy and no risks too great if success would thereby be attained. But there is not in present circumstances a reasonable chance of success.* That said, he was determined to overcome the challenges and encourage all to do their best 'as the eyes of the world were upon them'.

'We all went to the bridge and the bombardment began. The sight now was wonderful – never to be forgotten. A beautiful sunny morning, a glassy sea, on one side of the Peninsula and Asia Minor, apparently uninhabited, being pounded to bits, and in every other direction ships and ships and ships – British battleships round Helles, all the best of the pre-Dreadnought era, cruisers, destroyers, French battleships on the Asiatic coast, like top-heavy walnuts, all bumps and excrescences, the five-funneled Russian cruiser, the *Askold* and, in the background, the newest and mightiest, yet so symmetrical as to look quite small and low, 'Queen Bess', one funneled and one masted, with her eight 15-inch guns. All these ships had their allotted areas to bombard, some the coastline, some searching up the valley behind and some dropping their 12-inch and 15-inch shells that burst with mighty columns of smoke on Krithia and on the summit of Achi Baba.'

Staff Captain Clement Milward, 29th Division.

The sight of the naval bombardment was undoubtedly reassuring, but it was largely ineffective against the entrenched positions; not only did it end ten minutes before the Lancashires landed, but the flat trajectory of naval gunnery meant that most of the shells either exploded into the cliffs or fell too far inland.

When the bombardment stopped,

'...all was deadly still and silent, the engines of our ship hardly made a sound. One couldn't help pitying the men sitting there in their boats. It was indeed a hush before the storm. There lay the Peninsula with not a sign of life on it, but the Turks were there all right in their trenches watching our every movement.'

Captain Clement Milward.

The boats unknowingly approached the killing zone where, ninety metres from the beach, a fusillade of rifle fire was unleashed. Those that had not been killed or wounded in the boats gallantly jumped into the water. The men struggled waist-deep, exacerbated by the weight of their equipment, the trip wires and land mines. The Turks continued to fire down from the cliffs into the battalion, which was now held up by a deep belt of wire. Initially the Fusiliers could not retaliate as their rifle actions had become clogged with sand and salty water. The men frantically kicked open the bolts of their rifles in an effort to fire back.

'A very heavy and brisk fire was poured into us, several officers and men being killed and wounded in the entanglements, through which we were trying to cut a way. Several of my company were

10

with me under the wire, one of my subalterns was killed next to me, and also the wire-cutter who was lying the other side of me. I seized his cutter and cut a small lane myself through which a few of us broke and lined up under the only available cover procurable, a small sand ridge covered with bluffs of grass. I then ordered fire to be opened on the crests, but owing to submersion in the water and dragging rifles through the sand, the breech mechanism was clogged, thereby rendering the rifles ineffective. The only thing left to do was to fix bayonets and charge up the crests, which was done in a very gallant manner, though we suffered greatly in doing so. However, this had the effect of driving the enemy from his trenches, which we immediately occupied.'

Major George Adams, 1/LF

The commander of the Covering Force, Brigadier General Steuart Hare, who was leading the second wave into the shore, witnessed the Fusiliers' plight. He could see that a further landing on W Beach was senseless and, thinking quickly, he ordered the remaining boats to row to the left-hand side of the beach under the cover of the cliffs. Outflanking the Turks, Hare and his men scrambled up a steep slope through a gap in the defences, forcing the Turks to flee. Unfortunately, when nearing

The Lancashire Landing.

11

Hill 114, Hare was wounded; but through his initiative, and that of officers like Adams, a landing had been effected. By 8.00 a.m. W Beach had been tentatively secured.

'They all drank our health and the General (Hunter-Weston) said our landing was one of the finest deeds that had been performed, far, far finer than Quebec; in fact they treated us like heroes. He said that every man should have a VC if they had their rights.'

Lieutenant Douglas Talbot, Royal Navy

In fact six Victoria Crosses were eventually awarded to the Lancashire Fusiliers. In an unusual, but not unprecedented, military decision, the survivors were asked to elect six recipients for the award because it was felt that the Battalion comprised 'equally brave and distinguished people'. The 'six VCs before breakfast', as they famously became known, were awarded to Major Cuthbert Bromley, Captain Richard Willis, Sergeant Alfred Richards, Sergeant Frank Stubbs, Corporal John Grimshaw and Private William Keneally. Three of them would not survive Gallipoli. The cost to the battalion that landed with twenty-five officers and 918 men was fifteen officers and 411 other ranks; 55% of them became casualties. Their feat passed into the folklore of this English county and, as a testimony to the gallantry of the Fusiliers, Hamilton ordered W Beach to be named 'Lancashire Landing' in their honour.

The fighting above Lancashire Landing and X Beach lasted until the weight of British numbers forced a Turkish withdrawal. After 1/LF connected with 1/RF on Hill 114, reinforcements landed on the beach in the form of the 1st Battalion, Essex Regiment (1/Essex) and the 4th Battalion, Worcestershire Regiment (4/Worcesters). Both battalions pushed out from the beach and made their way towards V Beach and two landmarks, a lighthouse and Hill 138. The hill had been entrenched by the Turks, with the approaches protected in parts by wire. The 4/Worcesters, having cut paths through the wire, along with 1/Essex, made a series of bayonet charges against the redoubt, eventually capturing it. However, their path to the beleaguered men on V Beach was still barred by a second hill nestled about 300 metres behind, namely Guezji Baba. Mistakenly, 4/Worcesters believed this to be Hill 141, the hill behind Sedd-el-Bahr, and when they signaled its capture just after 4.00 p.m. on 25 April, there was some confusion at Divisional headquarters until the mistake was realised. Hill 141 would not fall until the following afternoon; but for now 1/Essex consolidated Hill 138 and 4/Worcesters Guezji Baba. Counter-attacks halted further movements towards V Beach and no resumption of the advance occurred until 2.30 p.m. on 26 April, a day behind schedule.

## V Beach

The landing at V Beach was undoubtedly the bloodiest of them all. Defensive trenches and wire once again had been placed to disrupt any advance from the shoreline, while a rifle company from 3/26 Regiment, supported by four 'Pom-Pom' quick firing 37mm Maxim-Nordenfelt anti-aircraft guns had established a semi-circular defensive position between Fort Ertuğrul (Fort No. 1) on the cliffs, along a ridge to Hill 141 and down onto the beach to Sedd-el-Bahr castle (Fort No. 3). Two of these guns were located in the castle, and two were near Fort No. 1. Reports on the 4 March RMLI raid at Sedd-el-Bahr had stated that four Nordenfeldts had been destroyed and so it is unclear if these guns were operational on 25 April. The Turkish defenders had a clear field of fire from this natural bowl-shaped amphitheatre down on to a 270-metres wide, narrow and gently sloping beach.

The plan was to land four battalions by 8.00 a.m., capture the village of Krithia by noon and to have taken Achi Baba by nightfall. At first light, HMS *Albion* would bombard the defences at V Beach, to be followed an hour later by the landing of three companies from the 1st Battalion, Royal Dublin Fusiliers (1/RDF), towed to the shore in six strings of rowing boats pulled by steam pinnaces. Five would land on V Beach whilst the sixth was directed to land at the Camber, a harbour that was nestled between the castle and village. The plan also included the use of a 4,000-ton converted steam collier, the *River Clyde,* which would be beached and then quickly disembark its hidden cargo of 2,000 men.

**River Clyde (Painting by Charles Dixon).**

13

The *River Clyde* was to be an extraordinary survivor; she was refloated from V Beach in 1919 and sold to a Spanish owner. Renamed *Muruja Y Aurora*, she sailed the Mediterranean until she was finally scrapped in 1966, over fifty years after its distinguished role in the events at Gallipoli. An unlikely candidate, she has become possibly the best-known ship that saw service with the Royal Navy during the war.

The idea of using a modern 'Trojan horse' was conceived by Commander Edward Unwin RN, who assumed command of the ship. Sally ports had been cut in her side to allow the men to disembark via gangways, protected under the covering fire of eleven Maxim machine guns of the Royal Naval Air Service (Armoured Car Division). In the hold were two battalions, comprising 1st Battalion, Royal Munster Fusiliers (1/RMF), two companies from 2nd Battalion, Hampshire Regiment (2/Hants) and one company of 1/RDF, supported by a platoon from Anson Battalion and a Royal Engineers field company.

The tows carrying the 1/RDF were meant to land at 5.30 a.m., but embarkation delays and a strong current running out of the Straits held up the Dublins' approach. As a result the *River Clyde* overtook them. Even the best laid plans rarely survive first contact with the enemy, but this one appeared to be unwinding even earlier. Commander Unwin, concerned that there would be hellish confusion if he landed first, or if both forces landed simultaneously, turned the Clyde around to allow the Dublins to land. With so many ships close by, this manoeuvre proved extremely difficult, although ultimately it was successful. He then headed his ship straight for shore, to the utter amazement of the Turkish defenders.

'There was a jar that quivered from end to end of the ship, and she was aground. Hardly had the ship come to rest when the little steam hopper with her tow of barges rushed out from under the Clyde's quarter and made for the sandy shore some eighty yards distant. Up till now not a shot had been fired from the shore, and indeed we had begun to wonder whether the landing was to be unopposed, but hardly had the hopper's bow appeared beyond her huge consort when the whole slope leapt into a roar of firing, and a tempest of lead poured down upon the devoted craft and her gallant crew. Disaster overwhelmed her in an instant. Nothing could live in such a torrent of lead and in a moment the middy at the wheel and every sailor on the deck of the little ship was shot down. Devoid of guidance, the hopper went astray and beached side-on while the barges all went out of line, the connecting ropes broke under the strain, and they came to rest in a hopeless muddle

lying about twenty yards from the shore. The bridge of boats had failed.'
Petty Officer David Fyffe, 3 Armoured Car Squadron, RNAS.

Landed by rowing boats, but pinned down on the beach, the Dublins' commanding officer, Lieutenant Colonel Richard Rooth, was already dead, and Father William Finn, a Roman Catholic chaplain, mortally wounded. As the boats drew nearer to the beach the awful hail of machine gun and rifle fire, together with shrapnel, took its toll. Those lucky enough to reach a two-metre high sandbank along the beach sheltered behind it, the only cover that afforded any protection against the ferocious Turkish fire. As more boats rowed to the shore, they were met with the same maelstrom of fire, cutting men down before they even reached the beach. Some were killed outright; others drowned or were pulled under by the weight of their equipment. Between the drowning men, boats floated helplessly in the water with their dead and dying crews.

'There were twenty-five in my boat, and there were only three of us left. It was sad to hear our poor chums moaning, and to see others dead in the boat. It was a terrible sight to see the poor boys dead in the water; others on the beach roaring for help. But we could do nothing for them. I must have had someone's good prayer for I do not know how I escaped. Those who were lying wounded on the shore, in the evening the tide came in and they were all drowned, and I was left by myself on the beach. I had to remain in the water for about three hours, as they would fire on me as soon as they saw me make a move. I thought my life was up every minute.'
Private Robert Martin, 1/RDF.

Of the 700, only 300 reached the beach and many of them were badly wounded. They sought shelter behind the sandbanks and under overhanging shore sections. Some of the Dublins who landed on the Camber came ashore with few losses, but ultimately this flanking manoeuvre failed; some of the Dublin men managed to fight their way into the village of Sedd-el-Bahr but were unable to retain a footing and were forced to retire. The survivors eventually fought their way around the fort and joined the rest of the battalion, who were still pinned down on the beach.

The grounded *River Clyde* was powerless, and the bridge of boats had to be formed manually if the men were to run down improvised gangways and over the boats to the beach. It was intended that the flat-bottomed steam hopper, *Argyll*, which was accompanying the *Clyde*, was to move to the ship's port side and move lighters into position. The hopper, commanded by Midshipman George Drewry, was stuck and his six Greek volunteer crewmen, understandably took cover in the hopper's bows. From the deck of the *Clyde*, Unwin appreciated the hopelessness of the situation and acted. Followed by Able Seaman William Williams, he jumped into the sea and got hold of the lighters and pulled them underneath the bow of the *Clyde* and began to connect them up. The closest piece of dry land was a rocky spit jutting into the sea, and it was towards this natural pier that the men steered the boats. There was no way to hold the boats together, other than by grim determination, so Unwin and Williams clung on while the call was made for the infantrymen to leave the ship. Immediately the men of 1/RMF opened the doorways cut into the superstructure and began to run down the gangways towards the lighters.

'We could hear splash after splash as the gallant fellows fell dead from the gangway. A few however reached the nearest barge, raced across her open deck and crouched for shelter in the adjacent open boat. One after another the devoted fellows made the dash down the deadly gangways until a considerable number gathered in the bottoms of the open boats or were lying prostrate on the deck of the barge. Then the order was given and up they leapt and rushed for the rocks while a hail of rifle and machine-gun fire beat upon them. Wildly they leapt from boat to boat in that gallant rush while

The carnage of V Beach. (Inset: Lieutenant Colonel Charles Doughty-Wylie VC)

we on the ship cheered wildly at the sight, until they reached the last boat, when they leapt down into the water and started wading towards the rocks that were their goal, holding up their rifles high above their heads. But to our horror we saw them suddenly begin to flounder and fall in the water, disappearing from view and then struggling to the surface again with uniform and pack streaming, only to go down again, never to reappear as the hailing bullets flicked the life out of the struggling men ... We almost wept with impotent rage.'

Petty Officer David Fyffe.

Lance Corporal George Smith, 1/1st West Riding Field Company, Royal Engineers, wrote:

'I landed with a crash on the first barge, bullets spluttering all over the place as our fire had not silenced all the rifles and machine guns on the shore. I lay down at on my tummy and looked around to get my bearings and a terrible sight met me as the barge was crowded with men who had died and lots of wounded men whom we could not help as we had to push on owing to the other fellows coming on behind. Eventually, after crawling along three barges, I came to the place where I could push my face over the gunwale of the last barge and make up my mind to jump into the sea. I managed it all right, clutching my explosives – I had lost the shovel somewhere – I managed to get to a place where no bullets could reach me and lay down under cover of a small sandbank and at last I was for the first time on the enemy shore.'

Captain Guy Geddes, a company commander in the Munsters, recalled:

'We all made, Dublins and all, for a sheltered ledge on the shore which gave us cover. Here were shook ourselves out, and tried to appreciate the situation, rather a sorry one. I estimated that I had lost about seventy percent of my Company.'

As Geddes made his dash to the right, Unwin and Williams remained chest-deep in the cold water securing the boats; but they were soon exhausted and with Williams now wounded they were forced to let go of the ropes holding the boats together and return to the *Clyde*. In Unwin's absence, Drewry had taken over and with the help of two other men a third lighter had been brought round from the *Clyde*'s starboard side and a bridge of sorts completed. Further attempts were made to land men and three further strings of boats, packed with infantrymen, made for the shore. This time more were able to land but a number were cut down by the burst of three shrapnel shells overhead. Men were sent from the beached collier, and more arrived on lighters, but all were forced to head for the sandbank so that by 9.00 a.m. a few hundred men were huddled there for protection. It was clear that the position was hopeless. The landing had failed.

For these extraordinary acts of self-sacrifice, there were six Victoria Crosses awarded to members of the Royal Navy that day at V Beach: Captain Edward Unwin, Midshipman George Drewry, Midshipman Wilfred Malleson, AB William Williams, Seaman George Samson and Sub Lieutenant Arthur Tisdall.

The dramatic extent of the disaster unfolding on V Beach was unknown to Hunter-Weston and his staff on board the *Euryalus*, who ordered the landing of the main body at 8.30 a.m. Using the limited boats that were still seaworthy, the men met with a similar fate; the dead included men of all ranks, among them Brigadier General Henry Napier (88 Brigade), who had personally led the assault, and his brigade major, who followed him.

'We received depressing messages telling us of the death of General Napier, killed on the lighters, and shortly afterwards of the death of Costeker, his brigade major. Colonel Carrington Smith, a fine soldier, of the Hampshires, had taken command, but he was killed on the bridge in the afternoon. Truly the casualties were staggering. General Marshall, too, was slightly wounded. They told us too of how 1,000 men of those on board the River Clyde had attempted to get ashore. About half had been hit in the attempt. So great was the depression that we had great difficulty in dissuading General Hunter-Weston from going himself to V Beach to lead the men to the attack.'

Captain Clement Milward.

Finally, at 10.21 a.m., Hamilton, who was following events from his command post aboard the flagship HMS *Queen Elizabeth*, ordered Hunter-Weston to suspend operations. It was decided to wait until nightfall before a further attempt at landing should be made. Word was sent to the fleet of the failure and the ships recommenced their bombardment of the slopes above the beach and Sedd-el-Bahr. The plan to link up with W Beach was halted, at least for the time being; 4/Worcesters were within spitting distance of V Beach, but that was still not close enough.

Only with approaching darkness could both sides take a breather and the wounded on V Beach be treated. As night finally fell the navy

18

**Doughty-Wylie leading the charge onto Hill 141 (Painting by WS Bulitulis).**

shone searchlights onto the Turkish trenches, dazzling the defenders and, protected by the dark, the men who had been pinned down all day long began to move. Officers began to collect their men and more troops, who had been bottled up in the *River Clyde*, made their way to the shore. By midnight over two thousand men had reached the stretch of sand with hardly a casualty. The Turks were not beaten. They did not withdraw but counter attacked. This ultimately failed, but shocked the British, who now believed that the numbers holding the beach defences were far greater than they actually were. In fact it was just handfuls of men who had successfully pinned the Irishmen and Hampshires to the beach all day.

Staff officers on board the *River Clyde* realised that it would take a coordinated effort to break this impasse. Colonel Weir de Lancey Williams and Lieutenant Colonel Charles Doughty-Wylie formulated a plan. Williams would lead a party under the lee of the cliffs on the left flank under Fort No.1, Major Arthur Beckwith would advance in the centre, whilst Doughty-Wylie would take a party along the right flank, through the Castle and up through the village of Sedd-el-Bahr.

Despite the bravery of soldiers like Captain Garth Neville Walford, a brigade major of the Royal Artillery who was killed clearing Sedd-el-Bahr Castle of enemy, and of Corporal William Cosgrove, 1/RMF, who despite being wounded stood up in clear view of the enemy to clear a path through the wire, the progress was slow and casualties were heavy. Doughty-Wylie led the remaining men through the village and up to a defended redoubt on Hill 141. This final objective was taken by 2.30 p.m. but at a high cost, Doughty-Wylie being killed at this moment of victory.

Doughty-Wylie, Walford and Cosgrove were awarded the Victoria Cross for their bravery on 26 April 1915. Despite all the courage shown during the daylight landings on V Beach and Lancashire Landing, and what only can be described as lost opportunities on S and Y beaches, it is all too easy to state in hindsight what might have been. What cannot be ignored is that the best part of the 29th Division was thwarted by the unexpected, dogged and determined resistance of the Ottoman 3/26 Regiment. Despite heavy casualties, they had stubbed out any British advance, admittedly aided by lack of effective British command and control. With the loss of so many senior officers, but still outnumbering the Turks, the British units were in bloodied disarray, and by nightfall were worn out, somewhat demoralised and in a confused state of shock. The cost of the V Beach failure should not only be measured in casualties, but also in time; it took over a day for the British to secure Sedd-el-Bahr and thus the plan's timetable had slipped. The advance on the first day objectives of Achi Baba would not begin for another forty-eight hours; after another eight months of the campaign this objective would still not be reached – or even seriously threatened.

**The wartime grave of Captain Garth N Walford VC.**

# Chapter 2

# Advance to Contact: The First Battle of Krithia, 28 April 1915

By the evening of 26 April, Hunter-Weston's 29th Division had established a narrow, precarious beachhead at Cape Helles. The ferocity of the Ottoman defence had melted away under the cover of darkness, having done its job by delaying, and almost preventing, the landing. Some weakened units of the Turkish 9th Division and the remaining forces from both the 26 and 20 Regiment were now hurriedly preparing new defences just south of the village of Krithia, desperate to be reinforced.

It was clear that the operation was not going to plan. Whilst the superficial causes were obvious, the underlying reason for the failure to capture any objectives was more fundamental. From the War Cabinet down to commanders of the MEF there was a belief that the Turk was an inferior military fighting man and thus their defence would just collapse. To be fair, this view was not without basis, given the relatively poor performance of the Ottomans during the First Balkan War just a couple of years earlier. This serious underestimation of the enemy would

**Achi Baba – The Helles Battlefield.**

last throughout the campaign, although respect for the Turkish fighter grew as the battles went on. The 29th Division reorganised itself after the initial shock of the landings and waited for orders to advance. Hamilton realised that he would soon need reinforcements, which angered Kitchener and was not well received by Lieutenant General Maxwell in Egypt, whose garrison was going to be robbed of men to fulfill the request. Major General Sir William Douglas's 42nd (East Lancashire) Division, a Territorial formation, and an Indian Army brigade were sent. The French also committed to sending General Maurice Bailloud's *156e Division* (renamed *2e Division*). But what was Hamilton or, rather, Hunter-Weston going to do with this fresh injection of men?

Now ashore, the focus at Helles was the capture of the prominent hill of Achi Baba, which still sat unthreatened on the horizon, its gentle spurs tantalisingly stretched out in front, luring the assaulting forces to its summit. Not far away were the white washed stone buildings of Krithia, which shone bright in the late April sun. The original plan should have seen Krithia and the 700 feet high cone-shaped hill named Achi Baba in Allied hands by nightfall on 25 April; but, already two days behind schedule, this did not seem to concern Hamilton too much. As long as both objectives had fallen by sunset on 28 April the overall plan could be salvaged. It was of the utmost importance that a further attack was quickly mounted before the Turks could recover and be reinforced. Achi Baba was key terrain, the capture of which would deny the enemy such a wonderful view of Hamilton's forces. It would also be the platform needed for his artillery for the next part of the operation: the capture of the Kilid Bahr plateau. Never during the campaign did a British soldier stand on top of either.

During the night of 27/28 April General Albert d'Amade's French *Corps Expéditionnaire d'Orient* (CEO), or rather elements of their *1er Division*, which had made a broadly successful diversionary landing at Kum Kale on the Asian shore on 25 April, began the move across the straits to Helles to hold the right of the British line. This comprised General Vandenberg's *1e Brigade Métropolitaine*, namely the *175 RI* and a Composite *Régiment de Marche d'Afrique* consisting of a battalion of *Régiment étranger* and two battalions of *2e Régiment de Zouaves* (*2 RMA*). Colonel Ruef's *Coloniale* Brigade disembarked next, which comprised *4e Régiment d'Infanterie Coloniale* (*4 RIC*) and *6e Régiment d'Infanterie Coloniale* (*6 RIC*). The division was supported by six batteries of 75mm field guns and three batteries of 65mm mountain guns. The artillery was supplemented by two 14cm (5.2-inch) naval guns that

**French artillery landing at Cape Helles.**

were unshipped from a French cruiser for the sole purpose of providing counter battery fire against the Turkish guns on the Asiatic shore.

With Hamilton's forces not only ashore at Helles but also Anzac, General Liman von Sanders, the German officer who had operational control, in response divided Gallipoli into two geographically separate combat zones. Whilst at Anzac Mustafa Kemal commanded what became known as the Northern Group, at Helles the command was given to a German colonel, Edouard von Sodenstern. Both these groups would fall under the central command of battle-hardened Brigadier Essad Paşa.

During the morning of 27 April, Hunter-Weston's forces was reinforced when parts of the French division began to land after executing their successful diversion at Kum Kale on 25 April. The French were given the right flank that included both Morto Bay and V Beach. This enabled the repositioning of the 29th Division: 87 Brigade on the left, 88 Brigade in the middle and 86 Brigade in reserve. Between the British and French and the opposing Turks was about three kilometres of uncontested ground. The Turks had pulled back to consolidate the next line of defence and were in just as much disarray as Hunter-Weston's recently landed forces.

During the late afternoon of 27 April Hunter-Weston ordered an 'advance to contact' that pushed the line forward from the beaches over

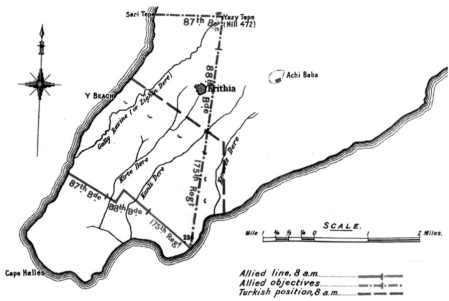

**First Battle of Krithia Objectives – 28 April.**

two kilometres inland and over a five kilometre width, from the mouth of Gully Ravine to Eski Hissarlik. Without opposition, the Allies were now astride the Peninsula. During the day, Hamilton felt confident enough to cable Kitchener about the progress and wrote that *thanks to the weather and the wonderfully fine spirit of our troops all continues to go well.* Hunter-Weston was confident of success, and Hamilton thought the worse was over. Far from it! The weather was cold and miserable and the men, still reacting to their shocking casualties over the last few days, were depressed and utterly exhausted. No one expected the welcome that the Turks had given them, and none were too keen to be thrown into another attack so soon.

The hastily prepared plan placed the 29th Division on the left and the French *1e Brigade Métropolitaine* on the right. The British 87 Brigade would advance on the left to their objective of Sari Tepe on the Aegean coast, and Yazy Tepe (Hill 472) to the north of the village. The British 88 Brigade, advancing in the middle, would then pivot, to capture Krithia from the flank and head in an easterly direction to come adjacent with the French at Kanli Dere. This would put the units within assaulting distance of Achi Baba. Even on paper this was an overly complex plan, which took no account of the intervening ground, most of it largely unreconnoitered. *It was necessary to take risks to reap advantage from the success already gained,* as one staff officer stated (Captain H. M. Farmar), as it was

24

thought that the Turks might make a stand and that Achi Baba could still be captured. Contrary to belief, the Turks had reorganised, reinforced and prepared themselves in the time that the British wasted between 26–28 April.

It is worth noting that the ground at Helles is not flat and whilst there is a mix of meadows, heath and arable land, this is intersected by deep rugged nullahs and numerous small water courses that form natural barriers. Whilst gentle, the advance would be uphill, onto the forward slopes of Achi Baba. This hill, 216 metres high, was vital ground and was shaped like the wrist of a hand. Like fingers, Achi Baba has five main spurs, divided naturally by four large ravines or nullahs. On the western side was Gully Ravine, which was separated from the Aegean shore by Gully Spur. Moving eastwards was Fir Tree Spur and then Krithia Nullah and then Krithia Spur. East of here was Kanli Dere and then the fields ran up to the Kereves Spur before the ground falls away into Kereves Dere, which flows into the Dardanelles north of Morto Bay.

The Turks were thus on the high ground, left free to observe all troop movements to the south. Turkish strength and dispositions were largely unknown. Brigade commanders were aware of the attack only six hours before, so there was hardly enough time for effective preparation for the action. None of this boded well for a successful advance. The only hope was that resistance would be light and the advance could reach its objectives relatively easily. This was not to be. Hunter-Weston of

**Lieutenant General Hunter-Weston, GOC VIII Corps.**

**Brigadier Essad Paşa.**

course knew the risks, but time was of the essence and working on the understanding that the Turks were weak and retreating northwards, this was the opportunity to advance.

The battle, which became known as the First Battle of Krithia, began at 8.00 a.m. on 28 April with a naval bombardment, supported by little more than twenty guns ashore. At 10.00 a.m. 87 Brigade on the left began its advance, encountering no resistance. On the right the *175 RI* had similar success as they followed the telegraph poles onto the ninety-metre contour line on Kereves Spur. For the first two hours all appeared to be going to plan as the thin British and French lines moved forward. On the left, 1/Borders and 1/Inniskillings reached the southern area of Gully Ravine, securing its mouth and Gully Beach with no resistance. The main thrust of the attack continued astride the ravine, with the Borders advancing along Gully Spur and the Inniskillings on the eastern side of the ravine, along what became known as Fir Tree Spur.

By about midday a Turkish strongpoint, near the abandoned Y Beach, was encountered that stopped the advance on both spurs. Only three days previously this area was in British hands; it would take another two weeks before this strongpoint eventually fell. The tired and battle shocked men from the landings needed no other excuse to halt, many collapsing in utter exhaustion. In defence were the remnants of Major Mahmut Sabri's regiment, recently reinforced by Colonel Halil Sami's 9th Division; the Turks now had thirteen battalions positioned in front of Krithia, three of which were fresh.

Hunter-Weston had fourteen British and five French battalions available for the attack, supported by a few field guns and the Royal Navy.

The advance of 88 Brigade, under the temporary command of Lieutenant Colonel Owen Godfrey-Faussett, in the centre of the attack and to the right of 87 and 86 Brigade, began well; however, although they did not have Gully Ravine to contend with, the brigade lost its cohesion, not helped by the complex nature of the terrain that is sandwiched between Krithia Nullah and Kanli Dere. This all led to fragmentation of this advance, with individual units acting independently of each other. It was not Godfrey-Faussett's finest hour;

Lieutenant Colonel Owen Godfrey-Faussett DSO, Essex Regiment.

he might have been a good battalion officer, winning the DSO in the Boer War, but in command of a brigade, for which he had no experience, he soon lost his grip of it, which quickly effected his brigade. He was criticised by General Marshall as being 'rattled' and there were comments that he made various excuses not to advance.

With a gap in the line, the situation became even more desperate when 1/Essex returned from the front, lost and unsure what to do. They were quickly returned to the line with a guide as Marshall's staff tried to reorganise this mess. Mutual support is key in an advance like this; command and control was failing. Godfrey-Faussett was relieved of command of the brigade (he was killed on 2 May and is buried in Redoubt Cemetery). By midday both the cohesion and momentum of the 29th Division's attack had been lost; any advances were timid at best against a Turk who remained defiant.

86 Brigade advance was spearheaded by 2/RF and 1/LF, with the Royal Dublin and Munster Fusiliers in reserve. Despite written orders for each battalion that named the point of direction (the white Mosque in Krithia), in reality the advance did not go well. The right flank of 88 Brigade ahead was lost when the French started retiring from positions they had gained earlier in the day. Some men from the Dublins and Munsters were sent forward in small groups, in artillery formation to avoid casualties from shrapnel, but became scattered. This in effect reduced the weight of 86 Brigade's attack, which floundered now two (admittedly very weak) battalions had effectively disappeared into the confusion. Despite the brigade major going ahead to try and collect these lost parties together, the momentum and any hope of advancing further was lost. Any training for mutual support in an advance and to conform to the movement had been lost.

That said, Twelve Tree Copse, through effective use of fire and movement, was captured. A small party of Lancashire Fusilier officers, a sergeant, a few men and the brigade major (Farmar), went through the wood, down a heathery slope and up onto a rise from where they could clearly observe the outskirts of the village and retreating Turks, less than a kilometre away. The wood itself was reported to be full of dead and wounded Turks. It was reported that shouts for the line to come forward were met with no response, this being put down to the exhaustion of the men, who were weighed down by their heavy packs and fatigued by the strain of the last four hours of fighting. It is thought that no one was aware that Farmar's little party was on the other side of the wood and so close to Krithia.

Captain Bromley attempted to bring on the line but after standing up was immediately shot through the knee. Eventually the line was brought forward, but by that stage the Turks were returning in force. The reconnaissance made their way back to what was now an empty wood and was fired on not only by the Turks but by the British on the other side. The retirement was ordered when the French pulled back on the right flank. This in turn caused 88 Brigade to fall back and the wood was lost. A mile of ground that had been captured that day was given up. It would take another month for the British to reach this wood once again. The wood and Krithia had been there for the taking.

Lieutenant Colonel JTR Wilson, commanding 5th Royal Scots (5/RS) had a lucky escape in this action, a story he would later tell Captain Albert Muir, who published it in his post war memoir *With the Incomparable 29th*. Wilson was wounded, fell unconscious and was left behind when 88 Brigade withdrew. When he came too, he was disorientated and found himself asking wounded Turks for directions. This produced no results and he then found himself walking towards a Turkish patrol. He ran and was chased but managed to hide, helped by the darkening sky as the sun was setting. Eventually he managed to get back to his own lines but his experiences showed that the Turks were not in great numbers and were coming forward from the village to find out where the British were. Wilson was lucky not to have ended up in Krithia as a prisoner.

Gains by 87 Brigade on the left were retained, the line now pivoting back to where 88 Brigade had withdrawn. A line was dug during that wet night of 28 April, later known as the Eski Line, which joined the British on the left to the French on the right. One long line was now dug

**General Vandenberg's recently landed *1e Brigade Métropolitaine* marching towards the front.**

to safeguard against an expected Turkish counter attack. Fortunately for the Allies, the Turks did not attack that night or the following day.

On the right flank, terrain had a significant influence on the attack. The French had only been ashore at Helles for a day and were unfamiliar with the ground. Ground appreciation for the British was little better as the line moved forward. Blocking the French advance was the Kereves Dere, a large, jagged edge ravine that ran from the Dardanelles in a north westerly direction, blocking the path to Achi Baba. The Turks had recognised the defensive value of this feature and had entrenched along the ridgelines and on the spurs that marked the way for the French towards it. The Turks also recognised the bright blue and red French uniforms topped with white cork helmets, severely handicapping their wearers and making them an easy target. When the French advance reached the ninety-metre contour line of Kereves Spur they encountered heavier Turkish resistance, especially before Bouchet Redoubt. The attack came to a standstill about 400 metres from the main Turkish defence line on Hill 300.

The Turks had rushed forward their Ottoman 19 Regiment, which had force marched to the area on that day. At 3.00 p.m. a counter attack was launched against 87 Brigade on the left. If it were not for the Royal Navy and their offshore gun fire support, the situation could have been dire. This counter-attack had the effect of stopping the timid advance and even in some places resulting in a partial retirement. Midshipman GMD Maltby described the scene off Y Beach, where HMS *Queen Elizabeth* helped save the day whilst in support of the tired Border Regiment, which at one stage broke in the face of a Turkish counter attack.

'At 12.30 the Huns [sic] could be distinctly seen rapidly advancing and firing from behind the farthest ridge. They came along in huge numbers, there being only a few of our men in the advance trench to meet them. These fellers [sic] became demoralized and many ran over the cliff, but the situation was partially saved by our 15-inch (13,000 bullets), which exploded bang over the Huns and those that it did not flatten out turned. These were wiped out by a salvo of our 6" shrapnel.'[1]

By 6.00 p.m. the fatigued and dispirited British were ordered to dig in. They had advanced just over a kilometre from their starting positions; the French on the eastern flank fared a little better; but when counter attacked at 5.30 p.m., they were forced back to their starting line. The First Battle of Krithia was halted and positions were consolidated.

The plan turned out to be overly complex and poorly communicated and so really had little chance of success. The 29th Division's advance also lacked cohesion and, although some blame had been put on Hunter-Weston for siting his headquarters too far back so that he had no control over the events that day, much of the problem lay in the tiredness of the troops and the sapping of morale that had occurred since the landing.

Brigadier General William Marshall was entrusted with the 86, 87 and 88 Brigade attacks; he not only lacked a headquarters but also had no field telephones to help coordinate the attack. Instead of moving as a unified body, some units became

**Brigadier General William Marshall.**

detached, veered off in the wrong direction and even crossed the paths of one another. Add the impact of enemy fire and it is easy to understand why the advance soon stopped, well short of its objective.

There were 3,000 casualties amongst the 14,000 troops that participated in the battle. Turkish casualties were also heavy, at nearly 2,500. The naval bombardment had been effective and inflicted heavy casualties on the Ottoman 19 Regiment whilst they were reinforcing the front lines. At no time were Krithia or Achi Baba threatened and the modest advance of the line that was made showed that a swift victory would not be forthcoming and that the Turks should not be underestimated. Further casualties amongst the Dublin and Munster Fusiliers meant that they had to be temporarily amalgamated into one unit, nicknamed the 'Dubsters'. Hamilton's hopes were dashed. In the words of the Royal Scots' history:

'After the battle of the 28th April only the incurable optimist could dream of Achi Baba being carried by a coup de main. A deadlock had been established and any possibility of surprise had vanished, or at least [it had] on the Helles battlefield.'

From the time of the landing the casualty figures were high: whilst the French had lost nearly 2,000 men, British losses alone totalled nearly 14,000: 177 officers and 1,990 other ranks killed, 412 officers and 7,807 other ranks wounded, thirteen officers and 3,580 other ranks missing. Most of the missing had in fact been killed. The officer casualties were particularly high. In comments to Captain RH Williams, the American military attaché, Turkish officers noted that *The English officers were brave but inexperienced, and did not seem to know how to command or to lead their soldiers into battle.*

## Turkish Counter Attack

It is worth noting that until the end of the First Battle of Krithia there were really no trenches to speak of; much of the field defences were merely shallow scrapings in the ground. Between 30 April and 1 May, 29 (Indian) Brigade and 2 (Naval) Brigade, RND, had been landed to supplement Hunter-Weston's weakened force. But this would not be enough.

Liman von Sanders at the same time created two new formations: at Helles a Southern Group, under the command of Colonel von Sodenstern; and at Anzac a Northern Group, under Essad Pasha. The Turks had defended well and now, reinforced by four fresh divisions, they prepared to launch counter-attacks at both Helles and Anzac whilst the Allies were at their weakest. The French *2e Brigade Mixte Coloniale* landed at Helles, only recently having made an opposed landing during which it suffered heavy casualties. Bolstering *Brigade Métropolitaine* and

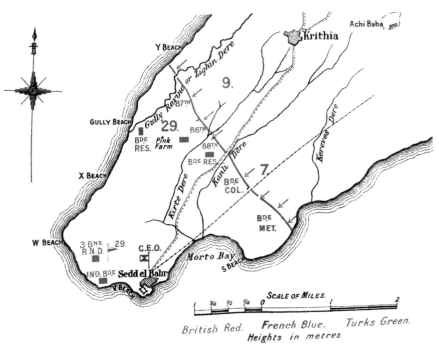

**Turkish Night Attack – 1–2 May.**

88 Brigade (29th Division), they were in unfamiliar territory and against an unfamiliar enemy. With little time to consolidate their positions or gain ground appreciation, the whole Allied front was vulnerable to attack.

At Helles Colonel von Sodenstern now had twenty-one battalions available across his divisions. Both the Ottoman 9th Division and 7th Division were severely weakened and the only fresh troops available to Sodenstern were the 11th Division, which had only just arrived from the Asian shore. These were supplemented by units from both the 5th and 3rd Divisions. The Turkish tactics were simple; they would charge out of the night on 1 May with the objective of pushing the Anglo-French forces back into the sea. Colonel von Sodenstern understood the urgency to strike quickly before the British and French had fully recovered from the shock of the landings and the First Battle of Krithia. With improved weather, supplies were now being landed on the beachhead in greater volume and the Allied morale was on the rise.

Colonel von Sodenstern issued his order to his troops for the forthcoming attack:

> 'Soldiers! You must drive the enemy, who are in at Seddulbahr, into the sea. The enemy is afraid of you; he dare not come out of his trenches and attack you. He can do nothing more than wait for you with his guns and machine guns. You are not afraid of his fire. You must believe that the greatest happiness awaits him who gives up his life in this Holy War. Attack the enemy with the bayonet and utterly destroy him! We shall not retire one step back; for if we do our religion, our country and our nation will perish! Soldiers! The world is looking at you! Your only hope of salvation is to bring this battle to a successful issue or gloriously to give up your life in the attempt.'[2]

His directive to his regimental commanders was delivered bluntly, the content of which does not indicate overwhelming confidence in his own men:

> 'Let it be clearly understood that those who remain stationary at the moment of attack, or who try to escape, will be shot. For this purpose machine guns will be placed behind the troops to oblige such people to advance and at the same time to fire on the enemy's reserves.'

At 10.00 p.m. on 1 May, Turkish artillery opened up on the Allied lines. *En masse*, over 15,000 of Sodenstern's men charged forward. In the British sector the Turks managed to penetrate the line to the right of Gully Ravine, albeit briefly, where the Dubsters (the amalgamated remnants of 1/RDF and 1/RMF) were defending.

Lieutenant Commander Josiah Wedgewood MP DSO, described the action of the 5th Royal Scots (a territorial battalion), who were in reserve in trenches astride Achi Baba Nullah and the Krithia Road, counterattacking to plug the line:

'Out of the night they came. "Where are the Turks that had got through?" and off they [5/RS] filed into the night. There was silence for perhaps ten minutes, and then the splutter of the rifles, the shouts of the charge. Off went the Essex after them – splutter, shouts. It was only midnight, and till 4.30 no man knew how that bayonet work on the left was faring, least of all those gallant Territorials, who could not tell from minute to minute whether they were charging fifty or 5,000.'

This critical situation was recovered by this counter attack and the lost positions recaptured. Elsewhere the British line held. The action was recorded in the diary of Sergeant Dennis Moriarty, 1/RMF:

'About 5 p.m. enemy started a heavy shrapnel fire on our trenches … 9 p.m. they started an attack, I am sure I will never forget that night as long as I live. They crept right up to our trenches (they were in thousands) and they made the night hideous with yells and shouting Allah! Allah! We could not help mowing them down.[…] My God, what a sight met us when day broke this morning. The whole ground in front was littered with dead Turks.'[3]

Some of those who fled when the line was broken were stopped at brigade headquarters and were led back into the line by Staff Captain Kane. The men redeemed themselves by carrying ammunition back into the line before taking their position once again in the ranks. Farmar stated that *the Irish were defending the weakest part of the line and bore the greatest weight of the attack*, so no blame should be put on the men who bolted. Captain Daubuz, Captain Wheatley and various gunners of 15th Brigade RHA (Royal Horse Artillery), did similar good work in helping to consolidate defences, organising men who had retreated under the heavy fire and shrapnel. Three bombardiers, Pawley, Love and Allpress, all of B Battery RHA, had remained in the forward trenches after the infantry vacated them and remained in contact with their battery.

**Graves of Lieutenant Colonel Smith, Captain Morgan and Gunner Payne.**

During the night Lieutenant Colonel Edmund Percival Smith, commanding 17th Brigade RFA (Royal Field Artillery) and his adjutant, Captain Frederick Harold Morgan, left their observation post to go forward to coordinate artillery fire from the trenches. Both were killed and are today buried in Redoubt Cemetery. Morgan had two brothers who also died in the war, one a RNAS pilot who was killed in a flying accident at Chingford, Essex in 1917 and another who, whilst attached to 6/South Lancs, was killed in action during the assault on Chunuk Bair, Anzac, on 9 August 1915.

**Lieutenant Colonel Edmund Percival Smith, 17th RFA.**

Wedgewood continued his account:

'... one prayed most to hear the guns of the Horse Artillery, an assurance that they were not captured. I do not know who makes the French ammunition; but they are above all men blessed. All night long, like clockwork, their 75 shells passed thumping ten feet overhead. One felt on hold on hope and sanity; one thing left solid; they would pump on through eternity and hold the fort. Each burst gave us a little light.

Allah! Allah! Allah! There must be another wave going through the French in the valley. "There is no God but God, and Mahommed is His prophet." "Train your gun more into the valley." "Don't you hear me, Rhys Evans, get your gun onto the valley." "He's dead, sir!" So in the black trench that brave dentist died with his thumb on the Maxim push and his eyes straining into the darkness beyond the parapet.

At last the dawn came red over Achi Baba. The black forms lying in the grass in front began to show up. Figures were moving away in the night. Till one could make out which way those figures were moving no one knew whether we were cut off or saved. To right and left they were in flight. The relief after that night's tension made one turn and solemnly shake hands. The Senegalese bayoneted the Turks on the right; the Lancashires and Essex were after them on the left; and the guns caught them on every skyline; and so the 2 May came up.'

The Allied recovery was quick and the lost ground recovered. Seizing the advantage, the British launched an immediate counter attack, which saw 87 Brigade gaining almost 500 metres of ground from the Ottoman 9th Division on the left. This, however, was only temporary, as the Turks subsequently pushed the British back. Casualties were heavy.

Liman von Sanders ordered a renewal of the attack for the following night, 2 May. A German colonel, Hans Kannengiesser, who had been in command of the 19th Division at Anzac, was sent south to support Sodenstern. Kannengiesser described the scene:

'By 10 o'clock in the evening I rode out from Serafin Tschiflik, and my guide was the sky, reddened as from an enormous conflagration. ...

The closer I approached the battlefield the more powerful was the impression on the eye and ear. I recognised the continuous flashes from the fleet that lay in a half circle round the Peninsula and bombarded the land with ceaseless fire, giving an impression of power and might which I can scarcely describe. ...

Even later, in August 1917, in the battles in Flanders, I did not have the same overwhelming impression of concentrated shelling as during this period.'[4]

To support the Turks, an Imperial German naval detachment of six Maxim machine guns were sent south to help Sodenstern. Still dressed in German uniforms, Sodenstern's chief of staff, Major Carl Mühlmann, describes an unexpected incident:

'I was stopped by Turkish infantrymen, who told me excitedly that they had captured English machine guns. My astonishment cannot be described as other than anger when I recognised that our six German machine guns from the *Breslau*, were in the midst of the so-called Englishmen. During the night they had already been stopped through non-recognition of their uniforms, roughed up and not allowed to proceed forward. And now, at this crucial moment, when the Turks had so few machine guns, our six good machine guns, well served, would have been able to achieve extraordinary results, but I found them to have been 'captured'. Of course, I immediately cleared things up & ordered them to continue to go forward into position.'[5]

For the Turks the front was divided into two halves by the Krithia road. On the left, facing the 29th Division, was the Ottoman 7th Division under Kemsi Bey. On the right, on the right flank of the 29th Division, was General Joseph Masnou's French *1er Division*, faced by the Ottoman 9th Division under Colonel Sami Bey. Including the mix of units from the 3rd, 5th and 11th Divisions, Sodenstern controlled a total of twenty-four battalions. Similar in strength to the British and French and whilst on paper this may look a sizable force, casualties had been heavy. In addition Sodenstern had no heavy guns, although he had sufficient field artillery and ammunition to support the infantry.

The 1/LF were in the line between the 2/SWB on the left and the 1/RMF on their right when this attack came. It has been a quiet night until about 1.00 a.m., when Lieutenant Dunn rushed over to Captain Richard Willis VC, saying that *the Turks are coming on in thousands*. At first Willis could not hear them as his position was in dead ground, nearer Gully Ravine, but this did not stop the 2/SWB and 1/RMF opening up a terrific fusillade on the oncoming Turks. The Lancashire Fusiliers' Annual noted that:

'Our men could distinctly hear the Turks exhorting one another with shouts of "Allah-a-din!" and the Yüzbaşı [captain] was having a difficult task as the Turkish did not like the ominous silence in their front. At last they plucked up their courage and after trying to draw our fire came on. Ten rounds, in two bursts of fire each, was enough, though a few got close up to our trenches. We gave them a taste of the machine gun, and then some wag called out "Are we down-hearted?" which made the men laugh … As it began to grow light the Turks began to sneak off up the nullah in spite of the efforts of their leaders. One German officer tried to stem the rearward movement with his revolver, but he was at once shot down. Willis's men had now a good target, as the Turks were still in a little nullah about thirty yards in front of them. However, they fought like trapped rats, and four good men were killed close to Captain Willis, all shot through the head. One bullet passed through Captain Willis's cap and one struck his periscope. This taught respect for their sharp-shooting.'

The Lancashire Fusiliers recorded that *next morning the Battalion buried the bodies of 163 Turks who lay in front of their trenches.*

This violent attack fell heaviest against the French, who endured the most sustained and committed part of these assaults. The Turkish bombardment had caught many of the French soldiers in the open, accounts noting that they had only been ashore three days, one of which was spent in landing and the other fighting in First Krithia, so little in the way of dugouts and trenches had been dug. The newly arrived *2e Brigade Mixte Coloniale*, situated between 88 Brigade and *Brigade Métropolitaine*, broke; one Senegalese battalion literally bolted and ran. The Turks exploited the gaps in the line of *4 RIC*, overrunning headquarters, artillery positions and even reaching as far as Morto Bay. Gunners fought as infantry and eventually the breach was contained and the Turks pushed back by a counter attack by elements of the *Régiment étranger, 6 RIC, 175 RI*. By dawn the line had been re-established and,

**French artillery in action at Sedd-el-Bahr.**

even though fighting continued until about midday, neither side held on to any gains.

Lieutenant Henri Feuille was encamped near Sedd-el-Bahr, waiting for his 150mm guns of the 52nd Battery to be disembarked.

'Fanatical Turks, good brave soldiers, were killed without mercy by our bayonets in the hand-to-hand struggle. In the course of the night they broke through almost to the cypress trees not far from our village. We could hear their shouts, their joyful cries in the certain belief that they were close to victory. We retreated, forced back by their savage efforts and faced, above all, by their heavy sacrifice of human lives. To cover the area of ground in front of us and above the cypresses, and to give the Turks the impression that the hill was occupied, I fired volleys of rifle fire. Nonetheless, the Senegalese were overwhelmed and fell back in disorder. To announce their advance so that their artillery could fire in support, the Turks lit red flares. Green flares marked out the trenches they had recaptured and they also had white flares, found on the corpses, which they also lit to illuminate our defeat, hopeful that at any moment their aims would be realised and, if the all-powerful Allah so wished, we would be thrown without mercy into the sea. The night passed in agonised anxiety as to the likely outcome of a hand-to-hand fight in which the fate of every life was in doubt. The dawn came at last, lighting up a scene of carnage; and the Turks retired to their trenches accompanied by salvos of 75mm shells. We have held the line but the dead and the wounded are legion.'

Lieutenant Joseph Vassal, Medical Officer, 6 RIC, described the aftermath of the Turkish counter attack during that night.

'The noise died down. We had the advantage. I got up at daybreak, stiff, tired, headachy, but ready for the day's work all the same. I went to the dressing station, then on to the plateau, where fighting had been in progress. I took an epaulette from a Turkish captain. Many dead. Horrible wounds. Bayonets used. Magnificent men, the Turks as well as ours. Turks, whites, blacks were all mixed up: men of the 175 RI, 6 RIC, 4 RIC, and Zouaves.

**Lieutenant Joseph Vassal, Medical Officer, 6 RIC.**

M. Huguenin was found dead, struck by many bullets. I went to the staff officers' camp. Nibaudeau or Simonin will command the *6 RIC*. The *175 RI* is commanded by a lieutenant, the only surviving officer. Not a single officer of the engineers remains. The graves of Lieutenant Huguenin and Captain Blanchard are marked. There are already other cemeteries for our regiment. That of the *175 RI* is a little further on, with no special boundary. Before leaving the graves I see a Senegalese bring some flowers (poppies); he puts them down on Blanchard's grave only. I imagine the suffering of their loved ones; and I move away so that these men may not see my tears.'

During the day of 3 May there was an unofficial truce and Turkish stretcher parties were left unmolested to recover their wounded, after which the Turks began bombarding the Allied trenches with shrapnel.

During the night of 3 May, Colonel Remsi Bey, commander of the Ottoman 15th Division, arrived with five battalions to support yet another attack that night. This time the 9th Division was to attack the British on their left flank; the 7th Division attacked down the middle, whilst the newly arrived 15th Division attacked against the French on the right. At 9.00 p.m. the attack was launched against the Allied lines, the Turkish infantry screaming 'Allah! Allah!' as they charged.

It started well against the French, where the 15th Division had not only breached the front lines held by *6 RIC*, but broke through the supporting lines and in places reached Morto Bay again and the outskirts of Sedd-el-Bahr. The lost ground was quickly retaken by a counter attack. On the British left flank the Ottoman 7th Division started well and, although held up by barbed wire in some places, small groups penetrated through the lines into the open ground beyond. In the middle, the 9th Division was stalled and, according to both Turkish and German accounts, performed poorly. By dawn and with ever increasing light these small groups of Turks, often without leadership, had no choice other than to withdraw. Casualties in the attack had once more been heavy and in the withdrawal these only increased. With the coming of light the Allies saw the danger and where the Turks had penetrated and could now concentrate their effort, including deadly naval gunnery support, to eliminate the threat. The Turks withdrew back to their starting line to lick their wounds. The 4 May otherwise passed peacefully, albeit with a battlefield now strewn with a new carpet of dead.

Sodenstern's night attacks had failed and had incurred heavy losses, amounting to some 5,000 casualties. Whilst British casualties were nearly 700, French casualties were particularly heavy, especially amongst officers, losing one brigade commander and two regimental officers. In total fifty-seven French officers and 2,520 other ranks were casualties. With French losses so high, General Albert d'Amade requested British support to help bolster his part of the line. This did not arrive in time and d'Amade's fear of another Turkish attack had been confirmed during the night of 3–4 May, when they attacked again. Once more the Senegalese broke, unable to hold against the ferocious onslaught, and the Turks flooded through the gap. However, with the help of French 75mm guns, reserves soon plugged the gap. Second Lieutenant Raymond Weil of the *39 Régiment d'Artillerie* wrote:

'We had made a veritable slaughter of the Turks, but we also had heavy losses. And I had learned of a terrible thing, namely that we had no more shells left. The artillery park was empty and all that remained at the batteries were empty limbers and that was it. If the Turks attack this night we are done for.'

The hard lessons learned as a consequence of these attacks caused Essad Paşa strictly to forbid any further frontal attacks. Colonel von Soderstern was replaced by Colonel Weber the same day. This front needed new leadership, a leadership that was familiar with trench warfare, as Weber was.

There was a natural gap in the fighting now as both sides were both exhausted and had suffered heavy casualties during the past week of fighting.

Observing the Turks developing their defences provided a dilemma for Hamilton. Should he wait for sufficient reserves and shells, or attack before their defences had been strengthened? Hamilton wanted to attack Krithia again and that quickly. In readiness for the next attack on Krithia, 2 (Australian) Brigade and the New Zealand Brigade, around 5,000 men in total, were transferred from Anzac. In addition 125 Brigade from the 42nd (East Lancashire) Division had just landed after its move from Egypt. The RND would also be available; whilst the 29th Division's contribution would once again be spearheaded by 87 and 88 Brigades (86 Brigade had been temporarily split between these two brigades due to their reduced numbers). In addition, five Australian and one New Zealand field artillery battery were landed at Helles, attached to 29th Division in support.

British and French troops remained jumpy during the following night. It would be the baptism of fire for 2 (Naval) Brigade, the Howe, Anson and Hood men. Ordinary Seaman Joseph Murray, Hood Battalion:

'Just before dawn, heavy firing broke out on the extreme left. The French on the right joined in and soon the whole line from the Straits to the sea was in turmoil but it died down shortly after daybreak. With the exception of sporadic outbursts, the line was comparatively quiet but the warships off-shore were doing a bit of shelling, We, however, are at peace but it is too noisy to sleep, even though we are all desperately tired but it's nice to know the ships are still there. Although we cannot see them firing, we can see their shells bursting on the slopes of Achi Baba. It must be uncomfortable up there for the Turks.'[6]

The outcome of the Turkish night attacks between 1 and 3 May had been a close run thing, leaving both Hunter-Weston and d'Amade deeply worried. On 4 May both generals sought to make the case for reinforcement and relief to Hamilton, whose own account shows how deeply concerned everyone was.

'Last night again there was all sorts of firing and fighting going on, throughout those hours peaceful citizens earmark for sleep. I had one or two absolutely hair-raising messages. Not only were the French troops broken but the 29th Division were falling back into the sea. Though frightened to death, I refused to part with my reserve and made ready to go and take command of it at break of dawn. In the end the French and Hunter-Weston beat off the enemy by themselves. But there is no doubt that some of the French, and two battalions of our own, are badly shaken – no wonder!

Both Hunter-Weston and d'Amade came on board in the forenoon, Hunter-Weston quite fixed that his men are strained to breaking point and d'Amade emphatic that his men will not carry on through another night unless they get relief. To me fell the unenviable duty of reconciling two contrary persuasions. Much argument as to where the enemy was making his main push; as to the numbers of our own rifles (French and English) and the yards of trenches each (French and English) have to hold. I decided after anxious searching of heart to help the French by taking over some portion of

**General Albert d'Amade, GOC Corps Expéditionnaire d'Orient.**

their line with the Naval Brigade. There was no help for it. Hunter-Weston agreed in the end with a very good grace. In writing to Kitchener I try to convey the truth in terms which will neither give him needless anxiety or undue confidence. The facts have been stated very simply, plus one brief general comment. I tell him that the Turks would be playing our game by these assaults were it not that in the French section they broke through the Senegalese and penetrated into the position. I add a word of special praise for the Naval Division, they have done so well, but I know there are people in the War Office who won't like to hear it. I say, "I hope the new French Division will not steam at economic, but full, speed!" and I sum up by the sentence that the times are anxious, but I believe the enemy's cohesion should suffer more than ours by these repeated night attacks.'[7]

The landscape was transformed as pick and shovel turned Helles into an elaborate trench system across the Peninsula. Fire support, and reserve trenches, with a few communication trenches running down to the beaches, now scarred the ground. In a way this was a confession of failure, as no one planned for what was now looking like a long drawn out campaign. The discomforts of Gallipoli, without question, far exceeded those on the Western Front; there were extremes of temperature, challenging terrain, the infestation of flies, poor sanitation, poor diet, water shortages and lack of sufficient war material to fight a campaign of this nature. In to this mix there was a well-trained, determined and formidable Ottoman Army.

'The one abiding solace was the beauty of Eastern scenery: Gallipoli at its worst was never monotonously drab like the low country of Flanders. The play of sun on land and sea drew many pictures of varied hues. Most dawns were a sheer delight to the eye. Shot by the gleaming streak of the rising sun, the soft morning mists floating over Achi Baba transformed the ridge into a delicate pastel of purple film. The illusion of dawn lasted for a few brief moments and the sun, dissolving the mists, poured over land and water a fierce white light in which every object stood out with tyrannic definiteness. The hard blue of the sea and sky contrasted sharply with the rich amber of the earth. Then towards the evening, when the sun began its westering career, a glorious chromatic architecture unfolded itself to the vision until the colours faded away, leaving the earth in inky blackness under the jewelled canopy of the Eastern sky.'

# Chapter 3

# The Second Battle of Krithia: 6–8 May 1915

Hamilton prepared his forces to launch another offensive; the Second Battle of Krithia. Due to the very significant casualties suffered so far, Hamilton had to reorganise his forces. Two brigades of the Royal Naval Division and the Lancashire Fusilier Brigade from the 42nd (East Lancs) Division had landed on 5 May, but the French *2e Division* only began disembarking on 6 May, after the attack had started. To supplement the numbers Hamilton also transferred two Anzac brigades to the Helles front and attached thirty machine guns from the RNAS Armoured Car Section. In total this gave him a force superiority of about 5,000 men.

Helles provided a distinct contrast to the country around Anzac; some observed that if were not for the war it might have been a nice place for a country walk. Private Cecil Malthus, Canterbury Battalion, NZEF, wrote:

'The country at Helles was in marked contrast to the savage ravines of Anzac. It was quite pretty and open, with fruit trees, olive and mulberry, elms, crops, streams, fields of poppies, lupins and daisies, old towers, cottages and wells. The roads were alive with traffic, including numbers of picturesque French and African troops, strapping Senegalese and colonial Zouaves with their broad red baggy trousers.'[8]

In the *History of the East Lancashire Royal Engineers*, the author, who was in the 42nd Divisional Signal Company, described the area as

'... a mass of bloom, and the air fragrant with the homely smell of lavender, wild thyme and other wild flowers more or less familiar. The linesmen often wandered knee-deep in the luxurious vegetation, fields of poppies, yellow and scarlet marsh mallows, cornflowers, clover and young maize, whilst the tree crossings were held up by the walnut, fig, mulberry or olive tree.

Wild life was plentiful, chiefly represented by numerous small birds, hares, tortoises, partridges, snakes, lizards and so forth, not forgetting a multitude of frogs. On a few occasions eagles, evidently from their eyries on distant Asiatic mountains, flew majestically over the Peninsula, surveying the invading army with distant curiosity.'

The battalions from the 42nd Division were split up for a period of acclimatisation, attached to the regulars of the 29th Division. The East Lancs men were not as well equipped as the regulars, but soon adapted. Lieutenant Robert Butcher, 5/LF, explained:

'It may be of antiquarian interest to note that the regiment took to the Peninsula the long rifle, the leather bandolier and belt with pouches, separate haversack and water bottle (and general Christmas tree effect), helmet (thrown away the first time in action – a number, however, subsequently recovered for protection from the sun) and knitted cap, different to the orthodox soft service dress cap. It was frequently impossible to know whether figures at a distance were British or Turkish because of the similarities of the knitted cap to the enemy's head-dress, and casualties were thus caused to friendly troops and so on.'

Lord Kitchener wrote to Hamilton on 4 May: *I hope the 5th will see you sufficiently reinforced to push on to Achi Baba at least, as time will enable the Turks to bring reinforcements and make unpleasant preparations for you.*[9] Hamilton's focus was to exploit the perceived Turkish weakness following the costly counter attacks; however, there was a serious lack of intelligence on the strength and the defensive positions of the Turks.

Hamilton suggested a night attack, but Hunter-Weston thought the risks were too high due to the shortage of officers, unfamiliarity with the terrain and the limited artillery support that could be provided in darkness. Hunter-Weston's daylight plan was agreed, although in reality this was little more than a replay of the first battle. After an artillery bombardment to soften up the Turks, the infantry would advance. The 29th Division would attack on the left flank and the centre, where they were supported by 2 (Naval) Brigade, and the French on the right. Little appears to have

Lieutenant General
Sir Ian Hamilton,
GOC Mediterranean
Expeditionary Force.

been learnt from the first battle. The Allies were not totally clear where the Turkish positions were, including their gun positions, and once again the orders arrived late on and so the infantry had little time to prepare. The Turks themselves had now been reinforced and had strengthened their defences around Krithia and along the spurs that run from the village. In this area the Turks had nine battalions from a mix of regiments from the 5th, 7th, 9th, 10th and 15th Divisions, and were supported by several field artillery batteries and at least one howitzer battery. The Turks had also been frantically digging trenches across the Helles front in anticipation of another attack and, whilst these works were far from complete, they could rely upon their snipers, concealed machine guns and hidden artillery batteries. Additional machine guns were added to the defence, manned by German naval crews from the cruiser SMS *Breslau*.

Even though this was a full-scale attack by some 25,000 British and French soldiers, supported by ninety-five guns, the shells (of which there was a woeful lack) would have little impact due to the fact that the Turkish positions were largely unknown. The weakened 29th Division, supported by newly landed 125 Brigade (42nd Division) and 29 (Indian) Brigade, would form the left of the line from Gully Ravine to the southeast edge of Krithia. The French, with their recently landed *2e Division* together with the attached British 2 (Naval) Brigade, were to attack the high ridge running north and south above Kereves Dere. This was key ground, whose capture would afford the best chance for the 29th Division's attack. In reserve Hamilton kept back 2 (Australian) Brigade, the New Zealand Infantry Brigade and 1 (Naval) Brigade, which formed a 'Composite Division'.

The attack would begin with a general advance of nearly two kilometres, at which point the British line would pivot in the area where Masnou's *1er Division* would be advancing towards the top of Kereves Spur. Krithia would be captured from the west of the village (from Gully and Fir Tree Spur). Once captured, the advance would begin on Achi Baba. This was a detailed and complicated plan, with three different key movements, each reliant on the others for success. The terrain was also challenging, as those who have been there will know. Whilst Helles, deceptively, looks flat and featureless, it is a complex landscape of spurs, nullahs and woodland.

The Second Battle of Krithia began on 6 May. A thirty-minute bombardment began at 10.30 a.m. and stopped promptly at 11.00 a.m., signalling the infantry advance. The French *1er Division* was over forty minutes late because of confusion over the role of 2 (Naval) Brigade and the frontage that they were going to attack. When they did advance

Above: Part of Lord
Rochdale's Lancashire
Fusilier Brigade being
shuttled ashore.
Right: 1/6 Lancashire
Fusiliers about to be
landed at Cape Helles.

it started well. *Brigade Métropolitaine* on the right encountered light
opposition until it reached the high ground overlooking Kereves Dere,
where its advance was stopped. In the French centre and left the situation
was similar for the *2e Brigade Mixte Coloniale*. As the French pushed
their advance further up Kereves Spur, resistance stiffened. The Turkish
defence here was bolstered by the German Naval Shore Detachment,
detached crewmen of SMS *Goeben* and SMS *Breslau*.

Lieutenant Wilhelm Boltz, who commanded these machine gun
sections, was in the front line with the 7th Division, described bringing
the French attack to a bloody halt:

'In thick columns, always fifty to sixty men all bunched-up,
they were death-defying in their advance, offering the Turkish
artillery and our machine guns an easy target. In rows they were
mowed down, but more and more columns were detailed to storm
forward. When our machine guns had completely expended all
their ammunition, the crews took rifles from dead Turkish soldiers

and continued to fire at them. It was not until 17.00 hours that the attack was halted. The enemy must have had tremendous losses on this day. The red trousers and red caps of the French offered excellent targets.'[10]

Even 2 (Naval) Brigade, with 1/LF attached, could not make much difference to the outcome, although they did push on a little further than the French and dug in. There was still confusion with the orders, so the Lancashire Fusiliers with Anson, Howe and Hood battalions dug in. Their right flank was exposed when the failed French effort, made worse by the loss of their commanding officer, resulted in a withdrawal. Ordinary Seaman Joseph Murray, Hood Battalion, recalled the moment he reached a ruined farmhouse, later known as the White House.

'There's no sign of the French. It was a beautiful morning. We got to a farmhouse, what was left of it, knocked about but serviceable. We were lying alongside the corner of a vineyard, a bush hedge, 3 or 4 feet high, a little ditch on the side. We started numbering. There must have been at least 50–60 men there. Then we were told to swing round behind the house and move forward. We found ourselves alongside another hedge of the vineyard. There was a big gap, about twelve feet wide, it looked like the roadway into the farm house. We lay there for a little then we were told to bear left, we were at the junction between the French and the British and we tried to keep connection with both flanks. We kept losing so many men that we couldn't do it. We could never locate these snipers. There were no trenches; it was open fighting. We had to rush along the front of the house and go through this gap. Only four people got through, we had to climb over the dead and the wounded. We got about ten yards in front, and down we went. The bullets were hitting the sand, spraying us – you were spitting it out of your mouth.'[11]

It was a bad day for Hood Battalion, which lost half its strength, including its CO, Lieutenant Colonel Arnold Quilter. Whilst several hundred metres of ground had been taken, the pivot point had not been reached and the white minaret of the village mosque was still some way off. The British attack on the left flank and centre stalled after advances of little more than 300 metres. The assault fell short of expectations and no objectives were reached during the first day of battle.

The British war correspondent, Ellis Ashmead-Bartlett, observed the battle and reported:

*'One of the most remarkable battles ever fought. Almost every detail could be followed with the naked eye. It was a battle of the old fashioned type, being chiefly conducted by the commanders from what they could see with their own eyes.'*[12]

He later wrote in this book *Uncensored Dardanelles* that *the whole scene resembled more an old-fashioned field day at Aldershot than a modern battle.*

The 29th Division's casualties had not been as heavy as the French, and so it was decided to continue the attack on the morning of 7 May. The plan was amended to remove the need to wait for the French to secure the pivotal point, but instead advance directly onto Krithia. Short of shells, only a desultory bombardment lasting fifteen minutes could be afforded, so ineffectual that no one really noticed it. Against unallocated targets its effectiveness was doubtful in any case and did little to support the renewed infantry attack at 10.00 a.m. The same concealed Turkish machine guns positions repeated their performance of 6 May.

On the left flank two ships, with the aid of a balloon ship, supplemented the barrage by shelling the machine gun post above Y Beach. The plan was that when the naval bombardment lifted, 5/LF of Lord Rochdale's 125 (Lancashire Fusilier) Brigade was to seize the machine gun post

**End of the line. The trench occupied by 1/5 Lancashire Fusiliers on 7 May, opening out onto a cliff.**

48

and once this had been successfully accomplished the remainder of the brigade was then to advance along the coast to capture Yazy Tepe, which was over two miles to the northeast. To make its attack the leading battalion had to move forward from its position in the support trenches to the front line, but this was fraught with difficulty due to the lack of communication trenches and thick scrub in the area that made forward movement in extended line difficult. The battalion came under fire almost immediately; even though some attempted to move forward along the cliff face, Turkish fire was too heavy.

George Bigwood's *Lancashire Territorials in Gallipoli* explains the situation that faced Lieutenant Colonel James Isherwood, the CO of 5/LF.

'The attack opened with a terrific fusillade at the stipulated time and developed rapidly, but at the end of four hours' hard combat no ground had been won. The intervening space between our trenches and those of the enemy was simply raked with machine-gun and rifle fire. Nothing could live above ground, and there was no evidence of life anywhere, except in the flight of whistling bullets. The only place offering any degree of safety was close under the traverse of the trench. But to take shelter here would not take Krithia.

Isherwood decided that even at great sacrifice a movement against the enemy's position must be made, and simultaneously he and Major Wood, the adjutant, leapt over the parapet of the trench and called the men to follow them across the lead-stormed terrain. Isherwood never doubted that where he led his men would follow, but the prospect of certain death in advancing over ground already covered with their own dead and wounded and a larger number of the enemy might, he thought, lead to some hesitancy. But the Bury men were not prepared to shelter all day behind earthworks.

The dry "Forward, my lads", is dimly heard above the rattle of musketry, and the men involuntarily raise a shout as they stumble among the dead bodies in the line of advance and fall into the advanced trenches, perspiring, breathless, and with an uneasy feeling that they cannot have faced that murderous fire unscathed. They had never before been so near the jaws of death. But all the men who began that fifty yards' rush (it seemed an endless journey) did not gain the trenches. Some lay in the open, wounded and afraid to move for fear of drawing the enemy's fire; others lay dead, their hands still grasping tightly their rifles, and wearing the grim, painful frown on their faces, like men who had fallen in the act of closing with the enemy.'

**Lieutenant Colonel Isherwood, Major Wood and officers after the attack.**

Even with the support of the Inniskillings and KOSB, no progress could be made and the Turkish front line trenches remained out of reach. The first action of the 5/LF on 7 May had cost nearly 200 men dead and wounded. Isherwood stated that *I think we were fortunate to escape so lightly, considering the heavy fire we had to go through. Several regular officers from France said that it was a picnic there compared with what we had here on that day.*

Elsewhere it was a similar story, with a few notable exceptions. Opposite Fir Tree Wood the 5/RS, and on Kereves Spur part of the French *2e Division*, did succeed in making limited advances. But the failure of the line on either side to conform left these forces isolated, forcing a withdrawal to the positions from which they had begun. But this would not be the end of the attack and a third day of fighting was planned.

With little change in the plan, Hamilton decided to renew the attack. A daylight assault began at 10.30 a.m. on 8 May against the same concealed trenches, machine guns and snipers. Whilst this might sound like madness, Hamilton was well aware that as each day passed the Turks grew stronger; a breakthrough was needed, not another defeat. Effective Turkish resistance held up 88 Brigade's advance on Fir Tree Spur, as did heavy fire against 125 Brigade and the RND brigade. 87 Brigade was held up by a machine gun near Y Beach on Gully Spur. On the right flank the French *1er Division* was still held up by Kereves Dere and their *2e Division* on Kereves Spur.

With 88 Brigade's attack stalled, the New Zealand Brigade was the first of the Anzac brigades to be called into action. They were moved up into the line at Fir Tree Spur and into an attack that was carried out amongst some confusion. In preparation for the attack, earlier that morning the brigade had been moved forward in broad daylight across open ground. Private Cecil Malthus, Canterbury Battalion, New Zealand Brigade, wrote:

> '"New Zealanders prepare to advance!" Where on earth were the enemy and what were our objectives? Hastily we threw off our packs and piled them in heaps – which were promptly looted by the Irishmen – and it was only in the act of springing over the parapet that we were told of another line of British still lying a hundred yards ahead of us. We sprinted the distance all abreast, in fine style, and thanks to our smartness it was only in the last few yards that the enemy woke up and loosed his fire. The tragedy of it was that from that moment he remained awake, and we were left with the certainty, in our next advance, of having to face a living stream of lead. This front line was held by men of the Worcester Regiment. They were even more dirty and woebegone than the Irishmen. They assured us it was madness to think of advancing, which certainly seemed to be dead right.'[13]

The New Zealanders reached the British front line and now readied themselves for the assault on the strongly held Turkish positions. The best part of nine Turkish battalions held Fir Tree Wood spur. The Wellington Battalion was on the left, nearest Gully Ravine, the Auckland in the centre and Canterbury on the right, bordering Krithia Nullah.

> 'For 200 yards we sprinted, thinking oddly how beautiful the poppies and daisies were, then from sheer exhaustion we rushed to ground in a slight depression and lay there panting. We had kept about ten yards apart, but soon the spaces were filled by those of our mates who managed to get so far. Now the storm was let loose, and increased every moment in fury, until a splashing, spurting shower of lead was falling like rain on a pond. Hugging the ground in frantic terror we began to dig blindly with our puny entrenching tools, but soon the four men nearest me were lying, one dead, two with broken legs, and the other badly wounded in the shoulder. A sledgehammer blow on the foot made me turn with a feeling of positive relief that I had met my fate, but it was a mere graze and hardly bled. Another bullet passed through my

coat, and a third ripped along two feet of my rifle sling. Then the wounded man on my right got a bullet through the head that ended his troubles. And still, without remission, the air was full of hissing bullets and screaming shells.'[14]

Unsupported, the New Zealanders had been cut to pieces, with little more than another 200 metres of ground gained. The nearest Turkish trench was still 450 metres in front; but it was the fire from Fir Tree Wood in the centre that proved so devastating to the Auckland Battalion and had stunted their advance, exposing the flanks of both the Wellington and Canterbury battalions.

By 3.00 p.m. the attack had clearly failed; but Hamilton had not given up and decided to make one last effort, ordering the whole line to attack again at 5.30 p.m. after a short naval bombardment. The Canterburys managed to advance another 200 metres on the right in what was a more coordinated advance, with less deadly Turkish fire. For the Aucklanders on their left, Fir Tree Wood and the large open field, covered in white daisies and red poppies, in front of it, proved deadly. Even with the support of the Otago men, the Aucklanders could not get any further, all advances being scythed down by deadly accurate machine-gun and rifle fire. The successful advance of the Wellingtons eventually assisted the Auckland and Otago battalions, who were able to advance again at dusk, enabling them to cross the Daisy Field and reach the edge of Fir

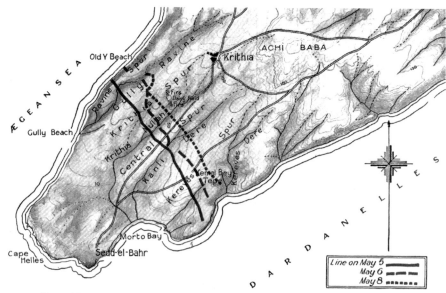

**Second Battle of Krithia – 6–8 May.**

Tree Wood. On the New Zealanders' right flank, the Australian Brigade was called forward to reinforce this final effort.

The objective for the Australians in this last push forward was simply described in the orders as *the ridge beyond Krithia*. No map coordinates were given. The 6/AIF (Australian Imperial Force) were on the left, in contact with the New Zealanders, 7/AIF on the right. Both 5/AIF and 8/AIF were deployed in support. Major Cass, the brigade major of 2 (Australian) Brigade, later recalled that the *old fool* Major General Archibald Paris, commander of the 'Composite Division', asked him

'... if we had bands and colours with us, remarking that they were to move forward with colours waving, and bands playing, and bayonets fixed, in order to drive the Turks from their position. As much use of the bayonet as possible was to be made in order to fully impress on the Turks that they had to go.'

Paris was, unfortunately, disappointed to learn that the Australians had no musical instruments with them.

Advancing in artillery formation, they were almost immediately showered with shrapnel but, luckily this time, it looked as if the Turkish gunners had poorly set the shells' fuses, as many burst close to the ground and inflicted few casualties. But casualties did mount the further they advanced; soon rifle and machine-gun fire was encountered. The Australians then reached what was later known as 'Tommies' Trench'. This had been dug two days earlier by the Lancashire Fusiliers and Drake Battalion, a surprise to the Australians, who had been taking increasing casualties over the last kilometre of ground and now realised that they had not even reached the British front line. There was no time to rest; the Brigade commander, Lieutenant Colonel James McCay urged his men out of this trench with the cry, "Now then Australians! Which of you men are Australian? Come on, Australians!" Private Harry Kelly, 7/AIF, described what happened next.

'Now casualties began in dozens and men could be seen falling everywhere and I do not think that there were many among us who expected to come out of the Hell alive. However, we pushed on and when I had almost reached the end of the advance [about 500 yards in front of Tommies' Trench] I got a violent smack in the left shoulder that knocked me over.'

Severely wounded, Kelly managed to get back after nightfall. Evacuated from Gallipoli, after medical treatment in Egypt he was eventually returned to Australia and discharged due to his wound.

'Leaving Tommy's [sic] Trench. The charge of 2 (Australian) Brigade'. McCay is on the parapet, spurring on his brigade (Charles Wheeler, 1927).

Major George Adams, 1/LF, witnessed the Australians being brought to a standstill about 200 metres in front of Tommies' Trench and crossed the Krithia Nullah with a company to support them. Adams reported to the Australian commander, Lieutenant Colonel McCay, who ordered the Lancashire Fusiliers into Tommies' Trench. Finding it overcrowded and *in a very disturbed state*, Adams decided to retire and formed a support line just behind it. The Australians tried to get forward again, advancing in short rushes, but only managed to gain another hundred metres at best.

Lieutenant Colonel (Temp Brigadier General) James McCay.

Although the Turkish lines were still 200 metres further on, Turkish skirmishers had come forward and, firing from concealed positions, stalled the Australian advance. A hailstorm of fire met anyone trying to go forward and so the decision was made to wait until nightfall, which was near, for any further attack. Those surviving this last assault paired up to scrape foxholes in the ground, one digging, and the other providing covering fire until the hole was deep enough. Many of these men had not even seen a Turk as the rough nature of the ground, its nullahs, undulations and clumps of trees, scrub and grass, made the area perfect for defence. Digging lying down was not easy:

'This was a difficult task and, combined with the groaning, screaming, and especially the mournful cries of the Turks, had a depressing effect upon all. Food and water were both short, but water was the most needed. Some managed to crawl down to the nullah. Drummer Bolton was one of the adventuresome kind. He came back with thirteen bottles [of it], only to fall by a Turkish bullet as he reached the brink of his dugout.'[15]

Private Robert Bolton, 1/LF, is listed on the Helles Memorial to the Missing. After surviving the mayhem of the landings on 25 April and both battles of Krithia, another to lose his life was Major Adams himself, ironically killed in a six-foot deep dugout by a stray bullet. Adams' body was carried down to the beach and buried in Lancashire Landing Cemetery. The Lancashire Fusiliers Annual states that

'...after the rest camp was reached the men went to the cemetery and planted his grave, which looks down upon Lancashire Landing, with iris. It was the only tribute these gallant soldiers could make; but it was one that came from the heart, one of affectionate respect.'

In the two weeks since the landing the Lancashire Fusiliers had suffered eighteen officer and 653 other rank casualties; only nine officers and 284 other ranks, including medical and transport men, remained. This situation was not unusual amongst the other battalions, now a fraction of their former size.

Casualties were also heavy amongst the Australians, especially officers. 2 (Australian) Brigade started the battle with 2,900 men but twenty-four hours later had suffered more than 1,000 casualties. Lieutenant Colonel McCay and Major Cass were wounded, also Lieutenant Colonel Walter McNicoll, commanding 6/AIF. Lieutenant Colonel Robert Gartside, 8/AIF, temporarily commanding 7/AIF was killed. Mrs Gartside received many letters of sympathy in connection with the death of her husband, including this tribute:

'Though no message from anyone can help you in the great sorrow that has come upon you by your husband's death, yet I feel I must write to tell you that he died as he would have wished, leading his battalion into battle. He was in command of the 7th Battalion, and on Saturday, 8th, we were ordered to advance. The 6th and 7th went forward first; I was near the 7th, and saw your husband, leading his men, brave man that he always was. There was a hail of shrapnel and bullets, and a little later Colonel McNicoll, of the 6th, was shot through the body, and my dear friend, your husband, was shot through the head, and died in a little while. You have this at least, the proud memory of a husband who died for his country in the forefront of the fight, fearless, doing his duty as always. For thirty years, I have known and loved Robert Gartside; I mourn for my lost friend, but I am proud of the brave soldier who gladly gave his life for his country; whom I trusted, whom his men had fullest faith in, and whose example on that fiery afternoon took his battalion forward with a dashing courage that every soldier envies who knows of it.'

The French on the right flank had made brave efforts to advance during 7 and 8 May, based on a simultaneous attack by both the *1er Division* and Simonin's brigade from the *2e Division*.

'At 6 p.m., with drums beating and bugles sounding, the whole French line surged forwards in a frenzy of enthusiasm. The red and blue uniforms of the French troops show up with terrible clearness and for a moment, to those watching in the rear, it seemed as if the whole spur, including the 'pivotal point' on the left flank, had at last been captured. But a minute later the Turks covered the ridge with high explosive shells. The trial was too severe. The left and centre recoiled ...'[16]

Initially it had appeared that the whole of Kereves Spur was carried; however, the Turkish gunners laid down such an accurate fire that it

An artist's interpretation of French colonial troops charging the heights.

AN ATTACK ON THE TURKS BY THE 'SINGALESE'

wrought havoc amongst the leading Senegalese tirailleurs, who were forced to retreat. Both General d'Amade and General Simonin, present in person, rallied the Senegalese and, with more support, took the fight back to the Turks. Simonin's *4e Brigade Mixte Coloniale* were within a hundred metres of reaching the top of the spur but ran out of energy, manpower and daylight to complete the attack. Simonin's brigade had only been ashore a day and were so damaged that they had to be removed from the line. In the French centre, Colonel Ruef's *2e Brigade Coloniale* captured the defences known as the Bouchet, a redoubt that had blocked the path on to the ninety metre contour line. On the right, General Vandenberg's *1e Brigade Métropolitaine* reached the southern face of Kereves Dere, an advance of over a kilometre, before being pushed back by counter attacks. It had been a day of mixed fortunes for the French, in what concluded their first battle of Kereves Dere.

Although an advance in some places of around 500 metres was made and retained, despite fierce counter-attacks, Hamilton, was still putting a brave face on a dire outcome, which continued to deny him Krithia and Achi Baba.

'This may not seem very much, but actually more had been won than at first meets the eye. The German leaders were quick to realise the fact. From nightfall till dawn on the 9th–10th efforts were made everywhere to push us back. An especially heavy attack was made upon the French, supported by a hot cannonade and culminating in a violent hand-to-hand conflict in front of the Brigade Simonin. Everywhere the assailants were repulsed and now for the first time I felt that we had planted a fairly firm foothold upon the point of the Gallipoli Peninsula.'

Despite exceptional bravery and self-sacrifice, the Second Battle of Krithia cost some 6,000 casualties. Once again reinforcements would be urgently needed. The French had lost over 12,000 men since the landing, whilst the 29th Division alone had lost 10,000 men. Lessons needed to be learnt, otherwise any subsequent attack using the same tactics would likely end up in failure and heavy casualties. Less haste would be needed to give the infantry more time to prepare. Orders needed to be less complex and the objectives defined clearly. Knowledge of the strength of the Turks and more importantly their defensive positions would be vital to the effectiveness of the bombardment. With the exception of the French front, the Turkish defensive positions were largely unknown and thus no artillery bombardment, regardless of weight, was going to be successful.

On the evening of 8 May Hamilton wrote to Lord Kitchener: *The result of the operation has been failure, as my object remained unachieved. The fortifications and their machine guns were too scientific and too strongly held to be rushed, although I had every available man in today.*[17]

The Allies had been ashore a fortnight now and, apart from wrestling a slightly firmer footing from the Turks, they had little else to show from these costly daylight frontal attacks. The stubborn Turkish defence had been a complete shock. The poor performing Ottoman army, as witnessed during the Balkan Wars, had been transformed into an organised, well-disciplined and tenacious fighting force that had frustrated and delayed the landings and had now stopped all Allied attempts to take Krithia and Achi Baba. Trenches were deepened, saps extended forward and communication trenches dug to help connect up this new chessboard of a battlefield. On the beaches wooden piers and stone jetties were constructed to aid the landing of stores and troops, whilst roads were constructed along the artery of nullahs and along the Aegean cliffs towards the Turks. The Turks carried out similar work, each side improving everything from their fields of fire to the logistical veins that fed and supplied the fighting soldiers in the front lines.

The British were desperately short of artillery ammunition and re-supply was vital. By 22 May it became so critical to the extent that GHQ ordered that a daily scale would be fixed for each calibre of gun. The 18 pdrs, 60 pdrs, 4.5-inch howitzers and 6-inch howitzers were rationed to only two rounds per gun. The naval 12 pdrs appeared to have had plenty of ammunition, so these were handed over to the Royal Artillery and proved invaluable in the forthcoming Third Battle of Krithia.

A chaplain from the Manchester Brigade wrote at this time:

'The country here is gorgeous. Wild flowers of exquisite beauty, moorland and streams, and sea and trees, as beautiful as one could wish for, and amongst it all men killing each other. I buried one of the 6th Manchesters yesterday. He was shot through the head and died just as he was going to the ambulance station. There I buried him in one of those beautiful fields. He was only a lad, and in his pocket was a letter to his sister. There are no coffins; the body was just laid in the graves as he died. I put some of those exquisite flowers in his hands, and there he lies in his soldier's grave.'

In a letter dated 10 May, a clear and graphic description is given of the positions and conditions under which the men fought and lived:

'I am still alive and in wonderful spirits – my knuckles barked by digging myself in at night. We made about 1,000 yards advance on the 8th inst., but with a big loss comparatively. An Australian Brigade did a magnificent advance, but omitted to fire very much, and so they suffered heavily; but with people being biffed all round one every minute one does not notice it much. Bishop (the CO) and I and the Adjutant live together in a hole by the firing line, and they bagged the Adjutant and the Sergeant Major both in one afternoon; but the former will be all right in a few days. The Peninsula ends for the last seven miles in a long slope with countless trenches and defences built on it, row after row, so before we get to the first stage and get to the main ridge guarding the point we have a long, costly and uphill bit of work. The Turks have countless snipers who hide in pits and trees and we lose men every few minutes; yet the men are strangely callous, and unless the sniping is very bad potter about like rabbits at their burrows. My poor old Company has been very much knocked about, but they are cheery as anything. Of course getting no regular sleep is very trying; one can't get out to wash or anything, and I haven't washed, shaved, or changed my clothes for ages. This is our eighteenth day in the firing line trenches. The dead Turks are rather trying, too. They snipe our burying parties and stretcher bearers so we can't get them all buried and the sun is very hot. All our kit has gone back to Alexandria in the 'Caledonia' with the wounded, so I have no kit and no change of clothes. There is a cursed sniper we have nicknamed Peter, who has a rifle or automatic gun trained on our burrow entrance. The Navy are most eulogistic about us, and send us tobacco and gifts.

We have a fight most days and every night; but never very serious, unless we make a strong advance. What I miss most is water. I can't wash or clean my teeth because once in the dark the whole plain zips with stray bullets. Of course one has to go about among them and trust to luck; but I can't ask anyone to bring up more than just drinking water. I have now got so hardened and tired that I can sleep through quite a large sized battle raging overhead, and unless a shell bursts very close I hardly notice it. The wounded are the most nerve racking people to put up with, poor fellow, one can't get them away for a day or so, the fire is so hot.'

It is interesting to note a story, related in the 42nd (East Lancashire) Division's history, about an incident during the lull in the fighting after 8 May. During this respite in battle it was a common sight to see bathing parties swimming off Lancashire Landing or Gully Beach, where there was some cover from the Turks, whilst others chanced their luck by swimming in Morto Bay in the French sector.

> 'General Bailloud informed General Douglas that his men were always shelled when bathing in Morto Bay until, soon after the arrival of the 52nd Division, a kilted battalion went down to bathe, and from that day the firing ceased. He concluded that the Turks were under the impression that the wearers of 'skirts' must be women, and, being of a gallant disposition, they refrained from shelling the bathers.'

The offensive spirit had to be maintained. During the night of 12 May, in a surprise attack, 6/Gurkhas pushed the line forward about 500 metres, capturing an important redoubt near Y Beach that had thwarted previous advances. This placed the British in a slightly better position for renewing the advance on this flank. Similarly, a series of four modest tactical night advances on 18, 23, 24 and 27 May resulted in the Allied line moving forward almost a kilometre with little loss, barely fifty casualties in all; quite a contrast to the 6,000 casualties paid for a similar distance during the last battle of Krithia.

During the night of 30 May *Le Fortin Le Gouez* was captured by a legionnaire battalion of *Régiment étranger* in another surprise attack. One assault was led by Captain James Waddell, who conducted the decisive bayonet charge that drove the Turks from the redoubt. Casualties were heavy as the legionnaire losses were twenty-one killed and fifty-three wounded.

Waddell was born in New Zealand; after leaving the British Army he joined the *Régiment étranger* as a second lieutenant in 1900. He was wounded on 21 July 1915; by the time that he retired as a lieutenant colonel he had served in Algeria, Morocco, Tunisia, Indochina, the Balkans and France. The *Régiment étranger* was an interesting unit, with many foreign volunteers, including British and Germans. In late July, to add to the international mix of the Allies, a battalion of Hellenic volunteers landed at Helles. It was nicknamed the Greek Legion and was commanded by Major Pantelis Karasevdas, a Greek

**Captain James Waddell, Foreign Legion.**

Olympic shooting champion at the 1896 Summer Olympics (it should be recalled that Greece was exercising a benevolent neutrality at this stage in the war).

The Allied line was thus moved closer to the Turks and on average less than 150 metres separated the two, thus reducing the large width of ground over which the men had had to advance during the last battle and which had contributed to needless casualties. Communication trenches were dug, sniper posts established and machine guns positioned; but whilst this all contributed to improving the defensive positions, it also played to Hamilton's fears of Gallipoli degenerating into a long and drawn out Western Front style affair. Open warfare had now given way to solidifying trench lines, meaning battles would soon be costlier in lives, munitions and resources for both sides.

Private Horace Bruckshaw RMLI, described this risky, gradual movement of the line forward:

'After dark [28 May] our supports made an advance through our line and carried on a distance of 200 yards in front of us. Arrived there, they immediately dug themselves in. I do not think that the Turks realized that an advance had been made until the chaps were in comparative safety. The 1/5 Manchesters who were on our left made an advance at the same time, but owing to some misunderstanding they only advanced 100 yards. This left a big gap between the two battalions with a very dangerous ravine in the space [between them]. Our company, being now in supports had to make our way up the ravine and dig a trench to connect up the two units. The Turks had now tumbled to the game and we had a devil of a warm time. It simply rained bullets and we dug until we got fairly exhausted. We had a fair number of casualties over the job. As soon as we had finished we got our heads down. I slept on until 12 o'clock noon. The enemy have started shelling us this morning. We spent the afternoon improving the trenches and dodging snipers, which are always bothering us. At 11pm the 1/5 Manchesters made another advance of 100 yards to make the line straight. The Turks however were not to be caught napping again and the advance was made under heavy fire. They still left a gap of about 50 yards between us, so we had to go and sap a trench between us. We got back to our own trench at daybreak fairly tired out.'[18]

On 24 May Captain Norman Dewhurst MC of the Munsters found himself in the line at Gully Ravine, relieving the 6/Gurkhas from the front line. He described the horrific scene that met him.

'There was a terrible smell all around coming from decaying bodies, and the parapet were I got my machine guns behind was partly built from piled bodies of the fallen, both ours and Turks. It was a hectic night, there was continuous firing from both sides with all arms. We also tried to make a start at clearing up the area of dead bodies but the barbs of the grapnel irons pulled out from the decomposing flesh. So they lay there in No Man's Land, covered with thousands of green flies as big as bumble bees. When disturbed these flies rose in swarms and were so thick around us that we had to eat with a cover over our heads to avoid swallowing them. We were in the sector for seventy-two hours, the Turkish line was only forty yards away and, what with the smell, the continual firing and the knowledge that it was a sticky place to be holding, we got no sleep at all during that period.'[19]

On the same day, 24 May, Hunter-Weston was promoted to lieutenant general and given command of the newly created VIII Corps, formed out of the 29th, 42nd and Royal Naval divisions. Major General Sir Beauvoir de Lisle arrived to take over the 29th Division; whilst General Henri Gouraud (who had fought an energetic campaign in the Argonne Forest in the winter of 1914–15) took over supreme command of the

**Hunter-Weston emerging from his HQ dugout on Hunter-Weston Hill.**

French forces from the weary and pessimistic General d'Amade, who was recalled to France. Gouraud immediately set about improving the French positions, repositioning badly placed machine guns, narrowing trenches and reducing the number of men in the front line, all lessons learned from his experience on the Western Front. He also requested (and received) two squadrons of aircraft, one fighter, one bomber, to gain air superiority over the Turks. Both commanders, Hunter-Weston and Gouraud, were natural thrusters and keen to launch another major attack, to which Hamilton finally agreed on 31 May.

Whilst the land battles were going on, the Allied navies were causing havoc to Turkish shipping in the shape of submarine warfare. British submarines had been running the gauntlet of the Dardanelles for some time and before the Gallipoli campaign got under way. The first naval VC, which also happened to be the first ever submariner VC, was awarded to Lieutenant Commander Norman Holbrook, who took the British submarine *B11* up the Straits, through the minefields and sank the Ottoman battleship *Messudieh* on 13 December 1914.

Submarine activity increased with the opening of the campaign. Lieutenant Commander Edward Boyle's *E14* successfully operated in the Sea of Marmara for three weeks, from the end of April, sinking two gunboats and two transports, the most important of which was an ex-White Star liner that had been carrying a battery of artillery and 6,000 Ottoman troops. Boyle was also awarded the VC. The loss of the French submarine *Joule,* which was sunk on 1 May with all hands, did not discourage Lieutenant Commander Martin Nasmith in *E11*, who navigated successfully through the Dardanelles on 19 May. Nasmith's ensuing patrol, which lasted two and a half weeks, became a wild rampage among Turkish shipping in the Sea of Marmara, culminating on 25 May when Nasmith entered the harbour of Constantinople itself at periscope depth and succeeded in sinking the large transport *Stamboul* just outside the Golden Horn. The effect on the Turks was electric, as the vulnerability of their capital to an attack from the sea sank home. Crowds rioted in the streets, all activity ceased on the docks, and reinforcements for the Gallipoli front were re-routed. Nasmith, too, was awarded the VC for his actions.

Before the end of the Gallipoli campaign thirteen Allied submarines took part in the Dardanelles operations and, although eight were lost, twenty-seven successful passages were recorded. Turkish losses included two battleships, a destroyer, five gunboats, eleven transports, forty-four steamers, and 148 sailing boats. Beyond the losses of ships and material, however, the effect on the Turkish supply lines was catastrophic. By the end of 1915 the Turks' dependence on tenuous land routes into the Peninsula meant that virtually all Gallipoli traffic was forced onto primitive roads along the shoreline of the Sea of Marmara or sent by a roundabout railway journey of some 600 miles.

The Allies were not alone in these limited naval successes, as both the Turks and Germans were able to create havoc in the Aegean. During the night of 13 May HMS *Goliath* was sunk in Morto Bay by two torpedoes from the torpedo boat destroyer *Muâvenet-i Millîye*. *Goliath's* commanding officer, Captain Thomas Shelford, along with 570 of her 700-strong crew were sent to the bottom with her. Then, on 25 May, HMS *Triumph* was torpedoed and sunk off Anzac by German submarine *U21*, commanded by Lieutenant Commander Otto Hersing. Two days later Hersing was to strike again, sinking HMS *Majestic* off Helles. Although losses were light amongst the crew of these two ships, it shocked the Royal Navy. De Robeck ordered the immediate withdrawal of all capital ships to the safety of Mudros Harbour. In the morning the army ashore looked out to sea and observed the end of their major naval support, inevitably adding to its low morale. The loss of two battleships in three days had a serious impact on the Gallipoli campaign, seriously reducing the amount of support the navy could offer the army.

HMS *Majestic* had taken up a position close to shore, protected by submarine nets and surrounded by a fleet of transport ships unloading supplies. It was hoped that this position would allow her to keep firing while protecting her against the submarine, which it was half-believed had been rammed on the previous day. At 6.45 a.m. this optimistic attitude was proved to be false. U-21 was spotted less than 400 metres from the ship. Moments later two torpedoes were fired through gaps in the lines of transports. Both hit the *Majestic* and in seven minutes she capsized. The loss of life was surprisingly low – it very quickly became clear that the ship was sinking, and the order to abandon ship was given. Of her crew of nearly 700, only forty-three were lost, mostly in the initial explosion but some when they became entangled in the submarine nets.

One of the official press journalists covering the campaign, Ellis Ashmead Bartlett, was aboard HMS *Majestic* at the time.

'I was aroused by men rushing by me and someone trod on, or stumbled against, my chest. This awoke me and I called out, "What's the matter?" A voice replied from somewhere, "There's a torpedo coming!" I just had time to scramble to my feet when there came a dull heavy explosion about fifteen feet forward of the shelter deck on the port side. The hit must have been very low down, as there was no shock from it to be felt on deck. The old

*Majestic* immediately gave a jerk over towards port and remained with a heavy list. Then there came a sound as if the contents of every pantry in the world had fallen at the same moment. I never before heard such a clattering, as everything loose in her tumbled about. You could tell at once she had been mortally wounded somewhere in her vitals and you felt instinctively she would not long stay afloat. The sea was crowded with men swimming about and calling for assistance. I think that many of these old reservists, who formed the majority of the crew, had forgotten how to swim, or else had lost all faith in their own powers.'[20]

Thanks to the swarms of small vessels that rushed in to try and rescue the crew the death toll was small. The great upturned hull of HMS *Majestic* would provide a grim monument just off W Beach until it disappeared during the winter storms later that year. The arrival of the U-Boats reset the equation of forces at Helles. The ships of war could no longer prowl night and day off the beaches; now they would only appear in special circumstances. Lesser ships, the destroyers, would take up much of the work of supporting the troops. Many of the troops ashore felt deserted and a little isolated after the battleships had gone.

The Admiralty deployed monitors as replacements for the capital ships; these were basically floating gun platforms, which, with their shallow draughts, were effectively immune to torpedo attacks. Once they arrived these would provide the necessary fire support for the

Farewell *Majestic*.

MEF. In fact in many ways they were an improvement, as they could deploy guns that acted more like a howitzer; but they would not arrive until August. Until that time the Allies' capital ships would only leave the safety of the protected harbour when an offensive was in progress. Land-based artillery would have to hold the ground in the meantime.

On land the Turks had used the relative calm of the rest of May to continue to fortify the slopes of Achi Baba and the ground around Krithia. Hamilton decided that another general attack was needed before the Turkish defences became impenetrable.

The night of 2 June was Lieutenant EM Lockwood's first experience of the trenches as the Hawke Battalion moved up from its rest camp to take over a section of the front line.

'I shall always remember my first night in the trenches in Gallipoli. The trenches were not by any means scientifically constructed, though they were good enough for cover. Trench boards were non-existent in those days, and sandbags hard to procure. However, considering that there was an absolute lack of, or, at any rate, great shortage of, all timber, sandbags, etc., the trenches were not to be despised as such. As soon as the outgoing troops had left us, we immediately started to look round and find good fire steps etc. for every man. Whilst I was busy doing this a message was passed down to stand to, and that the Turks were advancing against us. This was somewhat thrilling, as we had had no time to find out who our neighbours were or, indeed, our way about the line at all. We got the men standing to on the fire steps and threw up a Very light. I swore then, and still adhere to it, that some distance away I saw a line of men lying down facing us. Two or three of our officers and several of the men swore it also; but on another light being thrown up there was nothing to see. Being in the line, for the first time in an utterly unknown position, it was quite an exciting five minutes. One welcomes an attack when one knows exactly where everybody is, but I didn't even know where company headquarters was. To me it was, therefore, a distinct relief that it was a case of imagination.'[21]

Lockwood would be experiencing his first attack sooner than he probably thought.

Plans were well under way for the next assault on Krithia; and an opportunity was seen to close the gap in front by sapping forward. This eminently sensible measure threw up an example of the continued stubbornness of Hunter-Weston and his unwillingness to adapt to the grim necessities of circumstance.

**Members of Hawke Battalion, RND, in the trenches.**

Brigadier General William Marshall had been attached to 42nd Division to provide assistance to the inexperienced staff of 127 (Manchester) Brigade when he learnt the details of the proposal for the night of 2–3 June.

'A night advance was to be made on the night of 2 June and all the troops destined to carry out the attack were to dig themselves in within 200 yards of the enemy trenches. In front of the Manchester Brigade the line of the enemy trenches formed a re-entrant and, with an almost full moon, I would have preferred not to advance into this re-entrant, so I ventured to point out that the resulting casualties might be very heavy. However the orders were very explicit and had to be carried out. The result was the brigade made the advance successfully, and dug itself in all along the line within the stipulated 200 yards. Luckily the enemy fired high and the resulting casualties only amounted to fifty or sixty, nearly all being wounded cases. Hunter-Weston came down on the 3rd personally to congratulate Lee's Brigade on their successful effort; to me he said: "There you are! You see the thing has been done with no casualties". I gently murmured "Fifty" to which he retorted: "Well, that's nothing, it would have been worth doing if you had five hundred".[22]

# Chapter 4

# The Third Battle of Krithia: 4–6 June 1915

The battle plans for the next battle of Krithia were rather more realistic in the extent of the objective and more innovative; lessons had been learnt from the earlier failures. This time the objective was limited to an advance of about 750 metres only, so the notion of capturing Achi Baba was temporarily abandoned. The first step was to capture the Turkish trenches; the second was to advance a further 460 metres and dig a new trench line. There was also better intelligence of Turkish positions, some provided by aerial photography, so this helped the artillery to identify the defences to neutralise and the infantry in capturing these positions. To give the best chances of success to the infantry the width of No Man's Land was shortened by a series of night digs that sapped forward the line, bringing the jumping off point to within 230 metres of the Turks, as opposed to the previous 1,500 metres.

The Third Battle of Krithia started on a sunny but breezy 4 June, beginning at 8.00 a.m. with a systematic four hour bombardment of high explosive and shrapnel that would pause at 11.20 a.m., at which point the troops would make a *ruse de guerre*, in other words feint an advance by cheering and showing fixed bayonet, hoping to lure the Turks back into their trenches as well as getting their artillery to give away their

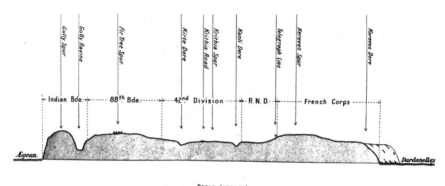

A topographical view of the lines attacked on 4 June.

positions. At 11.30 a.m. the bombardment of the Turkish front line would restart, hopefully catching the Turks manning their trenches and with counter-battery fire then suppressing their artillery. Field batteries were allotted either as 'wire-cutting batteries' or 'trench batteries' or 'approach batteries', whilst the counter-battery work was entrusted to the Royal Navy. At noon the guns would increase their range, whilst the first two lines of infantry would go over the top to capture the Turks' front line. A second wave would follow up at 12.15 p.m. to leapfrog the first and capture both second and third lines. The infantry were provided with improvised red emulation flags and shiny biscuit tin lids intended to show the artillery the infantry positions. In support of the infantry four RNAS Rolls Royce armoured cars would advance along the Krithia roads, providing supporting fire from their Maxim machine guns, and, mad as it may seem, they would drive up to the Turkish wire and by the use of grappling hooks literally tow it away. Whilst notable innovation is shown here it should be remembered we are still talking a 1915 battle here and the British Army was still near the bottom of the learning curve. Innovative yes, practical, maybe not.

The bombardment was less than effective. Although 17,000 rounds had been fired it was reported that several forward observation officers were hit during the first hour of the bombardment, limiting accurate targeting. In addition the battleships had difficulty with observation and had little effect in countering Turkish artillery fire that was pouring in to the British lines. One such position to suffer from the lack of shelling was a Turkish trench known as J.10, on Gully spur. Not only were the lines close together in this position, which caused its challenges, but the FOO had been wounded. The Lancashire Fusiliers Annual described the scene from the position of 1/LF, further over to the left of the line:

'Shells of every calibre were shrieking, moaning and humming around, over, short and in the trenches. The range of our fire trenches was so nicely gauged that in many cases the sandbags and loop-hole plates were hit direct, while one unlucky shot destroyed a machine gun and a whole team ... The guns did not cease fire at the time appointed for the 'ruse' and especially the Turkish guns made full use of the targets presented, and the rifle-fire fizzled out in a most unconvincing manner. Gun ammunition seemed by this time to have become scarce on our side, and it was evident to everyone on the spot that the preparation was a failure. About this time the armoured cars laboured up behind the 87th Brigade, but they met with such a hot reception that they very soon made off.'

**RNAS armoured cars in action.**

In one of those cars a survivor of the V Beach landings, who was on the River Clyde, Petty Officer Mechanic Geoffrey Rumming, previously a milling assistant in Wiltshire before joining the Royal Navy in 1914 and then was attached to the Royal Naval Air Service armoured car section. Highly decorated with the Conspicuous Gallantry Medal for his actions on 25 April, he had helped Sub-Lieutenant Arthur Tisdall VC in the rescue of soldiers in the water and who had been stranded on rocks under a hail of Turkish rifle fire. He had also been recommended for the Victoria Cross but was awarded the CGM instead. His bravery was repeated on 4 June, when Rumming took part in the armoured car attack and which left him seriously wounded.

Rumming was a spare driver and second machine gunner to Lieutenant the Hon. Francis McLaren. McLaren was a Liberal Member of Parliament, son of Lord Aberconway of Bodnant. Numerous MPs and their sons went to war, many paying the ultimate sacrifice, amongst them the sons of the King, the Prime Minister and the Chancellor of the Exchequer. McLauren survived Gallipoli but was killed later in the war whilst serving with the Royal Flying Corps. This attack was the first and last time that armoured cars were used on Gallipoli. Eight cars had been landed for this operation and were housed in specially prepared deep dugouts near Pink Farm. Manned by a crew of three, the cars moved off along the three roads under heavy shellfire as the infantry assaulted. Along Fir Tree Spur on the left, two cars were held up near the firing line by an unbridged trench and eventually had to return. On the middle Krithia Road, two cars could not cross a newly constructed bridge near the front line and in their attempt they partly ditched and came under shell fire. It was only on the right road that the cars reached the Turkish front line, but here again they were held up, this time by a high stone-faced parapet. When it became clear that the cars could do nothing to help the advance, they were withdrawn. Three officers were wounded. Rumming, who took a bad wound to the head, would later be discharged due to epilepsy, dying from his wounds in 1917. Although the cars had suffered minor damage, they could do no more in these conditions. Cars were not designed for trench warfare in terrain like Gallipoli's, so they were evacuated. The desert was to prove to be their ideal operating theatre.

From left to right the Allied troops were deployed as follows: 29 Indian Brigade would attack along Gully Spur; the 29th Division would attack the other side of Gully Ravine on Fir Tree Spur; the 42nd Division would attack astride Krithia Nullah; 2 (Naval) Brigade would attack up Achi Baba Nullah and Krithia Spur, and both French divisions would attack along Kereves Spur. Combined, Hamilton had 30,000 men in the assault, supported by additional artillery in the form of six French quick-firing 75mm batteries. Although this was the highest number of men ever allotted to a Helles attack, they were opposed by a much

**RNAS armoured cars in dugouts after the battle.**

**Part of the Manchester Brigade in Krithia Nullah.**

strengthened Turkish line that fielded similar numbers in well-prepared positions and with eighty-six guns in support.

Lieutenant W Horridge, 5/LF, who was positioned towards the middle of the British line noted that, *when the fire ceased, as ordered, at 11.20, a hail of Turkish bullets instantly swept over the trenches, giving a vivid impression of what might have been expected had an assault at this moment been made.* There was only hope now that the renewed bombardment would dampen this surprise response. As noon approached, the line made its advance in the face of an incredible fire, for the Turks were evidently waiting for the attack. In face of this murderous fire the first Turkish trench was captured, despite well-sited Turkish machine guns that scythed their way through the advancing ranks.

Brigadier General Noel Lee's 127 (Manchester) Brigade had an important part to play in the middle of the line in their advance astride the Krithia Road. Nearest to the Nullah were the 6/Manchesters in Ardwick Green Trench, with the 8/Manchesters to their right, jutting up to the Krithia Road. Across the other side of the road were the 5/Manchesters and on the extreme right, to the boundary with the RND at Achi Baba Nullah, were the 7/Manchesters. When they left the relative safety of their trenches at noon the Turks were waiting.

Private Ridley Sheldon, 6/Manchesters:

'The fellows in the trenches leaped over the parapet and away they went. It was their work to cut the barbed wire entanglement, if necessity required it, bayonet any resisting forces and take the next line of trenches. The enemy's fire was terrific in the extreme and most deadly in its effect and our men went down before it like chaff before the wind.'

Despite Turkish resistance, the Manchester's first wave captured the Turkish front line, where fierce hand-to-hand fighting took place.

At 12.15 p.m. the second wave left the British trenches, leap frogging over the captured Turkish front line and captured the second, third and fourth line of trenches and began to consolidate the gains. Sheldon, who was wounded in No Man's Land barely twenty metres from the British frontline, went on to say:

'It is, indeed, terrible the first step you take right in the face of the most deadly fire and to realise that any moment you may be shot down, but if you are not hit, then you seem to gather courage and when you see, on either side of you, men like yourself, it inspires you with a determination to press forward. Well, away we went over the parapet, with fixed bayonets – one long line of us, like the wind, but it was absolute murder.'

**The 1/6 Manchester Regiment going over the top on 4 June 1915.**

All of the Manchester battalions had success although it was at the loss of their general, Brigadier General Noel Lee, who was mortally wounded, whilst his replacement, Lieutenant Colonel Heys, was soon killed. The Manchester Brigade had captured over 600 metres of ground and was now within 500 metres of the village outskirts. But they were in a dangerous position, in a salient, ahead of all other Allied troops. Very quickly the Turks not only fired into the front of them but at both flanks as well. All they had to do was hold these positions until other parts of the line could obtain their objectives. The 5/LF's right flank now rested upon a branch of the Krithia Nullah known as West Krithia Nullah, at a point about 350 metres forward of the bifurcation. To the east of Krithia Nullah the Manchester Regiment had managed to get about forty metres beyond the bifurcation, and entrench in an easterly direction, following the branch known as the East Krithia Nullah. Separating these forces was a small strip of ground between the two branches that rose up into a dominant rise. Both 5/LF and 7/LF now began work on the western side of this nullah to consolidate their gains, extending them into the nullah itself and garrisoning them on both the left and also those on the right, captured by the 8/Manchesters.

Brigadier General Noel Lee, commanding 127 (Manchester) Brigade.

The 5/LF took on the task of clearing the captured trench.

'The trenches now held by our men were full of dead Turks and the bodies of some of them had been greatly lacerated by rifle and machine-gun fire. The conditions prevailing are indescribable. Men had to be detailed to bury the enemy's dead. The trenches were cleared after some hours of laborious and disagreeable work, but the intervening space between our own trenches and those of the enemy, fittingly described as 'No Man's Land', was covered with bodies in an advanced state of decomposition. It would have meant a great sacrifice of life to have attempted burial here.'

It was now time to wait for the inevitable counter attack.

To the left of the 42nd Division, the attack had not gone so well for the 29th Division and 29 (Indian Brigade), mainly due to the weakness of an artillery bombardment that left the Turkish wire largely untouched. Redoubts on both sides of Gully Ravine proved devastating to the advancing troops. The Indian Brigade, supported by 1/LF on Gully Spur, made little progress. The Gurkhas by the sea were stalled, as were the Fusiliers and 14/Sikhs in Gully Ravine, who had lost almost all of their British and Indian officers and 380 out of 514 other ranks. It was becoming clear that, despite the sacrifice and bravery of these men, getting further forward was proving impossible. This failure on Gully Spur also affected 88 Brigade's advance east of the ravine on Fir Tree Spur, which found its left flank wide open and enfiladed from across the ravine. It soon became clear to all that the attack was a failure.

To the immediate right of Gully Ravine there was initial success where the Turkish front line trench was taken. Major GMH Ogilvy of 1/KOSB, who was commanding C Company, was due to go over with the second wave at 12.15 p.m., to capture a Turkish trench named H.12. In his report Ogilvy described what happened.

'Owing to the fearful losses of the 1st wave our C.O., Major G. B. Stoney (afterwards killed), who was in the front line and to whom I reported, told me to wait till he gave the order. At 12.32 hrs he told me to move. My company got across into the first Turkish line without difficulty, though we had some thirty casualties, mostly owing to shrapnel. I pushed on and easily got into H.12, collecting about twenty-thirty prisoners and a Hotchkiss gun on the way. I could see both Worcesters and Sikhs on my left, while advancing. The trenches were littered with dead and wounded, but little damage had been done to the trenches themselves by our guns. H.12 was deserted.

On arrival in H.12, I collected what I could find of the Company and spread right and left. There was a communication trench about 150 yards long running out of H.12 to H.13. I sent a party of about twenty men along it to H.13. Both were then, at about 13.30 hrs., empty and this party stayed in H.13 about an hour whilst I consolidated and established a block in the communication trench behind them.'

The Turks had had to retire so rapidly under the ferocity of the KOSB attack that the German machine gunners had been overrun. Their officer, Sub Lieutenant Götz Friedrich von Rabenau, and Leading Seaman Peters were captured. Kannengiesser described the remarkable escape that Peters subsequently made:

'Amongst those taken prisoner with the Naval-Lieut. von Rabenau was Leading Seaman Peters. As he was being conducted to the rear he seized a favourable moment to knock the guard senseless. He then jumped down among the English in the trench who, in wild confusion, took him for one of themselves and wondered at his bravery as he suddenly jumped up and ran forward alone towards the Turks. But those, not recognising him, greeted him as an enemy. He had to throw himself into a shell hole, where he lay for two days and two nights without food or water, with a constant hail of bullets overhead. Owing to the heat he was almost dead of thirst as the Turkish counter-attack of 6th June freed him, more dead than alive. When praised for his coolness and bravery Leading Seaman Peters merely answered: "I have only done my duty".'[23]

For Ogilvy and the 1/KOSB it was all about to go wrong.

'About 15.00 hrs. a major of the Worcesters, I don't know his name, but he was killed later, came up and said he had orders to withdraw to H.11. I pointed out I had no such orders, and that withdrawal would leave my left in the air. I prevailed on him to remain till I could get definite orders. As it was quite quiet I went back myself and reported the situation to Major GB Stoney, whom I found near where I left him. He said he had no orders to withdraw and told me to hang on till he could get some definite orders.

I got back between 1600–1700, owing to the chaos and that I did not know the way, and found the Worcesters had withdrawn. I therefore extended to the left as far as H.12 went and covered the left with 2 M.Gs. These were then quite close to the gully.

About 1700 hrs the Turks began pouring in to H.13 and the communication trench and we killed a few as they dashed from one end to the other. A section of M.Gs of the Essex, who appeared from somewhere, were very useful and did some good shooting. Just before dark the Turks began to bomb the block and as I had no bombs I organised a counter-attack, covered by the Essex M.Gs. This was successful and we drove them right out of the C.T. [communication trench] into H.13, killing a good many.'

During the night, and early morning of 5 June, the Turks attacked the KOSB positions almost continuously, although in small numbers. The fiercest counter attack was launched just before dawn at 3.30 a.m., when the Turks managed to recapture H.12 and nearly H.11. In the fog of war,

**60-pounders of 90th Heavy Battery RGA in action.**

and believing that the Gurkhas were coming into the line from the Gully to support them, the KOSB withheld their fire until they realised that it was the Turks. Unable to break up the attack by machine gun, the defenders were quickly overwhelmed.

For an hour most of H.13 was held with no resistance and there were reports that some parties had got into H.14; however this success was not echoed elsewhere, where only small numbers of the brigade had penetrated into H.12.

Regardless of their gallantry, the 29th Division and 29 (Indian) Brigade struggled to reach the Turkish first line elsewhere, let alone push past it. Most fell onto the wire in front of the Turkish trench and the whole advance on Gully Spur was brought quickly to an abrupt stop. The 5/Gurkhas were practically destroyed in the first thirty minutes of the attack, as also the 1/LF to the right. The Dublin Fusiliers were brought up to the nullah but could not affect the situation. With no supporting fire being brought to bear on the Turks, little unchallenged forward movement could be made. The 14/Sikhs lost all but two of their officers in the attack and were forced to retire. The action around Gully Ravine ended almost as quickly as it had begun. To rub salt into the wound of this left flank attack, when some fourteen Lancashire Fusiliers who had been cut off in the attack made their return, a shell from HMS *Swiftsure* unfortunately burst amongst them, killing eleven.

Reverend Oswin Creighton, chaplain to 86 Brigade (29th Division), described the scene in and around Gully Ravine:

'The gully was in a perfect turmoil, of course, guns going off on all sides, and the crack of the bullets tremendously loud. They swept down the gully, and one or two men were hit. I cannot imagine anything much more blood-curdling than to go up the gully for the first time while a fierce battle is raging. You cannot see a gun anywhere, or know where the noise is coming from. At the head of the gully you simply go up the side right into the trenches. You see nothing except men passing to and fro at the bottom, and there is the incessant din overhead.

The place was very full of wounded, who were being got off on boats as quickly as possible. Everywhere, of course, I was hearing about the battle. The left had been held up, unable to advance. The centre had advanced. The casualties were heavy. The whole situation was terrible – no advance, and nothing but casualties, and the worst was that the wounded had not been got back, but lay between ours and the Turks' firing line. It was impossible to get at some of them. The men said they could see them move. The firing went on without ceasing.'[24]

The Royal Naval Division attacked between Achi Baba Nullah and Kereves Spur. Anson, Hood and Howe battalions were in the first assaulting waves. As the final minutes trickled away, Ordinary Seaman Joe Murray and his comrades of the Hood Battalion were readying themselves to go over the top in their packed trench.

'We were standing there, couldn't sit down couldn't lie down, just standing there. The fellow next to me was messing about with his ammunition, fiddling about, cleaning his rifle, looking in the magazine. Another fellow was sort of staring. The blinking maggots from the dead bodies in the firing line were crawling round right under our noses. Every now and again if a bullet hit the parapet there was a 'Psssst!' Wind – gas – it smelt like hell. The sun was boiling hot. The maggots, the flies – the stench was horrible.'[25]

The bombardment was suspended for just ten minutes at 11.20 a.m. to try and trick the Turks into believing that they were coming over. As the troops pretended to attack the Turks let them know exactly what they were in for with a storm of fire. When the bombardment reopened they all knew their likely fate.

**RND in the trenches with the French before the battle.**

'Honestly and truly the next half an hour was like an age. The bullets were hitting the parapet: 'Bang! Bang! Bang! Actually coming through the parapet, disturbing the dead bodies, the stench! Ooooh dear me! It was horrible! Between you and I, I said my prayers, "Please God, not only for myself but for my parents may I survive!" Lieutenant Commander Parsons, standing on the ladder, called out, "Five minutes to go men! Four minutes to go!" At that moment young Corbie, he'd be annoyed if I called him that, a young sub-lieutenant, only a youngster, he walked past me and said something to Parsons, so he missed Minute 2 and 3. The next time, "One minute to go men! Now men!" He blew a whistle and off we go.'

The Turks let them have it, and a storm of lead cut through the ranks of the Hood Battalion.

'Off we go and up we went over the ladder. The moment we started to leave the trench at this traverse, 10–12 feet long, where we were, there were men falling back into the trench or on the parapet. There was dead all over the place. My Platoon Commander got through, I followed him up there. Parsons had already been killed. We got into dead ground. The Petty Officer said, "Well, come on, lad! C'mon!" We moved again and then lay down to get a breather. He was an old reservist, his bald head glittering in the sun – he'd lost his helmet. He was up on the trench with his rifle and bayonet, "C'mon! C'mon!" Around his head he'd got a white handkerchief and blood pouring down his face just like the pictures in the *London Illustrated*. He was bleeding dreadfully. I wanted to keep up with him but he was now twenty yards ahead of me. I got to the trench and in I go – it was ten feet deep! There was one or two dead, nobody alive.'

Nevertheless the Royal Naval Division managed to get across No Man's Land and overran the Turkish front line. From there Murray could see the approach of the supporting troops.

'I looked back and I could see the Collingwood's coming up in fairly good line. They hadn't reached our first line, they were coming up in reserve. They were lying down and getting up again and they would seem to be getting quiet a bashing. When they laid down, whether they were frightened, injured or killed I don't know, but there didn't appear to be many getting up.'[26]

The seven hundred strong Collingwood Battalion took part in this second phase of the attack. At 12.15 p.m. the Collingwood's were supposed to take over the advance but the communication trenches were choked with stretcher-bearers and wounded, which delayed the Battalion's move forward. When the attack finally went ahead, the Collingwood's took heavy casualties, most from flanking fire on their right. Survivors, with parties of the Howe and Hood, pushed steadily forward and captured the brigade's second objective. But there, too, enfilade fire made the position untenable and by 12.45 p.m. the remnants of the brigade were back in their old front line.

The French had been given an impossible task, facing as they were the strong Turkish redoubts (*Le Rognon, l'Haricot* and *le Quadrilatère*) towards the head of Kereves Dere. The RND's right flank was exposed when the neighbouring French Senegalese troops were driven back by a counter-attack.

Murray recalled what happened next.

'I remember seeing two officers away to my left – Denis Browne was one – taking about fifty men forward. We went forward about half a dozen of us to a bit of a ditch – that was considered to be the third trench. All of a sudden the right flank started retiring, the Anson Battalion. We were forced to retire, hopped back and jumped over the second trench; then we scampered back to his

**An 18 pounder and limber from 368th Battery RFA, 29th Division.**

first trench. I thought, "Well now if we can stop here we can hold them here!" I kept on turning round and firing, but there wasn't much opposition from the front, I couldn't understand why we were retiring, we weren't being pressed at all.'[27]

Within 45 minutes the RND were back in their starting line; the Collingwood's were all but annihilated, suffering over five hundred men killed or wounded. As a battalion they ceased to exist after this attack; the survivors were transferred into the other RND battalions.[28]

Observing the RND attack through a trench periscope was Assistant Paymaster Harry Biles, 2 (Naval) Brigade HQ Staff. In the only surviving record of his time ashore is a remarkable letter he wrote to his brother, Arthur, a Ship's Steward, about a month after the attack. By the time Arthur received the letter, Harry was dead, killed by a Turkish sniper near Backhouse Post on 13 July.

'Our officers and men went down like ninepins and the poor old "Collingwood" Battalion who had only landed about 3 days previous, lost 16 officers killed and about 15 wounded, and about 350 men killed. At the roll call of the Collingwood, there were only 4 officers left – of those, one was the doctor, one a Transport Officer (who did not take part in it), the other two managed to get back safely.

I am not particularly anxious to watch another battle – the poor beggars who were wounded between the Turks' trench and ours were calling for help all night and next day, but our people dared not venture out for them, and so they were left; some managed to crawl to our trenches in the dark and the other poor chaps I'm afraid, died of exposure and loss of blood, and we have not been able to get them in yet. Only yesterday I was in the firing line and with a periscope could see numbers of them.

There was some big misunderstanding in the programme on that day, the scheduled time for our lines to jump out of the trenches was 12 noon, but for some reason, never explained, the French were all behind so that by the time our fellows had reached the Turks, they were enfiladed by the Turks whom the French ought to have driven out, and so the thing was a failure, and our men had to return to their own trench again, and in doing so, were again mowed down by the enemy's maxims. Had the French only gone forward with our men, we should probably have had the famous "Achi Baba" hill by now and should then have had a place to go to out of range of their guns, whereas they are still in possession of the hill and there is not a place in the peninsula we can fall back on for a rest without getting shelled by them.'

The French had failed in their initial assault on the far right and were ordered to renew their attack at 4.00 p.m. with the RND; however this had to be delayed an hour to 5.00 p.m. as they were not ready and by 6.00 p.m. they had still not attacked due to the grievous losses suffered in the first assault. Because of this it left the advance line of the 42nd Division dangerously exposed and prone to enfilade fire. At 6.30 p.m. there was nothing that General Douglas could do apart from ordering a withdrawal back to the Turkish front line due to these forward positions becoming untenable. The 42nd Division's history notes:

'The retirement was made with the greatest reluctance; indeed, the few remaining officers had great difficulty in making the men realise that the order to withdraw must be obeyed. The idea of giving up the ground they had won was almost unbearable for the four Manchester battalions had resolved to hold on to their gains, whatever the cost might be.'

All battalions suffered heavily; as an example, of the 700 men of the 6/ Manchesters who went into action that morning, only 160 were left.

Hamilton, observing this attack on HMS *Wolverine*, wrote in his diary:

'For the best part of an hour it seemed that we had won a decisive victory. On the left all the front line Turkish trenches were taken. On the right the French rushed the *Haricot*, so long a thorn in their flesh; next to them the Anson lads stormed another big Turkish redoubt in a slap-dash style reminding me of the best work of the old Regular Army; but the boldest and most brilliant exploit of the lot was the charge made by the Manchester Brigade in the centre, who wrestled two lines of trenches from the Turks; and then, carrying right on; on to the lower slopes of Achi Baba, having nothing between them and its summit but the clear, unentrenched hillside. They lay there – the line of our brave lads, plainly visible on a pair of good glasses – there they actually lay!'

The Manchester Brigade's objectives had already been taken; Achi Baba was not part of them. Without success elsewhere in the line, Achi Baba was no closer to capture as it was on the first day of the landings.

At 3.00 a.m., under the bright moonlit night of 4/5 June, the Turkish counter attack took place. The weight of the attack was directed on the ground by the Krithia Nullah bifurcation. From here the Turks dropped down into the two branches. On the east, this was between the second and third line trenches, so already the Turks had got in behind the British front line. Whilst this was happening Turkish riflemen fired down from the bifurcation rise. Under this weight of fire and the incursion from the nullah, it forced the withdrawal of the men guarding the right flank in the nullah itself and the front line, which was only a shallow entrenchment and thought untenable. The Turks had

The cost to the Manchesters. Of those shown in this photo, five were killed in the attack, four were wounded, one losing an arm and one later dying.

83

used West Krithia Nullah to gain a footing into the second line trench where it met the nullah; a barricade was quickly constructed. The situation was similar on the eastern bank, where the 1/8 Manchesters erected a barricade, thus protecting the trenches from another attack from the base of the nullah.

Lieutenant Geoffrey Kay, machine-gun officer for the 5/LF, positioned his guns in support of the 6/Manchesters in the communication trench by the nullah. He wrote:

'We piled up sandbags at the end of the trench and mounted one gun almost in the stream. The Turks kept on coming down the ravine and we got a good bag. The gun behaved splendidly, though we ran short of oil. The other gun was urgently asked for at the other end of the trench. Unfortunately the Turks got round and enfiladed the trench at that end, putting the gun out of action, killing two of our men and wounding three others. A sandbag barricade was hastily built – there was one Company of about seventy men in beside ourselves – which gave some slight protection. The losses, however, were heavy.'

5 June was comparatively quiet, with a little shelling. Another Turkish attack that night was repulsed successfully, Lieutenant Kay's guns being key to the defence until their positions were overrun and the guns captured. To the left of the nullah the Turks had got into the communication trench on the top of the rise and thus could enfilade those in trenches on the right bank. British efforts to recapture this lost trench during the night of 5 June failed; however the hard-won ground at the top of the nullah was retained, one of the few pieces of ground to be held in this attack. Horridge described the trench as

'...having become a very unwholesome one; at the outset it had been found necessary to clear the trench of the dead by throwing the bodies over the parapets. It was later found impossible to bury these owing to the vigilance of the enemy by day, and to the volume and accuracy of his fire by night. Earth for covering purposes was in many places also scarce, owing to the practice of the Turks of burying their dead in the floor of the trench. It would be no exaggeration to state that either within or beside the parapet in this portion of the line bodies were lying head to foot throughout its entire length. Seeing that we were in a hot country the effect can be better imagined than described. The flies also added to our discomfort.'

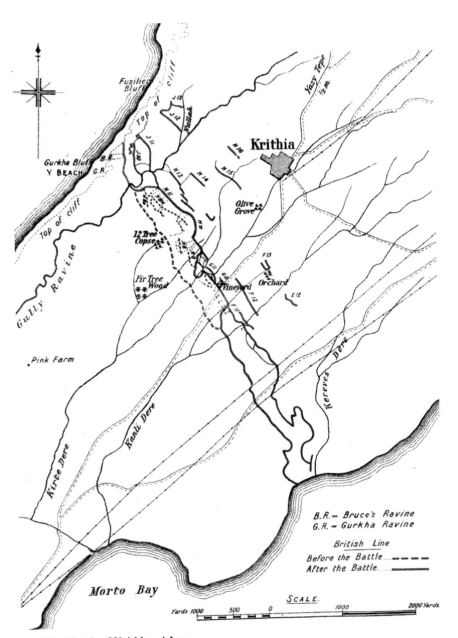

**Third Battle of Krithia – 4 June.**

To the left of the 42nd Division, the 29th Division was beginning to have problems, as evidenced in Ogilvy's (of the KOSB) account. The early morning attack on 6 June had finally managed to push 1/KOSB from their forward position in H.12 back into H.11. To the KOSB's left, the withdrawal of 4/Worcesters had left them dangerously exposed on the Gully Ravine flank and, to their right, 2/RF and the Hampshires had also been pushed back to H.11.

The 1/Essex had been split up to support these forward units, with X and Y companies supporting the KOSB and W Company supporting the Fusiliers. The Turks had got around W Company during the morning on the left flank and started bombing them from the rear. This forced the Essex to withdraw as they feared being cut-off, vacating the advanced position in H.12 and thus creating a gap in the line. When these men reached H.11 the whole second line broke on the right of H.11. They were soon rallied and the trench reoccupied, forcing the Turks out with bombs. Three companies of the Inniskillings were then sent to reinforce 88 Brigade, in particular the Essex, Worcesters and Royal Fusiliers. Whilst Y Company and the Machine Gun section fought to the last, only twenty-five men and one from the MG section reached H.11. Once the front line had reached H.11 this had a knock-on effect to those on the right who evacuated a considerable portion of H.11. The KOSB had to extend to the right to plug this newly created gap, whilst the men who were fleeing could be rallied and returned to occupy the trench. By 6.00 a.m. the whole of H.11 was back in British hands, with help of KOSB, bombing parties from 1/Essex and an 18 year old Australian born officer named Dallas Moor.

During the morning, Second Lieutenant George Raymond Dallas Moor, 2/Hants, witnessed a disorderly retirement of the Essex to the left of his sector, which amounted to panic for want of officers to control them. He realised the danger to his own battalion now that his left flank was in the air, and also the importance of returning to the position before the Turks could take advantage of it. Not only was the forward trench (H.12) lost, but the Essex had also pulled back from their second line (H.11). The whole line was thrown into panic. The Turks began to exploit this before the situation was restored by Moor, on the right of the incident. He led his men out of: *their trenches, and throwing forward a line against the left of the Turkish attack, and a second line at right angles back to their trench,* [they] *were able to enfilade and crush the enemy's advance.* He then dashed back almost 200 metres, stemmed the retirement, led back the men and recaptured the lost trench. Captain Beverly Ussher, a staff captain in 88 Brigade, witnessed what happened and wrote

'A poor young Second Lieutenant called Moor was commanding. The poor boy had been most gallant all that night leading his own and other men but by the time I saw him he was just about beat and rambling. I was only just in time to stop him going off his head. I think he will probably get something for his gallant conduct.'[29]

Ussher was correct. For this action Moor was recommended for the Victoria Cross by officers of 2/RF. His *London Gazette* VC citation reads:

'For most conspicuous bravery and resource on the 5th June, 1915, during operations South of Krithia, Dardanelles. When a detachment of a battalion on his left, which had lost all its officers, was rapidly retiring before a heavy Turkish attack, 2nd Lieutenant Moor, immediately grasping the danger to the remainder of the line, dashed back some two hundred yards, stemmed the retirement, led back the men, and recaptured the lost trench. This young officer, who only joined the Army in October, 1914, by his personal bravery and presence of mind saved a dangerous situation.'

The action actually took place on 6 June during the Turkish counter attack following the battle. Moor's VC would become the most controversial one of the campaign, if not the whole Great War. In the words of the 29th Division's GOC, Major General de Lisle, Moor shot *the leading four men and the remainder came to their senses.* De Lisle, in a commentary on Moor's VC action, said, *I have often quoted this young Officer as being one of the bravest men I have met in this War.* Balancing the desperate measures taken by Moor, it is certain that he prevented a wider rout that would have resulted in higher casualties had he not taken that action. Did Moor lose his head? It is interesting to note Ussher's

**Second Lieutenant George Raymond Dallas Moor VC.**

statement that he found Moor *was just about beat and rambling. I was only just in time to stop him going off his head.* Did he stop Moor shooting more men, or was his arrival just in time to calm him down from this most traumatic event? We may never know. Moor was invalided home soon afterwards, suffering from dysentery. He went on to gain the Military Cross and later a bar for bravery on the Western Front, but died of the Spanish Flu a week before the Armistice, in November 1918. He is buried in Y Farm Cemetery in France. Captain Beverly Ussher was later killed at Gallipoli on 19 June. He is buried in Twelve Tree Copse CWGC Cemetery.

**Captain Beverly Ussher, 88 Brigade.**

Twice in the afternoon the Turks tried another attack from H.12, but this was broken up by artillery, rifle and machine-gun fire, the Turks suffering heavily.

To the right of the British line the French attack did not go well in what became known as the Second Battle of Kereves Dere. Both *l'Haricot* and *le Rognon* redoubts were obstacles in the way of capturing the ravine, both thwarting each of Gouraud's assaults. Because the French could not advance their line it meant that the British right flank was exposed to Turkish enfilade fire. This made it extremely hazardous for the British to hold on to their costly gains, which on 6 June were lost to a Turkish counter attack. Like dominos, the British line collapsed from right to left and forced a withdrawal back to their starting positions. The Turks had withstood a massive Allied onslaught and, though the cost had been heavy, they had recaptured most of their previous defences. Whilst Kannengiesser reported that they captured *seventeen British machine-guns, a large number of rifles and ammunition as well as other booty*, it was not all good news. The Turks had exhausted themselves and Kannengiesser believed to another attack could not have been stopped in the same way, so he was relieved when it did not materialise. Even if the British wanted to attack, they could not as they had expended their reserves, both in manpower and ammunition. The Turks were not in a dissimilar position and they prepared themselves for what would certainly be another attack soon.

The French, the RND brigade and the 42nd Division made a promising start, but this early success was not to last. During the French advance the formidable *l'Haricot* redoubt was captured, but further advances were halted by the heavily defended, deep and wide Kereves Dere. A counter-attack on 5 June forced the French back, recapturing the redoubt and the ground that the French had just taken. With *l'Haricot* back in Turkish hands, and the French pulled back, it dangerously exposed the RND's right flank, into which the Turks poured murderous enfilade fire. When the RND's advance faltered, the next to be hit was the 42nd Division, which had made some deep advances. Then the 29th Division was hit and, with a domino effect, the once coordinated, broad attack front quickly collapsed. Most of the ground gained had to be relinquished, leaving the British with little more than a gain of 350 metres in a few places.

The cost was some 5,000 British (1,000 of which were from the RND's 2 (Naval) Brigade that had started the attack with 1,900 men) and 2,000 French casualties, including two of the latters senior officers, Brigadier General Marie François Ganéval and Brigadier General Marie Xertigny. Since the landings allied losses now totalled nearly 39,000 men. At the end of the battle, for example, 2/RF had only one officer left out of those that landed on 25 April, whilst an additional ten replacement officers had also been lost. This battalion was not alone: 2/Hants came out of the line with barely a hundred men, one of whom was Second Lieutenant Moor, who had prevented the rout of the Essex.

**French troops, exhausted from the recent fight, in the trenches.**

# Chapter 5

# Bite and Hold: the Fight for the Nullahs

It was apparent to the high command that attacking on a broad front, unless there was a certainty of success at all points, was probably going to fail. Reinforcements in the shape of the 52nd (Lowland) Division, under Major General Granville Egerton, brought some urgently needed manpower. What it did not bring was its guns. Prior to departure Kitchener informed Egerton that he would not need his artillery, the reason being that there were plenty of guns in Gallipoli. This was far from the truth, as there was not only a

**Generals Hamilton and Gouraud.**

lack of artillery but of shells as well. Even the 52nd Division without its artillery would not be enough to compensate for the previous losses. On 7 June, as the Third Battle of Krithia was being fought to an unsuccessful closure, Kitchener sent a telegram to Hamilton confirming the availability of three New Army 'Kitchener' divisions: the 10th (Irish), 11th (Northern) and 13th (Western) Divisions, all from 'K1'. This was excellent news for Hamilton who, whilst waiting for their arrival, ordered the pressure to be maintained on the Turks.

Out of failure comes ingenuity and later in June there were some limited successes. Hamilton authorised two attacks; one on the extreme right flank at Kereves Dere, the other on the left and Gully Ravine. These divisional attacks had the limited, local objective of biting out a key part of the Turkish line, and holding it against counter-attack. This new 'bite and hold' tactic proved successful and allowed Hamilton to neutralize key Turkish redoubts that had contributed to the failure of the recent Krithia attack.

## The Third Battle of Kereves Dere: 21–25 June 1915

On 21 June, Gouraud launched a French attack with two divisions, supported by mass artillery, with the objective of capturing Hill 83, on the crest of the Kereves Spur, and the head of *Ravin de la Mort*, an offshoot to Kereves Dere. This was going to be a divergence from the general advance in favour of a new 'bite and hold' tactic. It aimed to bite into a chunk of the Turkish line held by Lieutenant Colonel Hasan Askeri Bey's 2nd Division and then to use a wall of shells to assist the infantry in holding off the inevitable Turkish counter attack.

The French would attack on a very narrow front of just over 600 metres but it contained three objectives of great strength; not only the *l'Haricot* and *le Quadrilatère* redoubts, the latter being on the crest of Hill 83, but also the trenches overlooking the *Ravin de la Mort*. The artillery support was crucial and centred on the deployment of seven batteries of French 75mm guns, two batteries of Rimailho 155mm howitzers, trench mortars and seven British 4.5-inch and 6-inch howitzers to shatter the Turkish defences. At the same time six more batteries of 75mm guns were assigned to fire into the rest of the Turkish lines facing the French to keep them busy, while other French long-range batteries, accompanied by fire from the pre-dreadnought *Saint-Louis*, would try to suppress any interference from the Turkish guns on the Asiatic shore. This scheme provided a gun or howitzer for every ten metres of front to be assaulted. In the days leading up to the attack, the level of French fire increased as they tried to smash the Turkish trenches.

Second Lieutenant Raymond Weil, *39 Régiment d'Artillerie*, who was in a forward observation post, described what he saw.

'All along the French front the artillery raged. For our part we made our range corrections with a slow deliberation. Then we proceeded to methodically mop up every last fragment of the Turkish trenches that had to be completely destroyed. Each of our guns had its own pre-determined task but – in contrast to the last attack on 4 June – it was our Captain's orders which determined the changes in pace according to circumstances, rather than following a rigid plan laid out in advance.'[30]

The final bombardment opened at 5.15 a.m. and lasted for just forty-five minutes. At 6.00 a.m. the *176 RI* lunged for the redoubt, while to their right the *6 RIC* attempted to clear the *Ravin de la Mort*. The French had plentiful ammunition and during the attack expended over 30,000 shells on the narrow front. The dreaded *l'Haricot* was swiftly over-run by the *176 RI*, along with the Turkish second line. The *6 RIC* were

**A camouflaged French 75mm 'Soixante-Quinze' artillery battery.**

also successful in taking the Turkish front line but could get no further forward. The newly captured line had been severely damaged by the French bombardment and what was left was choked full of dead and dying Turks. However, there was little effective shelter in this trench causing the French many casualties after its capture, including the *6 RIC*'s commander, Colonel Noguès, who was badly wounded. After the loss of their commander and with growing casualties, confusion set in and by 7.00 a.m. the *6 RIC* had fallen back in disarray to their start line.

A young Turkish officer, Lieutenant Ibrahim Naci, 71 Regiment (Ottoman 1st Division), had been ordered forward with his regiment from reserve to support his hard-pressed colleagues trying desperately to hold back the French. In his first (and what turned out to be his last battle) he wrote a poignant final farewell in his diary entry for 21 June.

'7.00 a.m. The enemy attacked us the whole night. Now we are leaving. I hope the best from the Lord...

11.00 a.m. We went into battle. Millions of cannons and guns exploded...Now, my first corporal has been wounded.

Farewell.

11.15 a.m. I. Naci'[31]

'Johnny Turk' or 'Little Mehmet' was used affectionately to refer to the Ottoman soldier, an opponent that soon became respected amongst their foe.

Ibrahim Naci seems to have foreseen his end. He was killed that day. The diary was found by his company commander, Captain Bedri, who wrote a heartfelt epitaph: *You and your peers did not die. You were not buried into a pit made by some pickaxe strokes. You will continue to live in the heart of the great Turks and Islam with respect and dignity!* Bedri himself was killed on 2 July at Gully Ravine.

The fighting continued. Corporal Charles Thierry, *176 RI*, had been engaged in digging a sap when, at 3.00 p.m., he was sent forward with extra ammunition to the newly captured *l'Haricot* redoubt.

'The men go in threes: Legeay gets a shell fragment in the back, Legendre is wounded – many men fall! Our turn to go, a little shiver up the spine! I pass through a small communication trench, treading on the corpses of dismembered men, dry arms, one can no longer find anything human in these corpses. Only 25 metres across the open. At last I am in the first Turkish trench at the side of a wounded captain. We are subjected to a short bombardment. Surrounded by corpses we occupy the trench – I am almost alone in more than a hundred metres of front, all the men are wounded.

At every moment reinforcements are called for but none come; ammunition is also demanded but nothing comes. I attend to a wounded Turk in the trench. In gratitude he kisses my hand and lifts it twice to his forehead. I want him to write something in my pocket book but there is nothing to be done. The heavy shells from the Asian side rained down: Brumel is hit, Henriot as well. At about 6 p.m. an intense and well-directed bombardment from their lines warns us of a counter-attack, besides the situation demands it. But we enfilade them and they retreat swiftly. It is a veritable manhunt with our bullets. We throw our kepis in the air with shouts of joy. The bombardment is terrible; the shrapnel rains down. I lie down in the trench and a few moments later I am hit in the left hand. At last the bombardment stops.'[32]

In front of *l'Haricot, 176 RI* had improved their position and captured another trench, which positioned them closer to *le Quadrilatère*. The redoubt itself, perched on the top of Hill 83, was denied to the French despite their best efforts to secure it.

Gouraud ordered a final attempt to be made on the *Ravin de la Mort* before sunset; at 6.45 p.m. Senegalese from *1er* Régiment de Marche d'Afrique (1 RMA) recaptured it and this time held the line. For the first time the French had a position that could now overlook the Turks.

The fighting continued until 25 June with the French consolidating their gains, but capturing *le Quadrilatère* was proving both difficult and costly. On 30 June, whilst the Battle of Gully Ravine was raging on the Aegean side of the Peninsula, Gouraud launched a new attack, the Fourth Battle of Kereves Dere, this time using the fresh *7er* Régiment Mixte Coloniale. Not only did *le Quadrilatère* fall, but also several lines of trenches beyond it were taken. Unfortunately for the French, Turkish counter attacks recovered all the lost trenches but left the main part of the redoubt in French hands.

This attack cost the French 880 casualties and the loss of their commander. Whilst visiting the wounded from this attack in a V Beach field ambulance, Gouraud fell victim to a Turkish shell that landed nearby. The blast of the explosion hurled him over a two-metre-high wall; both his legs were broken and his right arm damaged, later amputated when gangrene set in. This was a severe blow to the French; under his command he had re-energised their efforts, raised morale and, through changes in tactics, had given them successes. These severe wounds, however, did not stop his progress up the chain of command; by the end of the war he was a notably successful commander of the French Fourth Army on the Western Front. General Maurice Bailloud took his place in command of the *Corps Expéditionnaire d'Orient (CEO)*.

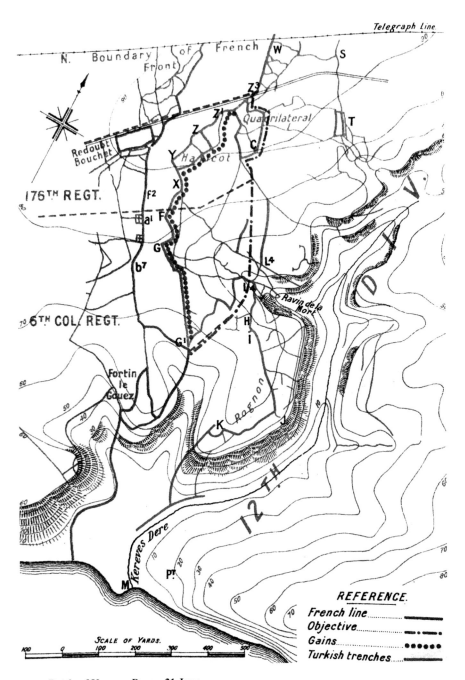

Battle of Kereves Dere – 21 June.

Turkish casualties were very heavy and were estimated to be nearly 6,000 men. Weber withdraw the weakened 2nd Division from the line and replaced it with the 12th Division. French losses were 3,200, including Colonel Ruef who, although wounded, refused to be evacuated. Despite the French successes, however, they still remained exposed to Turkish fire on their right flank and in the rear from the Ottoman positions on the Asiatic coast, a problem that they had to endure for the remainder of the campaign.

**General Maurice Bailloud, GOC**
*Corps Expéditionnaire d'Orient.*

## The Battle of Gully Ravine: 28 June – 5 July 1915

Following the success of the French attack, Hunter-Weston was encouraged to launch a similar 'bite and hold' attack on 28 June. Major General de Lisle's 29th Division had been much weakened, having been in the field continuously since the landings. To supplement the numbers, 29 (Indian) Brigade, and the newly arrived 156 Brigade from Major General Egerton's 52nd (Lowland) Division, were attached to it for the attack. The 86, 87 and 29 (Indian) brigades were to attack the J trenches along Gully Spur, including Gully Ravine; whilst 156 Brigade and 88 Brigade were to attack the H trenches on Fir Tree Spur. A diversionary attack was also to be made at Anzac on the same day, in the hope of diverting reinforcements that might otherwise be made available to reinforce the Turks opposing the main attack in the south. Opposing the British were the Ottoman 11th Division, under Colonel Rafet Bey. The idea was to advance on a frontage of 650 metres, a kilometre in depth, on either side of Gully Ravine. If successful this would position the British in a favourable position for a new assault on Krithia. The objective was to capture five lines of trenches on Gully Spur, up to J.13, nearest the sea, and two lines of trenches on Fir Tree Spur up to H.12 and H.12a, on the slope leading towards Krithia.

The opportunity needed to be seized; these trenches lay in an unfinished state because the Turkish flank was exposed to enfilade fire from British warships. Thus the defenders regarded them as a point of great danger and had developed a scheme to deal with the issue. The defences consisted of five, partially completed, notably narrow but already deep trenches, protected by well-placed machine gun redoubts.

This represented, even in its incomplete state, a formidable defensive position and would not be easy to carry.

The five lines of Turkish trenches were named J.9, J.10, J.11, J.12 and J.13, all positioned on Gully Spur, and were linked together by a long transverse trench called J.11a, which crowned the face of the cliff. The two furthest trenches, J.12 and J.13, formed the right flanks of an immediate trench system with H.12, H.12a and H.14 beyond, positioned on Fir Tree Spur.

The Turks had only begun working on these new lines recently and had been almost wholly unmolested by the British artillery. This was due to the British shortage of ammunition and the strict injunction that not more than two rounds per gun per day were to be expended except in the case of an attack. The Turkish wire was a lot heavier and thicker than the British wire, which caused problems with the standard issue British wire-cutters, which proved virtually useless in many cases. However, the wire's weight on top of simple wooden trestles often caused it to lie too close to the ground, enabling it to be fairly easily trampled over and, as little wire had been put out, this was not thought to be a major obstacle.

French 58mm Dumézil trench mortar bombs, fired from a Crapouillot, or 'Little Toad'.

The artillery was under the direct command of Brigadier General Sir Hugh Simpson Baikie, although de Lisle was free to express his wishes as to the distribution of the guns available. The allied artillery consisted of seventy-seven guns, including twelve British howitzers and nine 58mm French *Dumézil* trench mortars, nicknamed *Crapouillot* (i.e. little toad, because of its squat appearance) that were capable of dropping bombs, ranging from thirty to seventy pounds of explosives, almost vertically into the trenches but were restricted to a short range. There was further artillery support from the navy, with a cruiser, HMS *Talbot*, and two destroyers, HMS *Scorpion* and HMS *Wolverine*, all lying off the western coast. British ammunition reserves were meagre, with very few high explosive rounds available. Nevertheless, by sanctioning

97

the use of nearly a third of the total stock of ammunition at Helles for this one small operation, it was possible to allot a larger proportion of shells to the frontage of attack than in any previous British action on Gallipoli.

In fact the actual expenditure greatly exceeded the 12,000 rounds of ammunition allotted, totalling over 16,000 rounds; this total excluding shells fired by the navy, for which no records now appear to be available. During the Third Battle of Krithia, on 4 June, only 11,000 rounds were used, and these were spread over a far greater area. Earlier still, during the Second Battle of Krithia, on 6 May, twenty thousand troops were supported over three days by an average of six thousand rounds a day. In France, at the Battle of Aubers Ridge on 9 May 1915, 80,000 rounds in the course of a single day supported thirty thousand troops.

At this stage in the campaign one of the major issues facing Hamilton was not only a lack of shells but the War Office itself. No one had calculated the amount of ammunition for a prolonged occupation of the Gallipoli Peninsula. Hamilton was in dire need of shells and troops, but requests at this time tended to answered by London with the unhelpful injunction of 'push on'. The drain on stores and resources from fighting on two major fronts had become a critical issue for the War Office. Taking resources from one front to supply the other was not a solution. If, for example, the manpower and artillery support used during the failed attack at Aubers Ridge on the Western Front were to have been made available at Gallipoli, Hamilton would have had a better chance of 'pushing on'. It is undeniably true, however, that logistical support and the long line of communications inevitably told against the MEF.

The attack would commence at 9.00 a.m., with a preliminary bombardment by howitzers, heavy artillery and the fleet. At 10.20 a.m. the barrage would be joined by the field artillery, whose task was to concentrate on cutting the wire, whilst three batteries of machine guns were to concentrate their fire on the forward Turkish trenches. At 10.45 a.m. the artillery fire would lift off Boomerang Redoubt, opening the path for the 1/Borders to take this position. At 11.00 a.m. the entire artillery bombardment would lift and the main advance would begin.

The first phase of the main attack would then involve 87 Brigade taking the first three trenches on Gully Spur, J.9, J.10 and J.11 and including Gully Ravine up to this point. On the eastern flank the newly arrived 156 Brigade (52nd Division) was to capture the H.12 trenches. Units of 29 (Indian) Brigade were to occupy trench J.11a when it was captured and advance along the cliff to provide support to the left flank of 87 Brigade.

The next phase would commence at 11.30 a.m.; 86 Brigade would leapfrog 87 Brigade in order to capture trenches J.12 and J.13. They

**29 (Indian) Brigade – 14/Sikhs at rest in Gully Ravine.**

would then dig a new line from J.13 across to the Nullah, then extending it over to the eastern bank of the ravine to meet up with trench H.12. The Indian Brigade would continue support along the cliff tops, consolidating the length of trench J.11a and extending this line down to the shore. On paper the plan looked sound and was thorough in its detail.

The 29th Division's instructions for 156 Brigade were:

'The task of capturing the H.12 line has on previous occasions proved easy. Failure to retain possession has been due to want of support on the left of the line [i.e. Gully Spur], which will now be forthcoming.... It is anticipated that the artillery bombardment on this occasion, which is more intense than any in Flanders in support of our troops, will render the task of the brigade easy.'

This statement may have had some effect in giving the troops an added degree of confidence and encouragement, but it soon became clear that the artillery support for the attack on the H trenches along Fir Tree Spur was less concentrated than that provided for the assault along Gully Spur. The reason for this was that the task of capturing Gully Spur, with its five lines of trenches, was thought to be both the most difficult and the most important part of the attack.

No more guns were available to give 156 Brigade any further artillery support, whilst the support that they did have consisted only of four and a half batteries of 18-pdrs with no high explosives, just a limited supply of shrapnel. Shrapnel was good for dealing with infantry in the open, but less effective in destroying wire entanglements and entrenched positions. High explosives were the answer at the time. Hamilton later remarked in his diary that *Baikie is crying out to us for shells as if we were bottling them up! There are none.*[33] 87 Brigade were thus to take five lines of trenches with overwhelming artillery support, whilst 156 Brigade were to take two lines with practically none at all. The results were predictable.

All infantry battalions were to attack in three lines, consisting of an assaulting wave, support and reserve. The leading waves were ordered to attack with the bayonet in a quick rush, not to stop and fire; speed was of the essence. In addition to their fighting kit, every man was to carry two empty sandbags tucked into their webbing waist belts, to be used in repairing and reversing the parapets of the captured trenches and to help in barricading enemy communication trenches. Owing to the great heat, their heavy packs were not to be carried but were stacked out of the way.

At this stage of the campaign the British were still wearing their thick woollen serge uniforms, and had only been recently issued with 'Wolseley' sun helmets. Owing to the very high officer casualties, all officers were instructed to wear the serge 'Tommies' tunics, referred to as funk jackets, in order to blend in with the other ranks. To assist the artillery, every third man was to attach to his back a large piece of tin cut from either biscuit or kerosene tins, an idea developed by Brigadier General William Marshall. The 29th Division had an equilateral triangular piece with one-foot sides, and 156 Brigade a rectangular piece. These were to be connected by two loops of string to the shoulders, designed to flash in the sun to identify their positions. Each battalion was additionally to carry two red/khaki canvas screens each (red to face the British lines, khaki the enemy's), to be erected by day in the rear of a trench in order to request additional artillery support if required. Screens had been previously used on the Krithia attack on 4 June, but largely failed either due to the Turks counter attacking the trenches and the screens consequently being lost in these attacks, or because the men carrying them were killed or incapacitated. By night Very flare pistols would be used, although the field telephone was the preferred method of communication, which was fine so long as the lines were not cut. It was intended that the shining pieces of tin be placed on the back of a captured trench to show the furthest points penetrated. This would provide a problem, however, if newly won positions were lost under counter attack.

87 Brigade's orders were to assault the Boomerang and trenches J.9, J.10, J.11, including the gully up to this point, and half of J.11a. The

1/Border Regiment was to make the assault on the Boomerang, held by the Ottoman 2/33 Regiment. The Borders were to move up the left bank of the ravine in order to rush Boomerang Redoubt and the small portion of Turkey Trench still held by the Turks. This was the most advanced part of the Turkish line, heavily protected by a triple depth of wire, behind which were machine guns. This was a vital tactical point, from which Turkish fire could sweep all the surrounding area, especially Gully Spur. Because of this all earlier probes in the area had been unable to avoid huge casualties. Three attempts had already been made to capture this redoubt, all failing. A lot of emphasis was now placed on its

The field telephone was the preferred method of communication, which was fine so long as the lines were not cut.

capture, which was planned for fifteen minutes before the main assault. Unless this could be achieved immediately the whole advanced would be delayed, possibly causing the whole operation in this sector to fail.

When that position was captured, the Borders then had to clear Gully Ravine as far north as its junction with J.11. The 2/SWB were to capture J.9 and J.10 and the 1/Inniskilling and 1/KOSB were to leapfrog them and capture J.11 and the southern half of J.11a.

The advance of 86 Brigade was planned to begin at 11.30 a.m., half an hour after the first infantry assault. Under the cover of artillery, advancing across the open from the cover of Bruce's Ravine, the 1/RMF were to take the J.12 and J.13 trenches, whilst the Indian Brigade continued their advance up J.11a, protecting 86 Brigade's left flank. The 1/LF were to act as the connecting link between the 2/RF and 156 Brigade at H.12, advancing from Gurkha Ravine. The 1/RDF were to remain in Brigade reserve at Geoghegan's Bluff.

Three battalions (2/Hants, 1/Essex and 5/RS) of 88 Brigade were to be held in close support as divisional reserve. Its fourth (4/Worcesters) battalion held the old British front line between 156 Brigade and the left of the 42nd Division.

The role of 156 Brigade was to facilitate the advance of 87 Brigade by protecting its right flank. The brigade was to assault H.12a, H.12, H.11 and the Nullah northeast of H.11 as far as the communication trench joining H.12 at the bend of the Nullah. These trenches followed the general line of the ridge that dominated the western sector overlooking Gully Ravine. The frontage here was almost half a mile and the trenches had to be taken with what amounted to no artillery support. This was something that the Brigade did not realise, believing that the bombardment would be of equivalent force to that on Gully Spur. The Brigade deployed its battalions so that the 4/RS (Queen's Edinburgh Rifles) were on the left and the 8/Cameronians (Scottish Rifles) on the right, whilst the 7/Cameronians (Scottish Rifles) were held in Brigade reserve. In the centre were the 7/RS (Leith Rifles), which consisted of only two companies, a consequence of the Quintinshill Railway Disaster that occurred near Gretna in Scotland before they left home shores; three officers, twenty-nine NCOs, and one hundred and eighty-two men were killed. A further five officers and 219 other ranks were left injured,

**Due to the shortage of bombs, grenades made from jam tins were fabricated behind the lines.**

or suffering from shock. To bolster this weakened battalion a company from the 8/Highland Light Infantry (HLI) were attached.

The Boomerang Redoubt bombardment began, with the first bombs from the French *Dumézil* mortars falling on the redoubt with deadly accuracy. Petty Officer FW Johnston, a machine gunner in the Royal Naval Armoured Car Division, RNAS, recalled viewing the mortars in action:

> 'Their flight was easy to follow & was wonderfully fascinating. Reaching a height of, perhaps, two hundred feet and appearing to be directly overhead, it [the bomb] slowly turned over & still more slowly (it seemed) began to descend. It almost imperceptibly drew away from us and landed with a dull thud on the outer works of the Boomerang. A remarkable silence followed & then tons of earth, sections of entanglements, bodies, clothes and limbs were sent into the sky. A terrific explosion of unparalleled violence, causing the earth upon which we stood to tremble & spreading its pungent fumes, like a mist over everything & everyone, was the result. Its terrifying roar re-echoed along the ravine until drowned by the ships' guns at sea. Before the air was clear another torpedo [sic] was fired.'[34]

At 10.40 a.m. the order went along the Borders trench line to fix bayonets as the artillery barrage reached its crescendo.

> 'One further minute and the word 'Ready' is passed along. In that one minute we unconsciously take one look at the sun and the sea and involuntarily commend our bodies and souls to our Maker – and then before we realise it a hoarse shout of 'Over' and we are up the ladders and racing like the wind for the redoubt about 200 yards distant.'[35]

The bombardment lifted off the Boomerang Redoubt at precisely 10.45 a.m., opening the way for the Borders to attack. Second Lieutenant LR Grant recorded the moment:

> 'At quarter to eleven we heard a faint cheer and knew it must be the Border Regiment on our left storming the "Boomerang" Redoubt. We peered excitedly over the parapet and could dimly distinguish through the smoke figures running across the open.'[36]

Three open lines emerged from their trenches, bayonets fixed, advancing through the lingering dust cloud of the bombardment. The heavily fortified Boomerang Redoubt was quickly captured, along with almost a hundred dazed Turkish prisoners. Little return fire had been given by the surprised defenders; however Turkey Trench caused the Borders a lot more trouble. About forty metres of the trench, towards the rear of the enemy's barricade, was found to have been filled in. This left the assaulting party in the open and exposed to a murderous fire, mainly from a previously unknown trench that ran from Turkey Trench to H.12. All ranks in the first wave assault were killed or wounded in crossing this ground. The support wave fared a little better, but suffered very heavily again from the hail of rifle fire and shrapnel. However, the few who managed to get across this ground successfully captured the enemy trench using bomb [i.e. grenade], bayonet and rifle butt. Sub-Lieutenant Frank Yeo, 4/Squadron Royal Naval Armoured Car Squadron, RNAS, who commanded a machine gun supporting the attack, wrote:

> 'The prisoners are fine looking men. Our Tommies are extraordinary, they are now giving them cigarettes and shaking hands with them ... I can't understand it after seeing the sights we have seen – men's eyes gouged out, ears cut off and some propped in doorways and burnt ...' [37]

The Borders' casualties were fairly light, largely thanks to the effective bombardment by the British 4.5-inch howitzers and the two loaned French *Dumézil* trench mortars.

The British at this stage had only six 'Japanese' trench mortars. These arrived in mid-May 1915 from Japan, along with the instructions, unhelpfully only printed in Japanese. There was a very limited supply of ammunition for these mortars, and by early June 1915 Hamilton remarked that the War Office had let the stock of bombs run out 'because some ass has forgotten to order them in advance'. New bombs would have to be ordered from Japan, and it would be months before they arrived. In any case, of the six Japanese mortars on the Peninsula, four were up at Anzac,

A prisoner of war – 'The prisoners are fine looking men. Our Tommies are extraordinary, they are now giving them cigarettes and shaking hands.'

leaving only two on the Helles front for the June attack. Howitzers and trench mortars were very scarce and yet were in greater demand than any other gun type at this time.

At 11.00 a.m. the artillery lengthened their range according to the programme. A Turkish counter bombardment was already falling on the British trenches, now filled and congested with three waves of men awaiting the whistle to attack. On the hour the first line of troops scaled their trench ladders and left their trenches. The bombardment of Gully Spur had been so intense that the first two lines of Turkish trenches were effectively annihilated, leaving the occupants either dead or wounded. The main resistance on Gully Spur came from a machine gun on the right flank, in the Boomerang. Even though the Borderers had attacked fifteen minutes before the main assault, some elements of the Turkish garrison still held out in the redoubt and its satellites. This stubborn resistance inflicted a number of casualties on the 2/SWB, who were attacking to the Borders' left. This fire did not stop them, however, and the first few trenches were quickly captured.

Sub-Lieutenant Frank Yeo, 4/Squadron Royal Naval Armoured Car Squadron, RNAS, witnessed the SWB attack at 11.00:

> 'One place a little in advance of the Turkish trench was a sort of redoubt with several machine guns and from which the Turks threw bombs into our trenches – this was left for the South Wales Borderers to take. At 11 o'clock the SWB jumped over their trenches with fixed bayonets and charged the redoubt – it was dreadful to see them getting mowed down but a few reached the redoubt and then there was some battle! You could see them sticking the Turks like pigs and the Turks putting up their hands and yelling "Allah"! They took the redoubt and about eighty prisoners...The SWB charge was great, they must have some pluck, if they are really Welshmen I take off my hat to them. Really our soldiers are wonders and you people in England can't do too much for them – the whole lot deserve VCs.' [38]

With the exception of casualties here, the first two trench lines were taken with very little loss. Reverend Creighton was at his post with the 89/Field Ambulance Dressing Station in Gully Ravine.

> '...soon the wounded started to pour in. First the slight cases able to walk, in crowds. Everything seemed to be going well. The Turks were on the run and we had got a line or two of trenches. Then later on in came the stretcher cases, and they kept coming all night and the next day.' [39]

**Some of the booty captured on 28 June 1915.**

Hamilton had come over from Imbros in the destroyer HMS *Colne* for the battle, observing that:

'The cliff line and half a mile inland is shrouded in a pall of yellow dust, which, as it twirls, twists and eddies, blots out Achi Baba himself. Through this curtain appear, dozens at a time, little balls of white – the shrapnel searching out the communication trenches and cutting the wire entanglements. At other times spouts of green or black vapour rise, mix and lose themselves in the yellow cloud. The noise is like the rumbling of an express train – continuous; no break at all.'

Watching the men advancing, with the tin triangles on their backs, Hamilton went on to say:

'The spectacle was extraordinary. From my post I could follow the movements of every man. One moment after 11.00 a.m. the smoke pall lifted and moved slowly on with a thousand sparkles of light in its wake: as if someone had quite suddenly flung a big handful of diamonds on to the landscape.'

The bombardment of the line opposite the 4/RS and 7/RS achieved a fair degree of destruction, but nothing like as great as that to the left, on Gully Spur. Second Lieutenant LR Grant, 4/RS, wrote:

'The minutes passed and we looked anxiously at our watches. The men were all standing ready with bayonets fixed at five minutes to eleven. Excitement ran high and a certain tense nervousness. It was the supreme test of all our months of training. Would we stand the test? Three minutes more, two minutes more. The rattle of the rifle fire had become more pronounced and bullets were smacking on the parapet and hissing over our heads. "One minute more, boys" then, "over you go lads!" and, with a yell that thrilled the very marrow in one's bones, the men hurled themselves over the parapet and dashed forward into the inferno of flame and smoke, bursting shells and zipping bullets.'[40]

At zero hour the Royal Scots moved forward with great zeal and gallantly charged forward. Out of this inferno they managed to capture both the first and second Turkish lines. At the sight of this determined advance, many of the Turks in the front trenches bolted, and those left were quickly dispatched with 'cold steel' in the *mêlée* that followed.

However, the losses to the Scots were appalling, many of the casualties inflicted by an undetected machine gun nest towards the position of H.13 on the Scots' extreme right. This Edinburgh sacrifice cost the lives of many good officers and men, including Lieutenant Colonel Spottiswoode Robert Dunn, 4/RS's Commanding Officer. Dunn was mortally wounded just before reaching the first objective of H.12a, falling between the British and Turkish lines, where the majority of the casualties fell. Dunn, aged fifty-two, died later on a hospital ship and was buried at sea the following day.

Piper Major Andrew Buchan was another casualty of the advance across No Man's Land, [with] *rifle in hand, he continued to encourage forward a party of young Royal Scots, although he had twice been wounded. Hit for the third time, he fell dead on the parapet of the first Turkish trench.*[41] Both men are commemorated on the Helles Memorial to the Missing.

A small party under Company Sergeant Major DM Lowe of C Company, 4/RS, advanced a further hundred metres to the final objective, the second trench line at H.12, later to be known as the Eastern Birdcage. His party of about sixty men came under heavy enfilade fire from the western banks of Gully Ravine and the Nullah, owing to his party getting ahead of 87 Brigade's advance on the left. However, the sudden dash took the Turks completely by surprise, enabling the attackers to capture this last position successfully. From this vantage point Lowe's men poured heavy fire into the Turks retiring up the gully. The ravine at this point is like the depression of a shallow saucer, with little cover

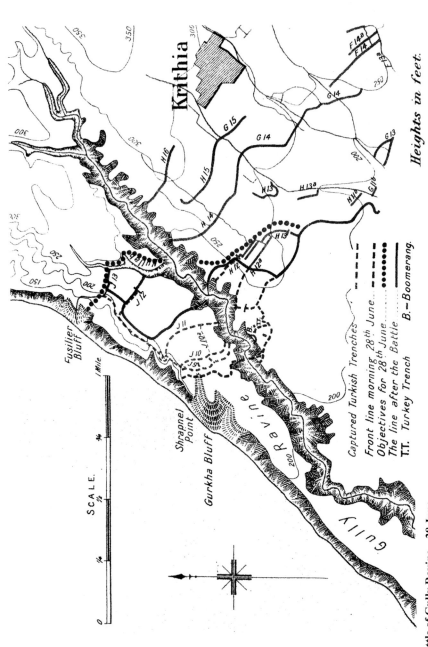

**Battle of Gully Ravine – 28 June.**

*Heights in feet.*

Krithia

Fusilier Bluff

Shrapnel Point

Gurkha Bluff

Gully Ravine

SCALE.

Captured Turkish Trenches ............
Front line morning 28th June ............
Objectives for 28th June ............
The line after the Battle ............
T.T. Turkey Trench B.—Boomerang.

to offer anybody who should pass through. In front of Lowe's party no more Turkish trenches were observed, only the summit of a small ridge, beyond which nobody knew what lay. The party was too small to exploit the situation further and they quickly set about consolidating their gains.

Not all went to plan, as the fate of one battalion on Fir Tree Spur shows all too clearly. The majority of the artillery bombardment was to fall on Gully Spur to give 87 Brigade the best chance of success. An anonymous officer eyewitness observed, *during the bombardment not one shell fell on the objective on the right of the 156th Brigade, and not more than six on the left.*[42]

Major James Findlay, 8/Cameronians had only taken command of the battalion a week before, but already was to lead them in battle.

'The artillery bombardment, which took place from 09.00 to 11.00, was, even to a mind then inexperienced in a real bombardment, quite too futile, but it drew down upon us, naturally, a retaliatory shelling. How slowly these minutes from 10.55 to 11.00 passed! Centuries of time seemed to go by. One became conscious of saying the silliest things, all the while painfully thinking, "It may be the last time I shall see these fellows alive!" Prompt at 11.00 the whistles blew.'

Over the top went his men, to be met by a deadly stream of fire. Findlay soon realised that the attack was breaking down in No Man's Land and requested reinforcement. Captain Charles Bramwell, with his signals' officer, Lieutenant Tom Stout, tried to get forward.

'Bramwell and I then pushed our way up the sap, which for a short distance concealed us, but got shallower as we went along, until first our heads, then our shoulders, and then most of our bodies were exposed. We soon arrived at Pattison's bombing party, which I had sent up this sap. He had been killed and those of his men that were left were lying flat; they could not get on as the sap rose a few yards in front of them to ground-level, and the leading man was lying in only about eighteen inches of cover. In any case they were still some fifty yards from the enemy trenches. Bullets were spattering all around us, and we seemed to bear charmed lives, until just as we arrived at the rear of this party Bramwell fell at my side, shot through the mouth. He said not a word and I am glad to think that he was killed outright. I made up my mind that the only thing to be done was to collect what men there were and make a dash for it. I told this to Stout, and, stooping down to pick up a rifle, I was shot in the neck. At the moment I didn't feel much, but when I saw the blood spurt forward I supposed that it had got my jugular vein. I stuck a handkerchief round my neck and tried to get on, but I was bowled over by a hit in the shoulder.'

Badly wounded, Lieutenant Tom Stout and another tried to carry Findlay back, but they had not gone a few metres when Findlay was wounded again by a bullet. Then a shell burst and shrapnel killed Stout and the other man. Findlay wrote *Gallant lads! God rest them!* Findlay finally managed to stagger back to the lines, one of the lucky ones. His battalion had suffered 448 casualties and twenty-five of the twenty-six officers had been hit, all for a few insignificant gains. Captain Charles Bramwell, Lieutenant Thomas Stout and Second Lieutenant Robert Pattison are all commemorated on the Helles Memorial.

**Brigadier General William Scott-Moncrieff, commanding 156 Brigade.**

Although more attempts to advance were ordered during the day, none were successful. The 156 Brigade also lost its commander, Brigadier General William Scott-Moncrieff, who went into a forward sap to observe the attack and was sniped.

Turkish shelling increased quickly, shells falling profusely in and around the gully. Fearing a further advance up the ravine, thus stopping British reserves coming up, the Turks could not afford to lose any more ground. The shelling almost immediately set the dried grass, gorse and the scrub ablaze. Many of the wounded that lay helpless, unable to move, were burned alive. Added to this inferno of shell, bullets and fire, the sun was now blazing down pitilessly onto No Man's Land, heaped as it was with corpses, interspersed with the wounded that were trying to crawl away.

The elements of the Cameronians that had taken H.12a set about consolidating their gains as quickly as possible. Seeing that the advance on their right had failed, a sandbag block, later known as Southern Barricade, was hastily built across the captured trench. A further barricade, to become known as Northern Barricade, was constructed along trench H.12.

Whilst the above was taking place, the attack over on Gully Spur continued to go as planned. By noon, just before the Cameronians went over the top, 2/RF had taken J.12 and J.13. The Gurkhas, to the left of the Royal Fusiliers, had cleared J.11a and were in occupation of the spur running down to the sea just in front of J.13; a point later known as Fusilier Bluff. In Gully Ravine itself, 1/LF moved successfully along its western banks in order to join up the line with 156 Brigade in H.12. Sub-Lieutenant Frank Yeo recalled:

'We bagged a lot of Turks with our guns as they were retreating. Unfortunately, out of the four men I have with my gun I have already lost two in a few hours, one killed and one wounded in the shoulder. I had a narrow shave when the bullet that killed my No.2 just grazed the gun I was firing at the time. It went over my shoulder and hit my man, who was looking over it. It covered me with dirt and some got in my eye. I wondered what had happened. We have several wounded in the trench here. Two R.F men are just beside me now, one has his leg shattered and I have given him some opium [morphine] pills so he is now quite happy. The other is only slightly wounded … I expect the Turks will counter attack tonight and I ought to get some fine targets. This is better than blowing up pheasants at Holme Park…'[43]

At 2.00 p.m. the Turks launched several fierce and determined bombing attacks against their lost positions near the gully on Fir Tree Spur and the eastern ends of the J trenches at the Nullah.

At the Southern Barricade a Turkish bomb fell into the trench. Lance-Corporal A. Ross, 7/Cameronians, with no thought for his own safety, at once put his foot on it just as Private Young was leaning down to throw a coat over it. Throwing a coat over a bomb had a smothering affect that suppressed the explosion, thus retaining the force within the coat. The bomb exploded, wounding Ross terribly in the feet, legs, hands and face; but he undoubtedly saved several lives by his self-sacrifice. He survived, both Cameronian men receiving the DCM for their gallantry.

On Gully Spur a large party of Turks approached the barricaded ravine. shouting *Lancashire Fusiliers!* and waving a white flag. This *ruse* did not work, and they immediately attracted heavy fire, leaving over forty bodies behind. Bombs were an advantage the Turks had over the British. They had large quantities and put them to good use. Allied supplies were very limited and those that were available were used up very quickly. These local bomb attacks forced the British from the eastern halves of both J.12 and J.13 and pushed back the majority of the

Lancashire Fusiliers to the western bank of the gully. The Turks had not yet accepted defeat. Two of the Lancashire Fusiliers amongst the 'six VCs before breakfast' became casualties as a result of these attacks, Lance-Sergeant William Keneally and Major Cuthbert Bromley.

About 6.00 p.m. 5/Gurkhas and 1/RMF were ordered to retake the lost portions of J.12 and J.13. Although this was eventually done after much hand to hand fighting and bombing, by nightfall the Turks counter attacked again, and had recaptured both the eastern ends of the trenches. During the time of the Gurkha and Munster attack, the 1/RDF were ordered up to the barricade made by the 1/Borders, later called Border Barricade, near the junction of H.12 and Gully Ravine. They then advanced up the Gully towards the Nullah and the eastern end of trench J.12. Heavy fire met the Dublins, who made little progress. They did try digging a trench on the western side of the ravine to connect to J.12, but fierce Turkish opposition forced them back to the line at J.11a. Lieutenant O'Hara of the 1/RDF wrote that we *were in a condition bordering on lunacy* when it was all over. The Munsters' history describes how the men were in a very bad state from exhaustion and want of water and food after thirty-six hours of fighting and digging. Many literally collapsed, finding it difficult even to get out of the trenches without help.

After Brigadier General Scott-Moncrieff's death, General de Lisle had put command of 156 Brigade in the hands of Lieutenant Colonel Cayley of 88 Brigade. In the late afternoon, supported by only a few guns, 1/Essex and 5/RS tried an assault on H.12, but this again proved impossible, meeting with the same result as that suffered by 156 Brigade. The Turks were expecting the attack to be renewed and thus maintained heavy shelling on the British lines. Not a single person reached H.12, all being cut down immediately after leaving the cover of the trenches. Incredibly, a further attempt was made towards the evening, but this fared no better. Turkish fire was accurately directed from trenches still untouched by British artillery. After dark the 2/Hants began relieving the Royal Scots and the Cameronians in the western end of H.12 and H.12a. This proved a difficult and confusing process as the narrow trenches were still littered with the dead and dying and debris from the morning's battle. During this relief the Turks made two fierce counterattacks on the line, both repulsed with heavy loss to the Turks. When dawn came, the relief complete, the front of the line had a new carpet of dead, now littered with the interspersed mounds of Turks from the night before. 156 Brigade was now fully relieved and in the reserve trenches near Twelve Tree Copse. The Turkish trenches at H.12 and H.12a on the right remained in the Turks' possession for the rest of the campaign, as did the Nullah and the eastern ends of J.12 and J.13.

The wounded lay where they had fallen in No Man's Land, the trenches and the saps. Many were in exposed positions so could not be rescued until nightfall; many would not live that long. They were not only exposed to the enemy, but also to the scorching sun, that was likened to a blazing death star, an enemy crueller than the Turk. It was not long until the scrub and sun-browned grass caught fire again, devouring anything in its path. Those wounded who were helpless perished, burnt to death in the blaze. A blood red sunset closed a bloody day,and night came mercifully to cloak the scene of horror.

The following message was received by Major General Egerton, 52nd Division, dated 29 June, congratulating the troops:

'General de Lisle wishes to express how much he valued the help given to the 29th Division in yesterday's attack by the 156th Brigade. The attack by the 156th Brigade was almost entirely successful – the 4th and 7th Royal Scots succeeded in every detail in the task imposed upon them. The 8th Scottish Rifles met with enormous resistance owing to the fact that our artillery had not prepared the Turkish position in front of them quite so successfully as in other places. The 8th Scottish Rifles were gallantly led. This position was unsuccessfully attacked twice by the 88th Brigade (29th Division) with great gallantry. General de Lisle does not blame the 8th Scottish Rifles at all for their failure. He much regrets the death of Brigadier General Scott-Moncrieff.'

Egerton, who was powerless to intervene, because during the action his brigade was under the command of de Lisle, was heartbroken to see the destruction of his brigade. He was also furious to hear Hunter-Weston's comment of being *delighted to hear that the pups had been so well blooded*. The losses by both battalions of the Cameronians were so severe that after this battle, on 1 July, they were forced to form a composite battalion, the 7/8th Cameronians, sufficient to supply only three companies of survivors. Likewise the 4th and the 7th Royal Scots, who were equally devastated by the heavy losses during the recent battle, were obliged to amalgamate on 7 July.

The Turks were extremely concerned at this stage, as the advance along Gully Spur seriously enfiladed their positions on the eastern banks of Gully Ravine. Five lines of trenches were lost and now Krithia looked in grave danger of being lost too. The Turks began a series of desperate counter-attacks to win back their lost territory and make good their poor position. During the night of 30 June two Turkish Regiments crept along the cliff tops to the northernmost British positions at Fusilier Bluff. The

**Captain O'Sullivan and Corporal Somers in the act of gaining the Victoria Cross.**

mass of Ottoman infantry was soon detected by the searchlights of HMS *Scorpion*, whose guns destroyed the advance in minutes. When dawn came all that was to be seen in front of the trenches were 300 Turkish bodies lying in heaps upon the ground. Some 180 prisoners belonging to the 13th, 16th and 33rd regiments were taken when they were found hiding out in the scrub.

**Captain Gerald Robert O'Sullivan VC.** **Corporal James Somers VC.**

Fighting reached its crescendo on 2 July as the British did their best to consolidate gains and fight off further Turkish counter attacks, spearheaded by the Ottoman's 1st Division, under Lieutenant Colonel Cafer Tayyar. During the course of the Gully Ravine action three VCs were won for conspicuous bravery; two were won by the 1st Inniskillings. Captain Gerald Robert O'Sullivan and Corporal James Somers were instrumental in recapturing trench J.12. A report by Lieutenant Colonel Buckley stated how the two men responded to the knowledge that J.12 was in Turkish hands:

'[Captain O'Sullivan] immediately attacked, leading the storming party. Accompanied by Cpl Somers, he advanced in the open along the parapet of the trench, bombing the interior as he regained it. The Turks bombed back and from where I was I could distinctly see the flashes of the Turkish bombs, generally two to Capt O'Sullivan's one. We had only the jam-pot bomb ... while the Turks had quite a useful bomb.'

Sergeant James Somers wrote to his father:

'I beat the Turks out of our trench single-handed and had four awful hours at night. The Turks swarmed in from all roads, but I gave them a rough time of it, still holding the trench … It is certain sure we are beating the Turks all right. In the trench I came out of, it was shocking to see the dead. They lay, about 3,000 Turks [sic], in front of our trench, and the smell was absolutely chronic. You know, when the sun has been shining on those bodies for three or four days it makes a horrible smell; a person would not mind if it was possible to bury them. But no, you dare not put your nose outside the trench, and if you did, you would be a dead man…'

For more information on these men and their London Gazette citations, see *Gully Ravine* in this series of Battleground Europe books on Gallipoli.

The third VC was won by Second Lieutenant Herbert James, 4/Worcesters, who at the time was acting as a liaison officer with 5/RS. Using his own initiative, James led the Royal Scots in two advances and then single-handedly kept the Turks back at a makeshift barrier until the trench was secured.

Over the next day several frontal Turkish counter attacks were made but all were defeated by the combined firepower of the Navy, artillery, machine gun and rifle fire. There was a lull in the fighting

**Second Lieutenant Herbert James VC.**

during 3 and 4 July, but this was just the lull before the storm.

The Turks had suffered enormous casualties and the threat of losing their Southern zone seemed to them to be imminent. Unknown to them, however, the British had achieved their more limited objective and were consolidating their gains. Liman von Sanders sacked his II Corps commander, Brigadier Faik Pasha, for his failure to expel the British, and appointed Brigadier Mehmet Ali Pasha in his place. The Turks brought in three extra divisions to the area during the evening of 3 July: the 5th Division from Anzac, the 4th Division from Bulair and the 3rd Division from Kum Kale.

They were given time to reorganise on 4 July; on the morning of 5 July a huge Turkish counter attack was launched, the biggest seen so far at Gallipoli. The 3rd Division was to assault the 'J' trenches, the 5th Division the 'H' trenches, whilst the 4th Division was to be held in reserve. The attack was to be extended along the whole southern sector by the other formations already holding these positions. From the

Turkish perspective it looked like the whole Helles defence was about to crumble.

The heavy Turkish bombardment that began before dawn on 5 July took the British completely by surprise. The Turks were soon observed massing for an attack, which prompted the British guns to throw down a counter-bombardment, concentrating on the Turkish trenches and the Nullah. HMS *Wolverine*, using her searchlight, was able to illuminate Turkish troops advancing across the cliff tops and shell them to a devastating effect. At about 4.15 a.m. the Turks began their attack, to be driven back with heavy loss, as in the previous assaults. At about 6.00 a.m. the Turks again attacked: *thousands of Turks in a bunch, so the boys say, swarmed out of their trenches and the Gully Ravine. Well, they were stopped dead. They lie, still. The guns ate the life out of them.* British shrapnel and rifle fire had done it again; only about thirty Turks actually reached the British parapet. These attacks were far greater than any other experienced by the British.

> 'Flares, shot up by our officers, showed the Turks advancing in regular parade formation in line of columns. As soon as the Turks saw that they had been observed, they charged, yelling their war cry: "Allah, Allah!" The Gurkhas waited patiently, lining the trenches as thickly as they could stand. They allowed the Turks to approach within fifty yards of them and then opened such a hurricane of rifle and machine-gun fire that the Turks were absolutely crumpled up in ranks as they stood.'[44]
>
> 'On came the Turks, line after line, but not a single man reached the parapet of our front-line trench. They were literally mown to pieces, and the dead were heaped one on top of the other. The rifles of the men in the firing line became so hot that it was necessary to pass up rifles from the supports whilst the men in support kept the firing line rifles while they cooled and recharged the magazines.'[45]

The Turkish attacks continued all over the southern zone, but by midday they had exhausted themselves and failed, resulting in enormous Turkish casualties. [There were] *...line upon line of Turkish dead, silent witnesses to the terribly accurate fire poured into them ... They are brave fellows, those Turks, and it was a sad sight to see so many gallant men laid low.*[46] British losses in comparison were negligible.

Turkish sources put their losses between 28 June and 5 July at over 16,000. 'Little Mehmet', the Turkish equivalent of Tommy Atkins, fought with a steadfast courage that won him the respect of the Allied

**29 Indian Brigade - 6/Gurkhas in trenches at Helles.**

soldiers. The Turks stated that the battle of Zighin Dere, as they called it, was the most costly action they had yet fought on the peninsula.

The killing fields of Gully Ravine had taken their toll on both sides. *By July 5th,* wrote Second Lieutenant Savory, 14/Sikhs, *the Indian Brigade had shot its bolt. All its four battalions had been decimated ... we were no more than a band of survivors.* This left the 14/Sikhs with little more than ninety men, who were amalgamated with 10/Gurkhas, who themselves had only a subaltern in command. Similar to the Royal Scots and Cameronians, 5/Gurkhas and 6/Gurkhas were in a like state, and were also combined. Even if the British wanted to, they had no men left for a renewed attack on Krithia despite the appearance that they had it in their grasp. The battle of Gully Ravine was never for Krithia, but it shocked the Turkish forces.

Turkish morale had suffered terribly in this attack. A Turkish order by Colonel Rifaat, commander of the 11th Division, stated:

'There is nothing that causes us more sorrow, increases the courage of the enemy and encourages him to attack more freely, causing us great losses, than the losing of these trenches. Henceforth, commanders who surrender these trenches, from whatever side the attack may come, before the last man is killed, will be punished in the same way as if they had run away. ... I hope that this will not occur again. I give notice that if it does I shall carry out the punishment. I do not desire to see a blot made on the courage of our men by those who escape from the trenches to avoid the rifle and machine-gun fire of the enemy. Henceforth, I shall hold responsible all officers who do not shoot with their revolvers all the privates who try to escape from the trenches on any pretext.'

On the morning of 7 July the Turks requested an armistice in order to bury their dead. A note was received from a Turk bearing the flag of truce, which was addressed in a sealed envelope to the British Commander in Chief. However it was believed at the time that the Turks were more worried about the effect the dead would have on the morale of their troops if ordered to attack over the bodies of their comrades than humanitarian or health reasons. Reports show that the Turks tried again during the next couple of days to request a truce, but this was either ignored or answered with a hail of bullets. Hamilton remarked that *dead Turks are better than barbed-wire, and so, though on grounds of humanity as well as health, I should like the poor chaps decently buried, I find myself forced to say No.*

The conditions in the captured trenches and in the newly taken part of Gully Ravine were indescribable. Doctor William Ewing attempted to do so.

> 'To the ordinary litter and filth to be expected where the Turks had been settled for weeks, were added the wreck and ruin wrought by the bombardment, the scattered remains of food, dishes, firewood, articles of clothing and kit, abandoned in the scurry and scramble of the flight before our bayonets. The mangled bodies of the dead, unburied, half-buried, or partially dug up by H.E. shells, under the fierce heat, with loathsome clouds of flies, could only be dealt with by fire. The valley, with its heaps of rotting refuse, its burning pyres and sickening stench, was a veritable Gehenna.'[47]

The burial parties had a dreadful experience in trying to dispose of the dead. In this nauseating atmosphere they did what they could in the prevailing conditions. It was impossible to burn the bodies at first, given the risk of attracting enemy shellfire, so the bodies were buried as best they could be. Later they were collected together, soaked in petrol and set alight. Colonel GH Edington (1/Lowland Field Ambulance) remarked that, *every here and there irregularities in the ground, covered with loose earth and sandbags, and giving off a horrible stench, marked where our men had buried Turkish dead.* Ashmead-Bartlett, who visited Gully Ravine after the battle, wrote that,

> 'All the way up that portion of the gully, only 24 hours before in the enemy's possession, there is a litter of debris of the camp and

of the great fight. Scattered bodies half protruding from the ground, hastily-dug graves, hundreds of rifles and bayonets, some broken, but the majority intact, thousands upon thousands of rounds of ammunition – we made a very big haul indeed in this last engagement – entrenching tools, loaves of bread, soldiers' packs, Turkish letters, a Mullah's prayer stool (a souvenir eagerly sought after), greatcoats and kits, blankets and old sacks, cooking utensils,and firewood, left just where the enemy abandoned them when our gallant infantry broke through at the bayonet's point. Great fires burning at intervals. They are avoided by all and give forth a horrid and sickly stench. On these the Turkish dead, who have been hastily collected, are being burnt, for it is all important to get the dead out of the way as quickly as possible in this hot climate.'

**Ottoman prisoners of war being escorted down Gully Ravine.**

The British casualties between 28–30 June, most of which were incurred on the first day, amounted to 3,800. 156 Brigade lost 1,353, close to half its total strength. *The Times History of the War* states:

'… no action since the first landing did more to cheer the British forces. It seems to promise further progress. A whole mile along the coast, five lines of Turkish trenches, about two hundred prisoners, three mountain guns, and an immense quantity of small arms ammunition and many rifles were captured during the operations on 28 June.'

In his diary entry for 28 June, Hamilton wrote that *Hunter-Weston, Gouraud and Braithwaite agree that – had we only shell to repeat our bombardment of this morning now, we could go on another 1000 yards before dark – result Achi Baba to-morrow or, at the latest, the day after.*

Later, Hamilton noted that Hunter-Weston and Simpson-Baikie explained

**The entrance of Gully Ravine.**

'... forcibly, not to say explosively, that on the 28th June the attack would have scored a success equally brilliant to that achieved by the 29th Division on our left, had we been able to allot as many a shell to the Turkish trenches assaulted by the 156th Brigade – Lowland Division – as we did to the sector by the sea. But we could not, because, there was not enough stuff in our lockers for the night. Such is war! No use splitting the difference and trying to win everywhere like high brows halting between Flanders and Gallipoli. But I am sick at heart, I must say, to think my brother Scots should have had to catch hold of the hot end of the poker. Also to think that, with another couple of hundred rounds, we should have got and held H.12. H.12 which dominates – so prisoners say – the wells whence the enemy draws water for the whole of his right wing.'[48]

After the failure of the May offensive in France, if a decision had been made to concentrate all offensive effort at Gallipoli, the success of 28 June might have been more than just a brilliant success.

### The Battle of Achi Baba Nullah: 12–13 July 1915
The success of Gully Ravine put the British almost within touching distance of Krithia, now barely a kilometre away; but the village was never the objective for this battle. Following the June battles, there was a naive expectation that the Turks would now offer little resistance and were, by July, low in morale. This was far from the truth and, although

the Turks were on the defensive and had suffered devastating casualties, they were a long way from conceding.

Whilst Hamilton waited for three new divisions to arrive, he needed to maintain the pressure for as long as possible: to gain tactical advantage; to maintain the moral ascendency; and to keep the Turks eyes fixed upon Helles, rather than Anzac. Offensive spirit would be maintained by an unceasing routine of trench raiding, sniping and mining, whilst he prepared for another offensive, this one the sequel to the action of 28 June. Hunter-Weston and Gouraud had seen the successful bite and hold advances on the left and right flanks as merely the first stage before a joint attack by the British and French to bring the lagging centre into line.

The importance of artillery was now clear; as the French artillery would not be ready until 12 July, this was the date chosen for the attack. The breathing space that Hunter-Weston inadvertently had to allow, gave the Turks time to recover, reorganise and strengthen their positions, but the delay was unavoidable. It was not only the Turkish forces that had been hammered in the recent Gully Ravine fighting; it had also reduced the offensive capability of the 29th Division, 29 (Indian) Brigade and 156 Brigade. Leaving these troops to hold the line, Hunter-Weston gave the responsibility for the attack to the newly arrived and recently 'blooded' 52nd Division. Hamilton had hoped to use Egerton's division at Anzac; but his desire to capitalise on any Turkish weakness following their crippling losses on 5 July meant that he sanctioned Hunter-Weston's plan. Between Achi Baba Nullah and *Le Rognon* the Turks had deployed the 7th, 4th and 6th Divisions.

The attack on 12 July had the objective of straightening 1,800 metres of line on the right-centre, between Achi Baba Nullah and the Kereves Dere, in an effort to bring it into line with the advances made at Gully Ravine. It was planned to take place in two halves, to allow the artillery to concentrate on each half in turn. 155 Brigade would attack first at 7.35 a.m. The Brigade was on the extreme right of the British line and were to advance in conjunction with the French. To the left of 155 Brigade, 157 Brigade were to remain in their trenches whilst the guns swung round and bombarded their objectives on either side of Achi Baba Nullah. In this area there was a Turkish fortified earthwork which, owing to its shape, was known as the Horseshoe. From this ran two trenches, both wired, E.10 and E.11, approximately 150 metres from the British front line. Unless a real opportunity presented itself, they were not to advance until 4.50 p.m. in the afternoon. 156 Brigade, battered and bruised from its previous fighting, was to be kept as divisional reserve.

All the troops in the initial attack were to advance in four waves, starting at the same time, one from each of the British trench lines. The objectives were strictly limited to the first three Turkish lines, although this later caused considerable confusion, as in many cases only two Turkish trenches had been completed. The bombardment opened up at 4.30 a.m. with the French 75s, as usual, causing devastation in the Turkish trenches. At 7.30 a.m., the gunners lengthened their range to block off the surrounding area in hopes of preventing the inevitable Turkish reinforcements being rushed to the scene.

The leading waves, in some battalions gallantly led by their pipers, began their advance across No Man's Land at 7.35 a.m., while 157 Brigade gave supporting small arms fire in an effort to keep the heads of the Turks down. The Scottish troops reached the first two Turkish trenches with minimal losses. Major D. Yuille, 4/RSF, wrote of the event.

'Unless one has seen it there is no imagination that can picture a belt of land some 400 yards wide converted into a seething hell of destruction. Rifle and machine-gun bullets rip up the earth, ping past the ear, or whing off the loose stones; shrapnel bursts overhead and the leaden bullets strike the ground with a vicious thud; the earth is rent into yawning chasms, while planks, sandbags, clods of earth and rugged great chunks of steel hurtle through the air. The noise is an indescribable, nerve-racking, continuous, deafening roar, while drifting clouds of smoke only allow an intermittent view of the damnable inferno.'[49]

If it was only these two lines that had needed capturing the attack would have been a complete success; but orders mentioned a third trench and it was this that threw the attack into confusion. 4/KOSB, for example, advanced past this 'dummy' trench in search of the third line. Not realising that they had already past it, they unfortunately drifted into the French *feu de barrage* on the Turkish reserve lines. Cut off, it was a long time before they could fall back on the captured trenches – and then only after suffering heavy losses. Intelligence in the pre-attack planning had identified a third trench from aerial photographs, although in reality it turned out to be barely a scrape in the ground, a shallow ditch that could not be captured or defended. In the midst of a maelstrom of lead, the efforts to locate and capture this non-existent third line caused many unnecessary casualties. In the confusion many of the soldiers were isolated in the 'third line'; one of them was Private Nixon, also of the 4/RSF.

'I managed to get to the furthest point, that was the third Turkish trench or dummy trench. It was about one foot deep, and we had to set-to and fill sandbags. We were packed together and enfiladed from the left. Our fire rapidly diminished, till there was no one left to fire. Then I was knocked out. When I came to, our little trench was occupied by a Turk to every two yards. Four or five of our men were lying across me, and I could not get up. I was bayoneted six times in the back whilst lying there. A Turk officer, at the point of his revolver, ordered the Turks to release me.'[50]

Despite much confused fighting and fierce Turkish resistance, the second line of captured trenches were held.

On the British right flank the French had advanced at the same time and managed to capture *Le Rognon*, driving the Turks back to the edge of Kereves Dere. How the Turks managed to hold on to this rather precarious position on the cliff tops of the ravine was an achievement in its own right. The French could now claim the capture of the whole of Kereves Spur. This time a link with the British right was maintained and avoided the sort of domino collapse that had so plagued the allies. Hunter-Weston and Bailloud decided to proceed with the afternoon attack: that by 157 Brigade on the left in conjunction with a renewed assault by the French on *le Quadrilatère* area and 'tactical advances' where possible by 155 Brigade.

The second bombardment opened up and at 4.50 p.m. 157 Brigade rushed forward under heavy fire to capture the first two lines of Turkish

Officers of the 4/KOSB before leaving for Gallipoli.

**French soldier from 175e Régiment d'infanterie carrying a wounded comrade.**

trenches, putting them in touch with 155 Brigade on their right; but again there was confusion, as no third line could be located. Now in the hands of the Scots, frantic efforts were made to consolidate these gains in preparation for the inevitable counter attack. The shattered trenches had to be turned round to make the parapet and fire step face Achi Baba, old communication trenches were barricaded off and new ones were dug back to the old British front line. Wounded could then be evacuated and supplies brought up, all this against a backdrop of chattering machine-gun fire, flares and shrapnel bursts. However, the French attack failed and no more gains could be made at *le Quadrilatère*. Their fifth, and last, battle of Kereves Dere had ended.

At 6.00 p.m., the 52nd Division was ordered to make the line good; it seemed to be fairly in the Allied grasp. All night long, determined counter attacks, one after another, were repulsed by the French and 155 Brigade, but at about 7.30 a.m. the right of 157 Brigade briefly gave way before a party of Turkish bombers. Support in the form of men of the battle-weary RND were then sent forward to make a fresh attack.

At 4.30 p.m. on 13 July, 2 (Naval) Brigade, less Deal Battalion, lunged forward. Chatham Battalion, in some confusion due to orders arriving late, did not attack, leaving the Nelson and Portsmouth battalions to attack alone. Nelson Battalion on the left valiantly advanced and made good the ground, well supported by the artillery of the French, capturing the line E.12b and E.11. The Portsmouth Battalion, pressing on too far, fell into precisely the same error and at precisely the same location as 4/KOSB the previous day. Casualties were heavy. Both Nelson and Portsmouth battalions lost their commanding officers: Lieutenant Colonels Edmund Evelegh and Frank Luard. Nelson Battalion reported only four officers and 120 men remaining, whilst in Portsmouth Battalion it was reported that most of the men *were at that time in the front line totally exhausted owing to dysentery, gastric troubles and continuous wear and tear*. The trenches were reported to be in a very bad state, with the rotting bodies piled in heaps, forcing the men to wear gas respirators to try and suppress the smell. During the following day the RND relieved the remaining elements of the 52nd Division. Egerton was far from happy with the outcome of the battle and later wrote:

'It seems to me that the fighting of this battle was premature and at the actual moment worse than unnecessary – I submit that it was cruel and wasteful. The troops on the Peninsula were tired and worn out; there were only two Infantry Brigades, the 155th and the 157th, that had not been seriously engaged. It was well known to the higher command that large reinforcements were arriving from England and a grand attack was to be made at Suvla. Was it not therefore obvious that the exhausted garrison at Helles should be given a fortnight's respite and that the fresh attacks from that position should synchronise with those at Suvla and Anzac? I contend that the Battle of July 12–13th was due to a complete want of a true appreciation of the situation. If the conception of the battle was wrong the tactics of the action were far worse. The division of the attack of two Brigades on a narrow front into two phases, no less than nine hours apart, was positively wicked.'[51]

After two days' of fighting the result was an advance of up to 350 metres; but it was at a cost of thirty percent British casualties, about 3,000 men. The French suffered less; however, General Masnou, the commander of the *1er Division*, was mortally wounded on 12 July, succumbing to his wounds a few days later. Turkish casualties were reported as being in excess of 5,000, some sources putting them at over 9,000.[52]

Lieutenant Charles Black, 6/HLI, described the aftermath of this fighting.

'The 12th July had been awful but the days that followed were hideous. All around in the open lay our dead, whom no one could approach to bury by day or by night, for to climb out of the trench even in the dark was to court disaster. The trenches themselves were littered with the Turkish victims of our shell fire, in places piled on top of one another to the depth of several feet. The stench was indescribable. In one communication trench that had to be used for days until another could be cut, it was necessary to crawl on hands and knees for many yards over the reeking bodies in order to keep within the shelter of the parapet. The heat was stifling both day and night; water was almost unobtainable. It was hell!'

Some brave men did venture out, one of whom was Private James Cowan, 7/HLI, who showed *conspicuous gallantry and devotion to duty during the night of 12–13 July 1915, on the Gallipoli Peninsula, when he searched the ground up to the firing line and brought in under fire*

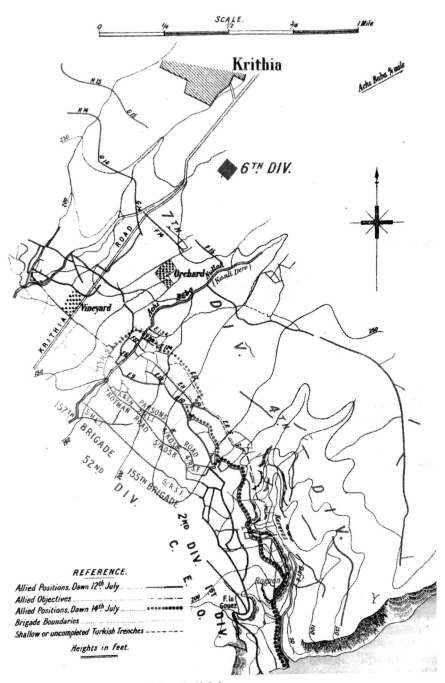

**Battle of Achi Baba Nullah – 12–13 July.**

*over fifty wounded men.*[53] Cowan was awarded the DCM but was killed in action on 4 December. He also received a posthumous Mention in Despatches from General Sir Ian Hamilton.

On 17 July Hunter-Weston fell ill from a mixture of exhaustion and sun-stroke, and a few days later was evacuated sick. He returned to Britain; and then went to the Western Front in March 1916 to command the re-formed VIII Corps. During the opening day of the Somme Offensive on 1 July 1916 his Corps suffered the worst casualties and failed to capture any of its objectives. Despite his prominent part in the Battle of the Somme, he was elected to the House of Commons in a by-election as the Unionist member for North Ayrshire (his predecessor, who had served from the outbreak of the war, died of his wounds in September 1916).

With the departure of this over confident, unrelenting and merciless man (though not entirely without attributes, including considerable personal bravery and, surprisingly perhaps, some empathy for the men), the tempo of leadership changed. On 24 July his place was temporarily taken by Lieutenant General Hon. Sir Frederick Stopford, who commanded VIII Corps while awaiting the arrival of IX Corps. The contrast between these two commanders could not have been more different, as will be seen. With Stopford ashore, plans were well under way for Hamilton's next offensive. A new landing was to take place at Suvla and an Anzac breakout was planned. Apart from a diversionary attack at The Vineyard, Helles, for once, would not be the main battlefront.

Whilst this was happening, the French were gearing up for their autumn offensive on the Western Front, in which the British contribution was to be the Battle of Loos commencing on 25 September 1915. The 'shell scandal' that had brought down Asquith's Liberal government in May was still a raw issue and the adequate supply of shells had still not been resolved. When Hamilton received a reply from the War Office regarding shells for Gallipoli, he was furious with the response.

'It will be quite impossible to continue to send you ammunition at this rate, as we have reduced the supply to France in order to send what we have to you, and the amounts asked for in the second part of your telegram could not be spared without stopping all operations in France. This, of course, is out of the question.'

Livid, Hamilton repeated the last two sentences to emphasise his disgust.

'"This, of course, is out of the question." "Stopping all operations in France" is the very kernel of the question. If half the things we hear about the Bosche forces and our own are half true, we have no prospect of dealing any decisive blow in the West till next spring. And an indecisive blow is worse than no blow. But we can hold on there till all's blue. Now H.E. is offensive and shrapnel is defensive. I ought to attack at once; French mustn't. Therefore we should be given, now, dollops of H.E. This talk does not come through my hat. Some of the best brains on the Western field are in touch with those of some of my following here. The winning post stares us in the face; my old Chief gallops off the course; how can I resist calling out? And then I get this "of course" cable (not written by K., I feel sure), which shows, if it shows anything, that "of course" we ought never to have come here at all! Simple, is it not? In war all is simple – that's why it's so complex. Never mind; my cable has not been wasted. We reckon the 1,100 extra rounds it has produced may save us 100 British casualties.'

Hamilton was seriously concerned.

'So far, so good. Bailloud and Hunter-Weston have carried two lines of Turkish trenches, an advance of two to four hundred yards. But the ammunition question has reached a crisis, and has become dangerous – very dangerous. On the whole Southern theatre of operations, counting shell in limbers and shell loaded in guns, we have 5,000 rounds of shrapnel. No high explosive – and fighting is still going on!'

And it was not just a problem with lack of shells to fight this campaign but also a lack of adequate and reliable artillery. For example, the 91st Heavy Battery RGA landed between 22 and 23 July, bringing into action four 60 pdrs. By 6 August, i.e. only about a fortnight later, there were all out of action owing to excessive recoil. None of this boded well for the future.

**French corpses by the Turkish wire entanglements in Kereves Dere.**

# Chapter 6

# The Vineyard: The August Offensive

Whilst there was never really a quiet period on Gallipoli, the VIII Corps action at the Vineyard would, albeit unknowingly, be the last significant offensive at Helles. Planned as a diversion to aid both the Anzac attack and the new landing at Suvla, it would also continue as part of the wider offensive. In the planners' eyes the areas chosen was selected to give maximum benefit to the British and French in the continued advances towards Krithia. Brigadier General Harold Street, one of the architects of this action, spoke *grandiloquently of the capture of Krithia and Achi Baba.*[54] This was rather optimistic, but it was a strategic objective nevertheless if a broader and deeper breakthrough was to occur. Since the attack on 4 June and the subsequent actions at Gully Ravine and Achi Baba Nullah, the new front line between these positions had assumed a dogleg shape. It was this ground where an opportunity was seen for two objectives: to bite out the dogleg to get closer to Krithia and to focus the Turks on this operation whilst more significant events were happening in the northern sector.

For the British there would be two separate attacks over two days, with a follow up action dependent on the outcomes of these initial attacks. On 6 August 88 Brigade (29th Division) would attack on a front of almost a kilometre from Worcester Flat to Krithia Nullah, aiming to take the remaining 'H' trenches in Turkish hands. Three battalions, almost at full strength, would be used; from left to right they comprised 1/Essex, 2/Hants and 4/Worcesters. To the right of 88 Brigade and on the Worcesters' flank, 5/Manchesters would attack the bomb stations at H.11a and H11b, both of which overlooked Krithia Nullah. Neutralising these bomb stations was important as they would pose a threat to the 42nd Division's assault the following day. If 88 Brigade's attack were successful, 86 and 87 Brigade would be available to follow up on 8/9 August. The attack on 6 August would start at 3.50 p.m.

The second attack would be on 7 August and would be spearheaded by the 42nd Division's 125 (Lancashire Fusilier) Brigade and 127 (Manchester) Brigade. Their objective was to the right of Krithia Nullah and 88 Brigade and 5/Manchester's earlier assault. The plan for 127 Brigade was that, left to right, 9/Manchesters and 7/Manchesters

**Krithia Nullah.**

were positioned to advance up either side of Krithia Nullah and, to their right 1/6 and 1/8 Manchesters, now amalgamated because of earlier casualties, would attack the 'G' and 'F' trenches. 125 Brigade were stretched from the left of the Vineyard, across the Krithia Road and beyond for another 250 metres towards Achi Baba Nullah, in order 6/LF, 7/LF, 8/LF and 5/LF. Both 127 and 125 Brigades' attacks would begin at 9.40 a.m. 126 Brigade would be in support. To their right the French *2e Division* would attack *le Quadrilatère* again and to their right the *1er Division* would attack two Turkish trenches by Kereves Dere.

The bombardment of the 'H' trenches and the flank began at 2.30 p.m., supported by naval gunfire, preceding the infantry advance. The Turkish guns replied in their normal retaliatory fashion, ranging their shells to drop on the support and reserve positions with such effect that several of these trenches became untenable and the troops had to be moved. The trench mortars, borrowed from the French, were reported to have done great execution in the strong points on left front and totally demolished the parapet in several places; but on the whole H.13, H.13a and H.13b were relatively undamaged. At 3.15 p.m. British machine-gun fire added to the crescendo of battle, the Turkish lines almost invisible in the dust of battle.

The objective for 4/Worcesters was the H.13 trench. The Battalion's War Diary recorded.

'At 3.40 pm the range of the guns was lengthened and the first line went over the parapet, followed almost immediately by the second. The fourth line entered the trench to assist the third line

131

over the parapet. The first line had now covered about 200 yards but were already thinned considerably on the left by machine-gun fire, notwithstanding the haze of dust which partially obscured them. Many men were now forced to stop for breath and when they again advanced came under a heavy enfilade fire. The second line suffered terribly from machine-gun fire when about half way across and only isolated groups reached the slope to the Turkish trenches. The third and fourth lines encountered a murderous machine gun and shell fire immediately they left the trench and, though none turned back, only a small section in dead ground on the right succeeded in getting more than 50 yards from our trench.

On the extreme right our men were enfiladed by a terrible machine-gun fire that increased in intensity when the attack on our left failed, and the only survivors from this flank were those who were hit on leaving the trench and fell or scrambled back.

Detached parties of the first and second line had entered the enemy's trench and thrown the tin disc over the back parapet to show the sections occupied. On the right a continuous stretch of 30 or 40 yards was occupied by about 30 men and one Sergeant.

The attack on both flanks had failed and the only approach was across the open. It was owing to the failure of these attacks that our men were subjected to a terrible enfilade machine-gun fire, which was continuing even after the last line had nearly all been shot down, being brought to bear together with shrapnel on the groups of wounded until scarcely a man was left alive.'

Very few unwounded men actually reached the enemy's trenches and those that did were attacked by large numbers of Turks. The Essex and Hants lads had a similar experience; the Essex captured their part of H.13 but were later pushed out by counter attack, the Hants were cut down by concealed machine-gun fire before they even reached it. After one hour just thirty men and a heroic sergeant from the Worcesters remained in a captured fragment of H.13, against unbelievable odds. They remained there all day; just twelve survivors returned to their original line after midnight. The attack was a failure.

Casualties amongst the officers and men were heavy. One such was Captain Howard Field of the Worcesters, killed in this attack. He was one of three Field brothers to die in the Great War. His younger brother, Second Lieutenant Cyril Decimus Field, was in the same battalion and was killed on 4 June, the same day that Howard was wounded. Recovering from his wounds, Howard returned to his battalion just prior to the August offensive. There was a third brother, Clifford, a

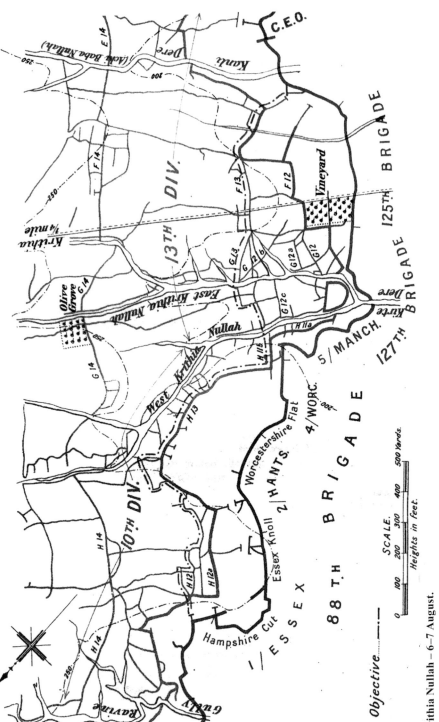

Krithia Nullah – 6–7 August.

captain in the Royal Marine Light Infantry, who was killed in 1914 when HMS *Aboukir* was sunk. This was a great tragedy for a family that had lost three sons in one year of the war.

Amongst the other rank survivors was Private Ben Tromans; a letter to his wife in Cradley was printed in the *County Express*, describing the intensity of the Turkish fire that the 4/Worcesters experienced:

> 'It was not fit for a fly to get out of the trenches, for the shot and shells were flying everywhere, knocking the sand bags off the top of the trenches which we had to mount to get at the Turks. For five days it was like that, and we had to advance in it. When we started we could see the men falling like rain, but when we got into the trenches it was our time. Then we started mowing them down. It can't last much longer here.'

In the action Ben was wounded in the knee and evacuated to hospital in Alexandria, Egypt, from where he wrote: *Let me know if Harry has got through, for I did not see him after we made the charge on August 6th. I can't hear how he got on, and am very anxious to know.*

Harry Tromans was his brother and they had both enlisted together at the Stourbridge Recruiting Office, which was housed in the Labour Exchange. Harry was reported missing after the attack, and his body was never found. Ben was evacuated back to England from Alexandria, only to die on 19 April 1916 of an internal complaint after undergoing two operations. His body was returned home by rail to Cradley Heath Station and he was given a military funeral at St. Luke's, Cradley Heath.

A letter from Private Christopher Whiley, 4/Worcesters, also a Cradley man, described his experience of the day:

> 'On August 6th, about 3.30 p.m., we went into the firing line, and had to charge right away, only having time to fix bayonets. We had to charge about 350 yards, and never shall I forget that dreadful time and also the bullets which were whistling all around us; but I succeeded in reaching the Turks' trenches without a scratch. We were afterwards treated to a taste of rifle and maxim fire, and nearly all my pals were either killed or wounded, but thank God I came out unscathed.'

Whiley survived the war.[55]

There was hope that Private John Gardiner, the son of the late John and Abia Gardiner, was one of the survivors until news was published in The Malvern News in June 1917: *News has been received in Birmingham*

**Guests of the Sultan. British PoWs captured during August 1915.**

*that Pte John Gardiner, Worcestershire Regiment,* whose home was at
4, Woodland Cottages, West Malvern, and was reported as a Prisoner of
War, *is now reported as having died on the 6th August 1915 or sometime
later. He has two other brothers serving in France.* Gardiner, if the
reports of him being a prisoner of war were true, did not survive to have
his details taken by the Red Cross. Of the 4/Worcesters' casualties that
day, at least three officers and sixty-eight other ranks were captured,
mostly from X Company, who found themselves spending the rest of the
war in Turkish PoW camps.

After dark an officer's patrol was sent out to try and locate the sections
of trench H.13 that were believed to be occupied by the battalion but, after
an hour of thorough reconnaissance, it returned to report the news that
the whole trench was back in Turkish hands. Many wounded men were
brought in during the night and at dawn the battalion returned to Gully
Beach for reorganisation, having lost sixteen officers and 752 other ranks
in the attack. These were shocking statistics, especially when one realises
this was merely a diversionary attack to support the Anzac and Suvla
operations. This was the worst single day's casualties of any battalion at
Gallipoli; its 768 casualties in one day amounted to 93 percent casualties
killed, wounded or missing. The other two assaulting battalions suffered
442 (1/Essex) and 448 (2/Hants) casualties in the same attack.

The second attack was by the 42nd Division the following day,
7 August. Two attacking waves would be used, the first to capture

135

the front line; the second, which would attack ten minutes later, was to leapfrog through them to capture the second line. During the day and preceding night preparations were made for the assault; scaling ladders were placed on the parapets, kit was adjusted and weapons cleaned. Lastly the wire entanglements were brought in. All of this activity provided clear signs to the Turks that something was about to happen. The bombardment began early on 7 August and continued until 9.40 a.m., when the infantry went over the top. A tremendous fusillade of fire met the advancing battalions, showing that the Turks were ready, waiting and apparently unaffected by the bombardment.

Three battalions of the Manchester Regiment showed dash and determination in their attack either side of Krithia Nullah, but their efforts were only partially successful due to the intricacies of the ground around the Nullah and the associated Turkish trench system. Several bodies from the Manchesters were discovered in the nullah when this ground was finally captured by the 52nd Division at the end of December 1915; their bodies were identified and cremated in the Nullah.

When the evitable Turkish counter attack was launched at 4.30 pm against these partially occupied and exposed positions the British were forced back to their original line. The Turks seemed content with recapturing their trenches and did not push the attack any further, both lines settling back to their positions of that morning.

125 (Lancashire Fusilier) Brigade had more, if still only partial, success attacking the Turkish lines by the Vineyard and astride the Krithia Road. The advance of 6/LF and 7/LF to the left of the Krithia Road and in front of the Vineyard was successful. Initially the attack to the right of the Krithia Road went well, the 8/LF and 5/LF capturing the first Turkish trench, F12. However this front line Turkish trench was found to be shallow and was exposed to enfilade fire. The trench had probably not been completed because of the July Achi Baba Nullah attack, which had captured the salient on the right flank.

All the first line of attackers could do was to fling themselves down behind the fourteen-inch high earth parapet, which gave them more cover than the trench itself. From here they began firing into the second Turkish line in support of the next wave, which was due to follow ten minutes later. Despite this support, few in the second wave could get past this first position, eventually taking cover themselves alongside the men of the first wave. Superior numbers and a murderous enfilade fire soon ejected the few parties that reached the second objective, G. 12. Meanwhile, in the new British line (the old Turkish front line), because of the low parapet, the Fusiliers had great difficulty in filling sandbags or digging deeper into the hard, sunbaked ground. Casualties mounted. The inevitable Turkish

**1/5 Lancashire Fusiliers looking through a trench periscope.**

**A two millennia old design. A Leach 'bomb-throwing' catapult in action at Helles.**

counter attack came at 11.00 a.m. which succeeded in recapturing the front line. The 5/LF and 8/LF in turn managed to eject the Turks once more, but only from part of the trench. Another Turkish counter attack at 1.30 p.m. was brought to a standstill by the artillery. It was only another counter attack, at 4.30 p.m., that succeeded in pushing back both the Manchesters and 125 Brigade. The Vineyard however, was held against all attacks, which continued into 8 and 9 August.

Casualties were again heavy in the Division. Twenty officers and 203 men were killed; thirty-six officers and 770 other ranks were wounded and twenty-four officers and 511 ORs were missing. For example, 1/6 Lancashire Fusiliers went into the attack with fifteen officers; eight were killed, six were wounded, and only one returned unhurt.

One of the few that reached the second objective was Second Lieutenant Eric Duckworth, B Company, 6/LF. A student of politics and economics, Eric was the son of one of Rochdale's wealthiest families who owned a grocery empire totalling over 140 stores. Like many, he volunteered for his local Territorial Army unit, Lord Rochdale's 6/LF, when war was declared in 1914. At 19 years of age he was the youngest officer in this battalion. On 6 May the battalion had distinguished themselves, Eric emerging as a fearless and greatly respected platoon officer, much admired by his men. On 5 August he wrote home to his mother:

'Little enough did I think 12 months ago today that on the anniversary of mobilisation I should be writing you from a hole in the Gallipoli Peninsula, not having seen you for ten months, to the tune of 75mm guns. However, you never know your luck, and I may see you in time to celebrate my 20th birthday at home, but as things look at present there is not much chance of that.'

**Second Lieutenant Eric Duckworth, 1/6 Lancashire Fusiliers.**

Eric's luck ran out on 7 August. Reaching the first line of Turkish trenches that had just been captured by A Company with little difficulty, he rallied his platoon to charge the second line. Only three men, Eric and Privates Norman Howarth and William Porter, made it to this objective, where vicious hand to hand fighting took place. Eric was shot through the chest and fell onto the parapet of this trench; Porter was then killed, leaving only the wounded Howarth to tell the story. Private Heywood, another survivor of the battle, later reported that Eric's last words to his platoon, on seeing the odds stacked against them, were: *Well lads, we are not going to a church parade today!*[56]

Private Thomas Ashurst, A Company, 6/LF also fell that day, probably in the capture of the Turkish front line. He was 25 years old and left behind a wife, Frances, and a child in their home on Regent Street in Rochdale. Like Duckworth, his body was not identified after the war and remains missing. His wife later produced a memorial silk with the verse:

'Nameless his grave on a battlefield gory,
Only a cross o'er a mound of brown earth;
Dead in the pride of his youth and his glory.
Far from his home and land of his birth.'

Eric Duckworth, William Porter and Thomas Ashurst are today commemorated on the Helles Memorial to the Missing (Panel 59–73).

There were many acts of bravery during the battle. One young artillery officer, Second Lieutenant BC Trappes-Lomax, went forward into the firing line to report on the Lancashire Fusiliers Brigade's advance. He established a telephone connection and sent back constant and accurate reports of the advance. In the afternoon he went up a sap to the left of the Vineyard to reconnoitre the whole of the newly captured line, visiting each barricade and relaying the information back through the rest of the day and night. On 8 August, he made another reconnaissance but could not send back any information as his telephone cables had been cut in several places by Turkish shells. He was unable to repair so many breaks in the line so instead laid out a new line to his advanced observation post, re-establishing contact just before midnight. He remained at his post, sending back important information and directing artillery support until he was relieved during the morning of 9 August. Trappes-Lomax was awarded a particularly noteworthy Military Cross and a Mention in Despatches for his bravery.

Another feat of great bravery was performed by Lieutenant (acting Captain) William Forshaw, 9/Manchesters, a former teacher at Manchester Grammar School. Forshaw recorded his part in the defence of the Vineyard:

'I and about twenty men were instructed to hold a barricade at the head of the sap. Facing us were three converging saps held by the Turks, who were making desperate efforts to retake this barricaded corner, and so cut off all the other men in the trench. The Turks attacked at frequent intervals along the three saps from Saturday afternoon until Monday morning, and they advanced into the open with the objective of storming the parapet. They were met by a combination of bombing and rifle fire, but the bomb was the chief weapon used both by the Turks and ourselves.'[57]

Next to Forshaw at the head of the sap was Sergeant Harry Grantham.

'There were all sorts of bombs. Round bombs and bombs made out of jam tins and filled with explosives and bits of iron, lead,

139

needles, etc. It was lively while it lasted. We could see the Turks coming on at us, great big fellows they were, and we dropped our bombs right amidst them. Captain [sic. Lieutenant] Forshaw was at the end of the trench. He fairly revelled in it. He kept joking and cheering us on, and was smoking cigarettes all the while. He used his cigarettes to light the fuses of the bombs, instead of striking matches. "Keep it up, boys!" he kept saying. We did, although a lot of our lads were killed and injured by the Turkish firebombs. It was exciting, I can tell you.'[58]

The bombs used by both sides lacked any great lethal capability; they could kill, but they lacked much explosive power or a proper fragmentation casing; they wounded and often inflicted numerous cuts from the hundreds of minute fragments that were the result of the blast. And they were dangerous if you were unlucky or over-ambitious, as Lance Corporal Thomas Pickford found out.

Lieutenant William Forshaw
VC, 1/9 Manchester Regiment.

'Bombs were bursting all around us. Some of the boys in their excitement caught the Turkish bombs before they exploded, and hurled them back again. They did not always manage to catch them in time and three of them had their hands blown off. What made the position worse was that as soon as we had entered the trench a bomb laid out six of us. I was one of them. I bandaged up my leg, bandaged the others and sent them back – I carried on.'[59]

The fighting continued for the best part of two days. Even when the 9/Manchesters were relieved, Forshaw insisted in staying on to lead the defence.

'I was far too busy to think of myself or to think of anything. We just went at it without a pause while the Turks were attacking, and in the slack intervals I put more fuses into bombs. I cannot imagine how I escaped with only a bruise from a piece of shrapnel. It was miraculous. The attacks were very fierce at times, but only once did the Turks succeed in getting right up to the parapet. Three attempted to climb over, but I shot them with my revolver. All this time both our bomb throwing and shooting had been very effective, and many Turkish dead were in front of the parapet and in the saps. The attack was not continuous, of course, but we had to be on the watch all the time, and so it was impossible to get any sleep. Fortunately, we had no fewer than 800 of those bombs, but we got rid of the lot during the greatest weekend I have ever spent.'

The physical and nervous exhaustion that followed in the aftermath of their eventual relief took a toll on Forshaw, despite his apparent insouciance, as Lance Corporal Samuel Bayley noticed.

'Myself, a few men and the Captain [sic. Lieutenant] held a trench which was almost impossible to hold, but we stuck to it like glue, in spite of the Turks attacking us with bombs. I can tell you I accounted for a few Turks. Our Captain has been recommended for the V.C. and I hope he gets it because he was very determined to hold the trench till the last man was finished. But we did not lose many. Our Captain has not got over it yet, but it is only his nerves that are shattered a bit.'[60]

An artists' impression of the 'Cigarette VC'.

Forshaw would be awarded the Victoria Cross for his forty-one hours of battle. His citation states that:

> '...he held his own, not only directing his men and encouraging them by exposing himself with the utmost disregard of danger ... when he re-joined his battalion he was choked and sickened by bomb fuses, badly bruised from a fragment of shrapnel, and could barely lift his arm from continuous bomb throwing. It was due to his personal example, magnificent courage and endurance that this very important corner was held.'

Because of the continual way he had to smoke cigarettes during this action in order to light the bomb fuses, he became popularly known as the 'Cigarette VC'. One Military Cross and three Distinguished Conduct Medals were also won by members of Forshaw's A Company.

Following his exploits at The Vineyard, his promotion to captain was confirmed. Captain Forshaw VC married a nurse in Ashton under Lyne a year later whilst he was on leave, and spent most of 1916 and 1917 touring the country and giving speeches to raise citizen morale. He joined the Home Guard during the Second World War; in 1943 he died, apparently from a heart attack, whilst cutting a hedge in the garden.

The first stage of the battle for the Vineyard came to an end on 9 August, with 126 (East Lancs) Brigade holding the division's hard-won gains; but the Turks were determined to regain the lost ground. During the night of 12 August they attacked in strength and were briefly successful in its recapture, only to be bombed out on 13 August, when the British finally consolidated the line and held it until the end of the campaign.

For an area of ground no more than 180 metres long and ninety metres wide, the Vineyard had been hard-won. The thought *that*

A sketch of William Thomas Forshaw by Henry Wright (The Westminsterian).

142

*the attack might lead to a complete breakthrough can be seen as a failure of intelligence, with this set alongside over-optimistic expectations for the 6/7 August.*[61] The French objectives were more optimistic and their attack was a complete failure, causing losses of 780 men. British casualties for the attacks were estimated at over 3,300; Turkish losses were believed to be 7,500. These were high casualties indeed for what could be argued as a tactically unimportant area of shell-blasted vines.

Hamilton sent a congratulatory message to the Corps Commander:

'Your operations have been invaluable, and have given the Northern Corps the greatest possible help by drawing the main Turkish effort on yourselves. I was sure you were ready for them to-night. Well done, 8th Corps.'

The diversion at Helles was to prove of no value to the operations in the north and it did little to straighten the line between the Nullahs.

# Chapter 7

# The End – The Evacuation

With the failure of the August offensive, the stark reality of the situation at Gallipoli began to sink in. Whilst large expanses of ground had been taken at huge cost at Anzac and Suvla, the tactically important high ground remained in Turkish hands. Even Achi Baba, the first day objective at Helles, remained a hill too far for Hamilton's force, whilst hope had gone for capturing Krithia. The MEF's fighting strength, physical ability and morale was dwindling by the day. Not only was there little hope of further reinforcements, but the Turks had continued to grow stronger in both manpower and the supply of munitions, both of which flowed steadily into the area in ever increasing numbers: it was reckoned that by this stage they had 315,000 men available compared to the MEF's 150,000.

On 6 September 1915, Bulgaria declared war on Serbia, joined the Central Powers and effectively opened a new front in Salonika, in north eastern Greece. The Greeks made a plea to the Allies for military support, which was granted. There was no possibility in the short term of finding the manpower required as on the Western Front a new joint Franco-British offensive (the Second Battle of Artois 1915; the Battle of Loos) was about to begin. Much to Hamilton's disgust, Kitchener ordered that men be sent from Gallipoli. Hamilton eventually released the French *2e Division* from Helles, and the 10th (Irish) Division from Suvla. Any future major operation at Gallipoli was now far less likely.

At Gallipoli there was more than one enemy for Hamilton's MEF. In the 42nd Division history it states that *the ravages of sickness had reduced the fighting strength of the Division more than had bullets of the enemy.* This was a common situation amongst all the divisions. Dysentery and jaundice were rampant and there was an epidemic of septic sores.

In September and October there was little break in the hot and dry weather and water was still in short supply. Wells had long since run dry or were poisoned, which meant much of the water had to be transported from distant places, including Egypt. The diet still largely consisted of tinned salted bully beef, Maconochies stew, dry biscuits, cheese, bacon and apricot jam, none of which helped quench the thirst. Helles was not

**Wire rests in front of the British trenches.**

a spacious battlefield and the men were confined largely to trenches or cramped in reserve areas where sanitary conditions were far from ideal. Along with the monotonous food, lack of sleep, lice, plagues of flies, Helles was one huge graveyard, many of the corpses, both friend and foe, lying partially or completely unburied. It was not surprising that sickness was rife amongst the weak and emaciated soldiers who garrisoned Gallipoli.

From September onwards Helles settled down to trench warfare, comprising sniping, patrolling, bombing, carrying parties, trench improvements and salvage duties day and night. Offensive operations were confined to mining and bombing, used by both sides to gain tactical advantages over each other. In September alone, for example, the Turks detonated six mines at The Gridiron, near Gully Ravine, damaging the British trenches.

In mid September Ordinary Seaman Joseph Murray of Hood Battalion was in Gully Ravine and was busy priming a British mine:

'We had made a recess in which were laid three 10lb tins of Ammonal. The sandbags that would normally have been carried away were left for us to use as tamping. The detonators had been placed on one of the sandbags so that there would be no danger of pulling them from the tin during the tamping. Dozens and dozens of sandbags had to be carefully packed to ensure that the least resistance would be upwards; otherwise the force of the explosion would simply blow them away and we would completely destroy our own gallery and do absolutely no damage to the Turkish firing line some twenty-eight feet above.

At almost 3 p.m. the men in the line were warned that we were going to blast and down went the plunger. With a terrific bang up went the mine and, with it, the Turkish front line. Our line trembled; huge chunks of earth fell everywhere from the cloud of dust that shrouded the entire sector. So for my part ended four very trying days, of which every moment had been a nightmare.'[62]

The following day, 15 September, Murray was on duty again and went down the same British gallery to clean up and make safe the roof when all of a sudden there was darkness. The Turks had fired a counter-mine and blown up the British gallery, with Joe and his friend Alec inside.

'I could not for the life of me understand how the Turks had managed to spring their mine so soon. Only yesterday we had blown them sky-high from this very spot. Alec and I groped about in the dark, looking for our candles and matches. We found neither, so decided to explore the gallery to ascertain where the explosion had occurred. The level part was reasonably clear. Several minor falls of roof had taken place but we had no difficulty in climbing over these obstructions to reach the rising part. From there we should have been able to see daylight, but we couldn't. We knew that we were entombed; but the gallery was still open. We groped our way up the rising gallery and at once realised we should not be able to go much further. Everywhere was broken up. Timber – not broken but dislodged – prevented any further movement up the slope and we did not know if this blockage was the seat of the explosion or only another fall. We tugged at the timber until we got it free. Quite a lot of earth came away with it, which told us we had no more gallery left and our only hope of survival would be to claw our way upwards through the broken earth, knowing full well that if it was too loose it would suffocate us. We estimated that we were at least twenty-five feet below the surface. I began to burrow, with Alex behind me heaving the lumps of clay down the eight feet or so of the sloping gallery. We changed over repeatedly and, as time passed, found it increasingly difficult to clear the earth away. The burrow behind us had closed in and the roof kept caving in. We were unable to extricate ourselves from the earth we had clawed away and the constant failing of the roof altered our direction. Twisting and turning in an effort to free my leg, I fancied I saw daylight from a fraction of a second. Alec did not see it, but believed me. With new hope we struggled on; our time was running out and we both knew it. Again and again we were completely buried but, in time, managed to clear ourselves.'

By dint of one, last, super human, effort both Joe and Alec miraculously reached the surface. Mining and countermining was to continue right up until the end of the campaign in a cat and mouse game that was not just confined to the British sector.

On the right, near Kereves Dere, Lieutenant Joseph Vassal, *56 RI* eluded to the beginnings of the underground war in a letter to his English wife.

'There is no need to put one's ear to the ground to hear the sound of picks. At daybreak everyone went to listen to the picks: General Bailloud, colonels, majors, men. A new sensation, but a rather disagreeable one! A fresh method of warfare has now begun for us. General Gouraud had feared it, but did not wish to be the first to begin. His successors were of the same mind. But now that the Turks had challenged us we must answer them. Time presses. At first it was a question of reciprocating by means of camouflets, that is to say, laying the sap open after blowing up the retaining wall with dynamite. I think the counter-mine has been adopted.'[63]

Life below and above the ground went on, the British in particular keeping up the offensive spirit with some minor tactical operations. Whilst mining was going on in the Gully Ravine sector, the 52nd Division were particularly active in the Krithia Nullah sector. Here the work of pushing forward various bombing saps at night was carried out several times in October and with complete success.

Corporal Archie Alexander, 5/RSF, 52nd Division, was a fresh faced, innocent, handsome and proud soldier from Ayr Road, in Irvine, previously an employee of the Glasgow and South-Western Railway. In an article, 'A Scotsman's Letter From Gallipoli and Egypt 1915–16', first published in *The Gallipolian*, the journal of the Gallipoli Association, Alexander wrote:

'I am in the firing line and having my short spell off, so I am pleased to use my time this way. No doubt things out here will be appearing quiet to folks at home, quite true in a sense but busy enough for those actually concerned. The Turk and his German advisors try to harass us as much as possible, keeping us very much on the alert and taking no chance. Trench warfare is [?]. We have a lot of mining, sapping and getting at him with Bombs and many an anxious time he has. I have just got over a short spell in a hot corner of a bombing sap after doing our best to oust some of their snipers from an awkward position. You would not know me I have not shaved my lip for over 2 months and have a fancy moustache, eh? We lost another of our old officers the other night – Chris Vivers [Captain John Vivers, a schoolmaster, was killed on 27 October 1915; he is buried in Redoubt Cemetery.]; a fine fellow he was too. Shot thro' the throat by a sniper in this part we are in now.'

On 11 October, less than a week after the 10th (Irish) Division began departing for Salonika, Kitchener cabled Hamilton with a worrying question. If Suvla were evacuated, how many casualties did he envision during the operation? Fearing the worst, Hamilton estimated at least 50 percent. The question enraged him, noting in his diary: *If they do this they make the Dardanelles into the bloodiest tragedy of the world! Even if we were to escape without a scratch, they would stamp our enterprise as the bloodiest of all tragedies!*

Kitchener was far from happy with the answer and recalled Hamilton to London the following week, leaving Birdwood in temporary command. The only hope the MEF had of winning was to push the Turks back so far that their guns could not hit the beaches. However, with the limited resources available and with no hope of receiving additional reinforcements, there would be little chance of this happening. The French had also determined that their resources were better employed at Salonika and were firmly opposed to reinforcing Gallipoli.

**Large stores dump on V Beach.**

148

The political scene in London was now influenced by the British journalist Ellis Ashmead-Bartlett, who had written a letter to Prime Minister Herbert Asquith to alert him to the reality of the situation. In this letter he criticised the management of the campaign and the conditions the men had to endure. Ashmead-Bartlett was a long-time critic of the campaign and had struck up a friendship with Australian journalist Keith Murdoch. He justified this action on the grounds that *the issue now is to try and save what is left of the army.* This letter was confiscated from Murdoch at Marseilles, so the latter rewrote it in his own exaggerated, although not wholly unrealistic, words; it duly reached the Prime Minister and was in time circulated amongst the cabinet.

Lieutenant General Sir Charles Monro arrived on 28 October to take command from Birdwood and two days later he visited all three sectors. He concluded that there was no realistic chance of capturing the Peninsula. He reported:

'The position occupied by our troops presented a military situation unique in history. The mere fringe of the coast line had been secured. The beaches and piers upon which they depended for all requirements in personnel and material were exposed to registered and observed Artillery fire. Our entrenchments were dominated almost throughout by the Turks. The possible Artillery positions were insufficient and defective. The Force, in short, held a line possessing every possible military defect. The position was without depth, the communications were insecure and dependent on the weather. No means existed for the concealment and deployment of fresh troops destined for the offensive, whilst the Turks enjoyed full powers of observation, abundant Artillery positions, and they had been given the time to supplement the natural advantages which the position presented by all the devices at the disposal of the Field Engineer.'

After further commenting on the problems posed by disease, shortage of competent officers, the Turks' ability to hold their positions with a reduced force while deploying in other theatres and, above all, with the lack of any hope of a successful advance, Monro's solution was direct and to the point.

'Since we could not hope to achieve any purpose by remaining on the Peninsula, the appalling cost to the nation involved in consequence of embarking on an overseas expedition with no base available for the rapid transit of stores, supplies and personnel, made it urgent that we should divert the troops locked up on the Peninsula to a more useful theatre. Since therefore I could see no military advantage in our continued occupation of positions on the Peninsula, I telegraphed to your Lordship that in my opinion the evacuation of the Peninsula should be taken in hand.'

It was not so much now a question of whether another British push were possible but rather if they could hold off the next major Turkish attack. Severely depleted or not, evacuating fourteen divisions (five of which were at Helles) in winter was going to be an extraordinarily difficult challenge to achieve without heavy casualties. Churchill, on learning of the suggestion, jibed at Monro: *He came, he saw, he capitulated.* These were strong and unwarranted words from a man who had once stated that it was impossible to secure the Dardanelles.[64] Kitchener decided to see Gallipoli for himself and sailed for the Peninsula in early November.

Kitchener conducted a three-day inspection of Anzac, Suvla and Helles upon his arrival. He was shocked by what he discovered. On 15 November he cabled the Dardanelles Committee that he had reached the same conclusion as Monro.

If the general conditions at Gallipoli were not intolerable enough, the winter storms arrived just over a week later. Gales and thunderstorms gave way to a short Indian summer before the beginnings of winter showed itself in late November with heavy rain storms and even snow. This was such a contrast to the customary blistering heat of the summer and the lack of water. The men positioned in the ridges meant that they were spared the floods' worst effects as water filled trenches and gullies. The deres and nullahs, which usually contained barely more than a thin trickle of water, were turned without warning into fast, gushing torrents.

When the temperature suddenly dropped there were reports of at least 250 British soldiers dying of exposure or drowning in the torrential downpours and flooded areas. Over 5,000 more had to be evacuated, suffering from frostbite and hypothermia. The Turks were no better off. The winter weather

**Lieutenant General Sir Charles Monro.**

150

was fickle and would be an important factor in any decision regarding evacuation.

Whilst British politicians in London prevaricated over the decision to stay or go, the consequences of Bulgaria joining the Central Powers had already been manifested by the supply of heavier artillery and more reliable ammunition to the Turks. The relative lack of modern Turkish artillery, shortage of munitions and the unreliability of what they had, meant that the MEF previously could continue to exist even though their rear areas were under the intermittent menace of shell fire. Now with a direct land line to their German allies, with the impact that this had on all manner of ordnance supplies, Turkish shells were now dropping on areas that had been previously considered relatively safe. It was evident that the Turks were being supplied with new and heavier guns and to counter this the British had no answer.

It was not surprising to anyone, therefore, that on 7 December the Committee finally decided to evacuate the Peninsula; but it would only be a partial affair. Suvla and Anzac would be evacuated; but Helles would be retained for several reasons. The Royal Navy wished to keep it to help restrict enemy submarine activity in the Dardanelles, whilst Committee members felt that evacuating the whole peninsula would *really* be admitting defeat. Retaining Helles meant that it could still be used as a base for a future operation. In any case, purely from a practical standpoint, there was not sufficient shipping available to evacuate simultaneously all the three sectors. Nevertheless, it was soon decided that Helles too would be evacuated, but as a second stage.

The initial challenge was to evacuate from Anzac and Suvla some 83,000 men, 186 guns and as much of their equipment and stores as possible. The evacuation plans envisaged either a fighting withdrawal to the beaches, secured by fresh defensive trenches close to piers, or a withdrawal based on deception and cunning. With the trenches in such close proximity to each other, the danger lay in the Turkish reaction to an evacuation, which would almost certainly bring increased shelling of the beach embarkation points as well as disruptive attacks across the whole of the front. Because of this risk the chosen plan favoured deception in order to try and conceal the evacuation until the very last moments.

The main architect of the Anzac and Suvla plan was Lieutenant Colonel Cyril Brudenell White, the ANZAC Chief of Staff. It was undoubtedly a brilliant piece of work that combined rigorously and detailed planning with a considerable imaginative effort to 'fool' the Turks. The evacuation was carried out in three stages: a preliminary stage to remove all surplus personnel, animals and vehicles not necessary

Helles Evacuation – 8–9 January.

for the winter campaign; an intermediate stage that would remove all personnel, guns, and animals that were not absolutely necessary for the defence of the positions; and a final stage (which required two nights), with the units in reserve and support evacuated on the first night while on the final night the rear-guard elements would follow. Throughout every effort would be made to maintain the appearance of normality in everything the soldiers did.

In order to facilitate the evacuation without giving the plan away, clever means were employed to simulate the presence of men, guns and stores where there were none. Indian muleteers continuously drove their carts, throwing up huge clouds of dust, so that it appeared as if a consignment of stores had just arrived. Rifle and artillery fire was to cease unless there was an attack, in order to get the enemy used to extended periods of relative silence, just as it would in the last hours of the evacuation. Trenches were held by as few men as possible, their presence supplemented by uniformed, scarecrow-like dummies made out of straw-filled old jackets and hats. On the beach the illusion of stacks of wooden ration crates was created by means of constructing an outer framework only, making it appear that the massive piles were solid. Stores that could not be evacuated were buried, rum jars smashed and water tins holed. Even games of football and cricket were played in the overlooked reserve areas to give the impression that everything was normal.

It worked and, even though the Turks were suspicious, they remained ignorant of what was occurring. The evacuation of Anzac and Suvla was completed during the night of 18/19 December 1915. But could the ruse that was played out so well at Anzac and Suvla be repeated? The element of surprise had now gone and all Turkish eyes would be looking at Helles.

With the unpredictability of winter weather, any lull in between the storms and rougher seas was used by the Royal Engineers to maintain the piers running off the essential W and V Beaches, as well as those off Gully Beach. All needed constant repair, as they were vitally important as these would soon be the main exit points off Helles.

Captain John Gillam, Army Service Corps, 29th Divisional Supply Train, wrote in his diary for 22 December.

> 'It is quite calm now and a fine day; thus we are given an opportunity of digging the mud out of the trenches and to work on a system of drainage. But we want roofing badly. Unlike "V" Beach, now a perfect harbour, safe against almost any sea, "W" Beach at the first heavy swell becomes impossible for landing any supplies.

Engineers are busy as usual on the piers, not on construction, but on the work of repairing the damage done by each spell of rough sea. The storm that we experienced at Suvla did not spend its fury on Helles, though they felt the outskirts of its force here so much so that the flimsy piers off "W" Beach were almost washed away, and for the time we depended on the courtesy of our French Allies to land stores and supplies on "V" Beach. No.1 Pier here, however, is fairly safe, for we have two small ships sunk at the end, set at an angle, forming a breakwater; but they are too small to make the harbour as secure as the one at "V" Beach. We should have sunk ships six times as large. All along the shore off "W" Beach lighters lie three deep, washed up by past spells of rough weather.'[65]

The shelling at Helles began to increase steadily as more Turkish batteries began to arrive from Suvla and Anzac, their gunners determined to make their presence felt. In support of the Turks the timely arrival of an Austro-Hungarian four-gun 15cm howitzer battery

**Evacuation – Lancashire Landing being shelled.**

and also a 24cm howitzer battery, the latter with 1,200 rounds[66], added to the daily hate. The Austro-Hungarian's opened fire for the first time at Helles on 24 December. Their presence known, this put paid to any idea of hanging on to Helles; with the Turks now able to focus their efforts, Helles would soon become untenable. Some of these large guns had been brought so far forward that even Sedd-el-Bahr was being hit by howitzer shells.

Alex Barclay, along with two companies of the 1/1st Ayrshire Yeomanry, was sent into the firing line to reinforce the Lanarkshire Yeomanry, who had been under a heavy bombardment since the previous day.

'... the enemy shellfire intensified and started much earlier in the day. From 10 a.m. onwards the shellfire was very heavy indeed and more accurate than previously; more shells were dropping in, or near to, the frontline and by mid-afternoon we were suffering the most intense bombardment that any part of the peninsula ever had to endure. It was estimated that over 1000 'coalboxes' (10-inch howitzer shells) exploded in the area of the Horseshoe during the day, in addition to other high explosive and shrapnel shells which came along with them. The trenches were being very badly wrecked but, surprisingly, we did not have a large number of casualties. At one stage a pair of trousers was seen to be blown high into the air – it transpired later that they belonged to one of our officers whose dugout had been hit – Luckily this officer was not wearing them at the time.'[67]

The British at Helles followed the same template as that adopted at Anzac and Suvla so successfully. Once again the number of men in the line was thinned and guns removed, leaving roughly half of the original force, 17,000 men, to be evacuated on the night of 8 January. But could they once more get away with it?

It had been decided that the French would be withdrawn entirely; it would make the final evacuation easier. It would leave only one nation's army, and not two, to be taken off the beaches, avoiding the complications and potential for misunderstandings in carrying out so complex an operation. On 4 and 4 January 1916 the French departed, leaving only a few artillery batteries and a small party of sappers, the latter charged with the task of dismantling the Decauville light railway. Sapper Gaston-Louis Giguel, *1er Régiment du Génie*, was one of the few Frenchmen who remained.

'The firing scarcely stopped all night at the front. I was a little afraid. We can no longer receive messages; things are getting desperate. How long must we remain here? We are being well shelled from Europe and Asia; the whistling and rumbling of the shells' passage followed on without a gap, falling more or less everywhere but mainly on the beach from which we must be evacuated. I envy my comrades who have already left.'[68]

After the French division had gone, the RND moved across to take over their old Kereves Dere sector.

A week later the 13th (Western) Division, after a week's rest from the line and already experienced by their evacuation from Suvla, was landed at the end of December 1915 at Helles to relieve the 42nd Division. At Helles there were now only four divisions remaining, the 13th on the left, the 29th and 52nd in the centre and the RND on the right. The replacement of formations was designed to look as though IX Corps was relieving VIII Corps, leaving the Turks with the impression that this was a routine rotation, albeit on a grand scale. Guns and troops were still landed during the day; but, unknown to the Turks, under the cover of darkness the garrison began to dwindle.

On a clear Christmas Day the semi-finals of the 'Dardanelles Cup', a VIII Corps football competition that had started back in October, continued to be played on the Corps football ground near Hunter-Weston Hill. This ground, which also doubled as the aerodrome emergency landing strip, was under the full observation of the Turks, who had a grandstand view from Achi Baba. Although a shell or two on occasion would bring a temporary pause to the match, on the whole the games continued unmolested. Alas, the final, scheduled to be played on Boxing Day, had to be postponed because of the evacuation, though it was eventually played, on 13 January 1916, on Lemnos.

The Christmas of 1915 at Helles was a strange affair. Preparations were being made for the final evacuation using the same successful tactics that made the withdrawal from Anzac and Suvla such a success. When the men found out that they leaving Gallipoli for good, emotions were mixed. Many felt that they had not been beaten and hoped that with the right level of support, a renewed attack could finally win them the Dardanelles. Others were totally disillusioned and could not wait to leave those fatal shores. But all shared the sacrifice and did not want to leave their 'chums' who were buried on the Peninsula. At Helles men spent time visiting the graves of friends for what, they assumed, would be the last time.

It was also a normal working day for the British tunnellers in the Krithia Nullah sector for what would become the last small scale tactical operation at Helles. The 52nd Division had had success in November with the use of mines and small bombing assault parties in the capture of trenches, G.11 and H.11a. Several frontal attacks had been made earlier in the year on these very trenches but without success, but a change of tactics and a little ingenuity had reaped rewards. The next target was G.11a, a Turkish strongpoint that was positioned on a tongue of land between the two branches of Krithia Nullah. VIII Corps planned two small-scale operations to take place on 19 December, not only to act as a diversion for the

**A dry spell in the trenches, December 1915.**

evacuation at Anzac and Suvla but also to improve the local tactical situation. Whilst the 42nd Division would attack the Turkish trenches at the Gridiron and Fusilier Bluff (with varying results), the 52nd Division would focus its efforts on the ground in the middle of Krithia Nullah, namely trench G.13a and the neighbouring G.12 and G.12a trenches on the eastern side of the Nullah.

157 Brigade were tasked with its capture and for this operation it chose to use small bombing parties from 6/HLI, 7/HLI and 5/AS&H to spearhead the attacks. Two companies from 7/HLI were to be immediate reserve whilst 155 and 156 Brigade provided fire support for the assault. At zero hour, 2.15 p.m., and without any bombardment in order to gain maximum surprise, a total of thirteen mines were detonated beneath the Turkish positions. Giving the important shock element, bombing parties quickly followed up the explosions to rush the craters and capture G.12 trench. To gain access on to the tongue of ground and G.11a between the nullahs, mine galleries were dug to exit into the nullah itself, from which bomb and bayonet men advanced up the slope, taking the Turks by complete surprise. G.12 was captured but only twenty-five metres of G.11a. The new gains were quickly consolidated into the British lines, despite numerous Turkish counter attacks to eject the Scots. Whilst it

is difficult to measure the impact of this attack in diverting Turkish attention to the south, it did improve the local tactical situation. The attack cost 157 Brigade 124 casualties.

Just over a week later, on 29 December, another attack was launched using similar tactics, this time by 155 Brigade. Mining continued, now supervised by the newly arrived 254 Tunnelling Company, with another charge being fired under the Turkish strongpoint that had prevented the complete capture of the tongue. This time the whole of G.11a was captured and barricades were erected in the communication trenches that stemmed from it. Despite numerous counter attacks and shelling that followed for the next few days, the gains were held. The brigade suffered casualties of 143 officers and men in the period 29–31 December; it would be the last offensive operation at Helles. One week later the British would be gone.

As well as attacks, the ruse of using silent periods was again employed. Any curious Turkish patrol that went forward into No Man's Land was met by the opposing trench line bursting into lethal life. What the British feared was an all-out attack, and their worst nightmares came true on 7 January, just thirty-six hours before Z-Day, the final day of the evacuation.

General Otto Liman von Sanders planned a large scale attack as he had noticed that the British were reducing their garrisons and removing artillery, as described in his book *Five Years in Turkey*.

'During the first days of January 1916 it appeared as though the fire of the land artillery at Sedd-el-Bahr was becoming weaker. But one gun was firing from several batteries, frequently changing its position, while the fire from the ships, including the largest calibres, sometimes grew to great vehemence. The removal of guns was observed from the Asiatic side. The scouting parties that were pushed forward against the hostile front at all hours of evening and night invariably met with strong resistance. Of the troops designated for the attack, the 12th Division had arrived in rear of the south front. The division was designated to capture a section of trenches projecting northward opposite the extreme Turkish right, from which the British artillery could have flanked the great attack we were planning. On January 7th I ordered the 12th Division to carry out the attack, planned on the extreme Turkish right after two hours of preparation by the heaviest artillery fire and explosion of mines.'

The bombardment fell remorselessly on the British trenches between Fusilier Bluff and Gully Ravine for nearly five hours; by that stage these positions were only held by a minimum of men from 9/Worcesters and 7/North Staffs and with precious few guns for support. Ordinary Seaman Joe Murray, who was in the trenches with the North Staffs, recalled the unexpected ferocity of the shelling, which fell

**Lieutenant Colonel Frank Walker, 7/North Staffs.**

'... on both sides of the Gully Ravine. It was soon obvious that this was the prelude to an attack. The question was, "How long did we have to wait?" As the hours passed, thousands of shells crashed into the empty support trenches and those that fell in the frontline took their toll. It was by far the most severe and prolonged shelling I have ever experienced.'

When the high explosive and shrapnel bombardment ended and two Turkish mines were fired on Gully Spur, there was no doubt that an attack would immediately follow. Fortunately it was only a half-hearted attack towards the North Staffs trenches. Some forty Turks left their trenches to be met by a withering fire from the Staffs and the supporting salvos of the Royal Navy. Opposite the Worcesters no Turks left the trenches.

'The Worcestershire lads for some wonderful minutes stood up on the firestep and jeered at the enemy, inciting them to come on. Captain Conybeare, in a fine battle-fury, leapt on to the parapet and stood there, shouting defiance and leading his men in derisive cheers; "All together now: One-two-three—Al-l-l-lah!"'[69]

Very soon the firing died away and again all was quiet. One of the casualties was the North Staffs' commanding officer, Lieutenant Colonel Frank Walker. His adjutant, Captain John Robinson, wrote to Walker's wife to tell her what happened to her husband.

'During all the bombardment your husband was in the firing line. Then the Turks attacked. Their trenches were, at one corner only,

159

from 10–15 yards away. Some four Turks got onto the parapet of our trench here and Colonel Walker, finding the bay empty, collected three or four [men] and rushed into the bay, into which the Turks were firing. I believe he shot two with his revolver and was then himself shot. But the Turks were driven off. That I think is the plain unvarnished tale. He fell down into the bottom of the trench and two of our men fell dead on the top of him. I feel sure he did not speak and that he felt no pain.'

Walker was buried in Border Ravine, close to his dugout, in a grave marked out with empty shell cases and a solid wooden cross edged in black, recording his name. Despite the efforts of his men, the location of the grave was subsequently lost and he is now commemorated on the Helles Memorial.

The British were enormously relieved that this attack had not been pushed home. On that day their total numbers at Helles stood at only 17,000, with sixty-three guns in support. Any sustained effort by the Turks would have surely broken through. Everyone feared a renewed assault and the tension remained excruciating. That night another 2,300 men and nine guns were evacuated. Still the Turks seemed oblivious as to what was going on.

All surplus stores and all horses and mules not required for moving the last guns were destroyed and the surplus ammunition was buried or packed into the natural caves at the back of the beach and fused, ready for detonation after the last men had left. All the wagons and vehicles that could not be embarked were parked on the cliff edge for destruction by naval guns. Positions were selected for a stand on Hunter-Weston

**All the wagons and vehicles that could not be embarked were destroyed.**

Hill, but the enemy did not take alarm and so these positions were among the last to be evacuated.

Luckily the weather had held again but, as the last troops began to make their way to the beaches, the wind began to pick up and there was a noticeable swell in the sea, threatening the evacuation of the last few men from the 13th Division. Designated to leave by two lighters from Gully Beach, the group included their divisional commander, Lieutenant General Sir Stanley Maude, who only narrowly escaped being left behind. The lighter that was allocated to evacuate the General and a rear section of men from Gully Beach accidently grounded due to the heavy seas. This left the General, members of his divisional staff and about 150 officers and men stranded on the beach. Eventually they made haste to Lancashire Landing but, when the main party reached this destination and boarded the two remaining lighters, the General and his staff were nowhere to be seen. A general could not be left behind!

At W Beach, Brigadier General James O'Dowda, the military commander of the beach party, found himself in a predicament. Not only was the firing line deserted and thus at any time the Turks could descend on them, more daunting was the fear of being blown up. The fuses to the main magazine dump had already been lit and were set to explode at 4.00 a.m.

'I packed up my dispatch case and, leaving my office, brought up the rear of the last party. Just at that moment a GSO, very disturbed, rushed up and told me that General Maude had not yet arrived. I asked what had happened and was informed that after they had left Gully Beach General Maude had discovered that his bedding roll had been left behind. He said that he was hanged if he was going to leave his bedding for the Turks, got two volunteers with a stretcher and went back for it. The time was now 3.50 a.m. and there was no sign of the missing General. I therefore sent an officer and a couple of men, who knew every inch of the beach, and gave them ten minutes to retrieve him. Fortunately, they found him almost at once.'

The crew and men on board the lighter were getting jumpy as the dumps along the cliff were already burning and they knew that the main magazine was set to explode. Maude's party was delayed as they came a different way and had been unable to find a gap in the wire until, luckily, a demolition party came along and showed them the way through. The last lighter left the jetty at 3.45 a.m. and was less than 200 metres from the shore when the magazine exploded, throwing up thousands of tons of debris into the sky. It was reported that a couple of men were wounded by the falling debris, and one was killed, a member of the lighter crew.[70]

General Maude's exploit became a legend soon after the evacuation when a verse was written about him refusing to leave until he had been reunited with his kit. Based on a parody of the Victorian-era parlour song, *Come into the Garden, Maude,* it became very popular with the troops.

> *Come into the lighter, Maude,*
> *For the fuse has long been lit,*
> *Hop into the lighter, Maude,*
> *And never mind your kit.*

When the Turks realized that the evacuation was in its final throws they began to bombard the trenches and beaches; too late, they were empty. The British warships responded with a last goodbye and gesture of defiance by shelling Achi Baba for one last time. The Turkish bombardment lasted until about 6.30 a.m., followed up by an infantry advance; but by the time they had got through the trenches, between which all gaps had been closed with barricades and blocked with mines and booby traps, the transports were already long gone. Helles was once again Turkish. Sanders noted in his book on the campaign:

**Lieutenant General Sir Stanley Maude.**

'The booty was extraordinary. Wagon parks, automobile parks, mountains of arms, ammunition and entrenching tools were collected. Here too most of the tent camps and barracks had been left standing, in part with all of their equipment. Many hundreds of horses lay in rows, shot or poisoned, but quite a number of horses and mules were captured and turned over to the Turkish artillery. Here, as at the other fronts, the stacks of flour and subsistence had some acid solution poured over them to render them unfit for our use. In the next few days the hostile ships made vain attempts to set the stacks and the former British tent camps and barracks on fire. It took nearly two years to clean up the grounds.'

**Lanarkshire Yeomanry packing up before leaving the Peninsula for good.**

All quite true, of course; but this account glosses over the fact that an enormous military and propaganda coup had been lost. Lieutenant Charles Black, 6/HLI, wrote that *no man was sorry to leave Gallipoli; but few were really glad.*

### Was Gallipoli a failure for the Allies and a victory for the Turks?

There are some key elements worth highlighting. To begin with commanders on both sides had demanded the highest sacrifices from their troops, much of which was in line with doctrine of the day and in lieu of sufficient artillery support to win the day. Attacks were ineffectually planned and unnecessarily pressurised, not giving troops enough time to prepare; this, coupled with exhausted and untrained men, were not a recipe for success. At Helles there was no space for troops to manoeuvre as the Aegean barred one side, and the Dardanelles the other, both with few suitable places for a new landing.

As the field fortifications grew with each passing day, achieving suitable operational conditions became increasingly difficult, all leading to pressure on both sides to make more hasty attacks. There was little time available to optimise defences, build up supplies, to devise and coordinate a workable counter-attack plan, and to instruct the officers and troops accordingly. The coordination of the available resources of land, sea and air power at this stage in the war that was in its infancy; in fact it was a learning experience that did not fully mature until the last year of the war, and even then it was only partially applied. At Gallipoli no side looked at concentrating resources on a single decisive point in a concentrated and decisive attack that might have given the best chances of success. Thus, whilst Gallipoli can only be described as an Allied failure, it – along with experiences in Flanders – did mark the beginning of a learning curve for the British Army, which was slow to adapt and quick to forget, providing lessons that in the end were instrumental in winning the war.

**The sun finally sets at Helles.**

# Helles – The Tours

1. **Behind the Turkish Lines**
2. **Helles Landings**
   - **Optional visit: French Gun Battery**
3. **Gully Ravine**
4. **Krithia Nullah**
5. **The RND Sector: Kanli Dere**
6. **The French Sector: Kereves Dere**
   - **Optional visit: Achi Baba Nullah and The Horseshoe**

Even though much of the area can be walked, the expanse of the battlefield really requires a car or similar vehicle if you are limited by time. Allow for four days to complete all of these tours.

Note: Please avoid walking through fields with crops; remember that most of this land is private property and must be respected. If you have to cross a field, always follow the field boundary, preferably a track if one is available.

Walking Helles.

*Getting to Helles*:

As most travellers stay in Çanakkale or Eceabat, the recommended route to Helles is mapped from these locations. From Eceabat it is about thirty kilometres to the tip of Cape Helles. The route will take you a southerly direction along the Dardanelles shoreline, passing Kilitbahr, Soğanlıdere, Behramlı and Alçitepe. It is best to refer to my Battleground Europe book *Walking Gallipoli* for places to visit on the way to Helles, including Kilitbahr castle, a gun battery and the Corporal Seyit statue.

# Tour 1

# Behind the Turkish lines

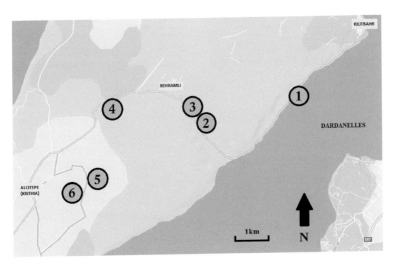

**Behind Turkish Lines.**

Leave Eceabat in a southerly direction towards Kilitbahr. About three kilometres beyond Kilitbahr is **Havuzlar Cemetery and Memorial (1) (40°07′56.0″N 26°21′21.0″E)**. Built in 1961, the memorial is dedicated to Staff Captain Kemal Bey, the Chief of Staff of the Ottoman 2nd Division, and his Regimental Aide, Lieutenant Ismail Efendi and seven other identified Turkish soldiers who were mortally wounded in the battle of Kereves Dere on 21 June. His last order to his men was *Let's charge, fall as martyrs, so our homeland will be saved.* Kemal Bey died in a hospital in Çanakkale on 26 June, 1915. If you look back down the road, on the corner is the Halil Pasha fountain, an important water filling point used by Ottoman soldiers in 1915.

Continue on for another five kilometres, where you will find the shoreline road sweeping sharply inland into the Soganli Dere, or Soğanlıdere. This is a deep, water rich and tree-covered valley that was located behind the Turkish lines at Helles. Soğanlıdere became an important logistical pipeline for the Turks. Here there was everything from field hospitals to dumps of all sorts of materiel that was needed to sustain an army in the field.

**Halil Pasha Fountain.**

**Havuzlar Memorial.**

About a kilometre into the valley, before you reach Soğanlıdere Cemetery, on the right side of the road are the remains of ruined buildings. This was once **Melek Hanım Farm (2) (40°6′57″N 26°18′18″E)**, whose buildings were used by the military from the times of the Balkan War. Converted into a Turkish field dressing station, it was one of at least four dressing areas and hospitals for the Ottoman 2nd, 7th, 12th and 15th Divisions fighting at Helles, particularly on the left flank of Kereves Dere.

Lieutenant Mehmet Sinan, a Turkish artillery officer, wrote that he passed Melek Hanım Farm, where he noted that the medical facilities got their fair share of the bombardments.

**The ruins of Melek Hanım Farm.**

168

'On 11 July 1915, my battery commander Mahmud Bey and I set off for Melek Hanım Farm. The sounds of bullets, infantry rifles, machine guns and bombs were becoming increasingly audible. The mild winds of the war storm were patting our face. Although fired some time ago, the holes made by the 35cm shells were quite horrific. Water had come out of some of these holes that were wider than 10 metres in diameter.'

Melek Hanım (seated on the right), who gave her name to the farm.

Another visitor was Lieutenant Ibrahim Naci, 71 Regiment, who was later killed at Kereves Dere. On 15 June 1915 he described the farm in his diary:

'I woke up at 3 a.m. I got food served. We got going at 4 a.m. We arrived at Melek Hanım Farm. I got the soldiers to set up tents. Then, I went to the 1st Company's tent and had tea. One hour later, the company was ordered to go to the disinfector. So we packed up again. On our way, we were informed that another battalion had occupied the disinfector. We sat on the roadside. I took out my book. I'm writing this under a group of oak trees. Right across (from) me, there are six bare hills, lined up parallel to one another in the shape of a semi sphere. Some of these hills have roads on them that look like white strips fading out in branches. The valley is pretty wide and half white from being trodden. Carriages, animals and people by the creek are idle and motionless. An animal, a carriage, a group is seen every now and then on some roads.'

Less than a kilometre along the road is **Soğanlıdere Cemetery (3) (40°6′57″N 26°18′18″E)**, constructed in 2005; symbolic gravestones designed as soldiers' helmets represent the home towns of those who are known to be buried here. Some original wartime graves with stone markers are located outside the new cemetery walls. The exact number of burials is unknown but it is thought to be a few thousand. Some 600 names have been identified.

**Soğanlıdere Cemetery, new and old.**

Leave the cemetery and continue on the road, passing Behramlı, for about four kilometres until you come to **Şahindere Cemetery (4) (40°07′18.7″N 26°15′38.6″E)**. Opened in 2005, its location close to the front made this an important field ambulance for the Krithia and Kereves Dere fighting. Of the 2,177 Turkish soldiers buried in this area, 1,969 names of the fallen have been identified. There is one identified grave within the cemetery, that of Lieutenant Mustafa Efendi, 30 Regiment (10th Division), who was killed on 18 September 1915. The Ottoman 10th Division is one of several commemorated on the Şahindere Memorial, which includes the 1st Division's 70, 71 and 124 Regiments; the 2nd Division's 31, 32 and 39 Regiments; the 5th Division's 13 and 15 Regiments; the 6th Division's 16 Regiment; the 7th Division's 19, 20 and 21 Regiments; the 10th Division's 29 and 30 Regiments and the 11th Division's 126 and 127 Regiments.

**Today's symbolic grave markers.**

Leave the cemetery and continue on for a further 2.8 kilometres, where you will come to a road on the left. Take this turning and follow the road for just over two kilometres to the summit of **Alçitepe – Achi Baba (5) (40°05'48.9"N 26°15'12.5"E)**, signed posted Alçitepe Baki Terası (Alçitepe Viewing Terrace). The viewing terrace of this 216 metre hill gives a spectacular bird's eye view of the Helles battlefield.

Achi Baba, as the British referred to this hill, was the first day objective of Major General Hunter-Weston's 29th Division on 25 April 1915. Hamilton needed to seize this key piece of terrain before his forces could continue an advance up the Peninsula and take the vital ground of Kilid Bahr, where he would link up with the Anzacs. Never captured in the campaign, it remained in Turkish hands until the end of the war.

From the viewing terrace you can see the mouth of the Dardanelles and the four-pillared Çanakkale Martyrs Memorial on the headland of Eski Hissarlik, to the east of Cape Helles. This latter position is also the location of De Tott's Battery and S Beach. If you look to the right you will see the lighthouse at the end of the Cape and the Helles Memorial. On the left of the Helles Memorial is V Beach; to the right is W Beach, the two main British landing beaches. Looking to the right is the Aegean and, hidden from view, are X and Y beaches.

The intention on the landing day was to capture the little village of Krithia. You can see the mosque in the middle of it in the bowl to your right. At the same time the first day objective was to capture the hill where you are now standing. To your north is Kilid Bahr Plateau, an even more formidable natural fortress that overlooks the Narrows. This was Hamilton's ultimate objective for the land campaign. Once

**Achi Baba Panorama.**

captured, and the Narrows defences neutralised, the fleet could proceed to Constantinople. Neither Kilid Bahr, Achi Baba or the village of Krithia were ever captured.

Depending on how much time you have available, after you have completed the other tours it would be a good idea to return here for another look, armed with knowledge of the lie of the ground and the significant features of the fighting at Helles.

Leaving Achi Baba, continue along the road for a kilometre until you arrive at the **Marshal Fevzi Çakmak (6) (40°05′48.9″N 26°15′12.5″E) Memorial**. This monument was erected in 1941 in the name of Marshal Fevzi Çakmak, commander of the Ottoman V Corps during the campaign. Çakmak arrived at the Gallipoli Front on 13 July, commanding during the battles at Kereves Dere, against the French. His younger brother, Lieutenant Mehmed Nazif Efendi, was killed during the August offensive at Chunuk Bair, Anzac. Çakmak was a candidate to become President of Turkey following Atatürk's death in 1938, but stood down in favour of İsmet İnönü. Marshal Çakmak died in 1950.

Carrying on along this road for about ten kilometres to the Helles Memorial.

# Tour 2

# The Helles Landings

This is a walking tour of eight kilometres over road, track, beach and field boundaries. Allow a full morning or afternoon for this tour, which starts and finishes at the Helles Memorial, where there is ample parking for a vehicle.

The purpose of the tour is to give you a feel of the landing beaches and the fighting that followed on 25 April 1915. For more information please refer to *Gallipoli: Helles Landing* in this series.

Park your vehicle at the **Helles Memorial (7) (40°02′44.6″N 26°10′45.0″E)**. From this vantage point you can view the whole Helles battlefield, from the entrance to the Dardanelles and across the killing fields to Achi Baba. To the west is Hill 138 (42 metres), later renamed Hunter-Weston Hill when he established VIII Corps' headquarters on its western slopes. From here the ground slopes down to Lancashire

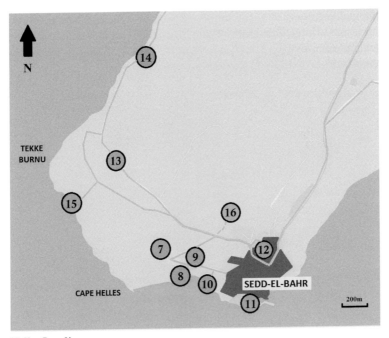

Helles Landing.

Landing before rising up onto Tekke Burnu and Hill 114 (35 metres). North of Tekke Burnu, along the Aegean coast line, is X Beach, Gully Ravine (now hidden from sight by a tree line) and Y Beach. Achi Baba (182 metres), the initial objective of the Helles landing, sits nestled in the centre, with the village of Krithia on its western spur. To the east is the village of Sedd-el-Bahr (Seddülbahir), with Hill 141 (43 metres) above it, behind which are the French sector and the Turkish Memorial. At six kilometres deep and three kilometres wide, Helles is not a large battlefield.

Designed by Sir John Burnet, the Helles Memorial was completed in 1924, and was described by TJ Pemberton, in his 1926 book *Gallipoli To-Day*, as

'A symbol of the triumph of human nature over fearful odds; a great nation's willing sacrifice for an idea. Having suffered this splendid failure, Britain has had the courage to ignore the defeat and commemorate in stone those who never questioned the worth or wisdom of the idea. The sacrifice and valour were things far greater than the un-acquired victory.'

The obelisk style memorial stands thirty-three metres high on a hill at the tip of the Peninsula, like a lighthouse for all ships that pass through the Dardanelles to see. The hill was known as Guezji Baba, and to the Turks as Gőztepe (Eye Hill). A redoubt originally stood on this position and, along with Hill 138 (Hunter-Weston Hill), temporarily prevented the forces on W and V beaches joining up as planned.

**The Helles Memorial.**

174

Guezji Baba was captured by 4/Worcesters on 25 April. The memorial is designed to serve two functions: as a campaign memorial and as a place of commemoration for the 20,763 British and Indian forces who died during the campaign and whose burial places are not known. It also includes Royal Naval personnel lost or buried at sea in Gallipoli waters, and those Australian servicemen who died in the Helles region and have no known grave. (Newfoundland's missing are commemorated at Beaumont-Hamel, on the Somme.)

Among those commemorated there are several Victoria Cross recipients, two of whom share the same citation: Major Cuthbert Bromley and Sergeant Frank Stubbs, both 1/LF (*Panel 218*). They were two of the six selected by their comrades for singular acts of bravery and devotion to duty whilst storming W Beach on 25 April. Stubbs was killed during the landing; Bromley was drowned when HMT *Royal Edward* was sunk on 13 August. Another landings' VC is Sub Lieutenant Arthur Tisdall, Anson Battalion. Tisdall was decorated for an action on V Beach for rescuing several men from the water under a murderous fire. He was killed on 6 May during the Second Battle of Krithia. Captain Gerald O'Sullivan VC, 1/Inniskillings, is also commemorated here (*Panel 98–102*). Killed on 21 August at Suvla, O'Sullivan was awarded the VC for actions at Gully Ravine during the night of 1–2 July, when he saved a critical situation by leading a party of bomb throwers to recapture a lost trench.

From the Helles Memorial walk down the slope 160 metres to **Ertuğrul Fort (8) (40°02'41.0"N 26°10'52.7"E)**. The fort, also known as Fort No.1, built in the 1890s, was one of five fortified emplacements

**Ertugrul Fort.**

guarding the entrance to the Straits, forming the outer defences of the Dardanelles. Ertuğrul and Sedd-el-Bahr forts were destroyed by the Royal Navy and subsequent Royal Marines' landing parties in February/March 1915. Rebuilt to their pre-war look, the original remains of one of the 24cm Krupp guns can still be seen. Ertuğrul was captured by 4/Worcesters just before sunset on 25 April.

Looking down from Ertuğrul, there are some magnificent views of V Beach, Sedd-el-Bahr Castle and its village. The systematic improvement of defences began in early 1915, when trenches were dug overlooking likely landing points. Barbed wire was stretched across the beaches; in instances where supplies were short, garden and agricultural wire was used. To disguise the new defences the work was done under the cover of darkness, although that scheme did not fool the British, who were certainly aware of – and rightly worried about – them. The rock spit is still visible where the *River Clyde* ran ashore, emptying its cargo of 1/RMF and two companies of 2/Hants. The narrow sandy beach where 1/RDF scrambled ashore through a hail of fire, and the high sand bank that saved so many lives, are both clearly visible.

Visit the adjacent cemetery and **Sergeant Yahya Memorial (9) (Yahya Çavuş Şehitlik ve Aniti) (40°02′42.7″N 26°10′57.3″E)** to the Turkish soldiers who defended this area. The statue depicts three Turkish soldiers with a flag unfurled above them, charging with rifles in hand. Sergeant Yahya, 3/26 Regiment, took over the company when its commander was killed. For most of 25 April the sergeant and other isolated pockets of Turks defended the area very bravely.

Well-aimed rifle fire pinned the British down on V Beach for the whole of 25 April, to such devastating effect that a RNAS pilot, Charles Samson, who was flying overhead, observed *the water simply whipped*

**Sergeant Yahya.**

*into foam by the shells and bullets ... lighters full of dead and the sea
stained red with blood all along the beach.*

With few exceptions the Turkish cemeteries you will see at Gallipoli
are all symbolic, meaning that there are no burials within their walls.
Sergeant Yahya actually survived the war.

Leave the memorial and, turning left by the post-war pillbox and
recreated trenches, take the steep road down the hill. After 150 metres
turn right, taking the sunken lane that leads you to **V Beach CWGC
Cemetery (10) (40°02′38.0″N 26°11′01.6″E)**.

The cemetery, beautifully situated on the beach, was started on
26 April and, with the exception of thirteen graves that were brought
in after the Armistice for burial in Row O, all the other graves date
from the landings. There are now 696 men buried or commemorated
in this cemetery, 480 of whom are unidentified; special memorials
commemorate 196 men known or believed to be buried among them,
nearly all belonging to the units that landed on 25 April.

They include Captain Garth Walford who, with Lieutenant Colonel
Charles Doughty-Wylie, led the survivors off the beach. Both won the
Victoria Cross but were killed during the fighting. Father William Finn,
who was the first RC chaplain to be killed in the war, ironically on a
Sunday, is buried here alongside his commanding officer, Lieutenant
Colonel Richard Rooth. Father Finn, in the same boat as Rooth, leapt
over the side and was almost immediately hit in the chest at about the
same time as Rooth. Although
badly wounded, Finn went to the
assistance of wounded and dying
men who were ashore. He was then
hit in the arm and leg but, despite

V Beach CWGC Cemetery.

In life and death, side-by-side –
Lieutenant Colonel Rooth and
Father Finn.

177

the pain that he endured, he was seen crawling about the beach talking quietly to the men and trying to give Absolution to those close to death. This was not without the greatest difficulty, according to one account, as he had to hold his wounded right arm up with his left. Suffering from loss of blood and exhaustion, he was eventually killed by shrapnel.

After visiting the cemetery you might wish to take a break and either sit on the beach or visit the Mocamp café, which is open in peak season and serves food, drinks, ice cream and has a customers' toilet. There are a few local shops in the village should you wish to supplement your packed lunch for the day. Leave the Mocamp and walk the 250 metres to **Sedd-el-Bahr Castle (11) (40°02′31.1″N 26°11′17.3″E)**.

In early 1915 the castle had ten large guns, antiquated but still effective. It was heavily shelled by British warships on 3 November 1914 and again on 19 and 25 February 1915, when it was finally silenced. Even though this objective posed no threat to the fleet during the attack on 18 March, it remained a threat to the British soldiers landing at V Beach. Defenders in these ruins could not only enfilade the men who had landed on the beach, but they also helped counter the smaller 1/RDF landing at the Camber. Two staff officers, Lieutenant Colonel Doughty-Wylie and Captain Walford, fought their way through the castle and up through the village. Walford was killed exiting the castle whilst Doughty-Wylie pressed on, leading the Irishmen to the fort on Hill 141.

**View of V Beach, the CWGC Cemetery and Sedd-el-Bahr castle from Ertugrul.**

Leave the Castle and follow the steep road that runs up to the northwest of the village. After 500 metres, you will reach Hill 141, where you will see a sign for **Doughty-Wylie VC Grave (12) (40°02′46.3″N 26°11′21.5″E)**. His grave is by the site of an old hill fort, once circled by a moat. On 26 April, increased rifle fire forced Doughty-Wylie's party to seek cover in the fort's moat. Doughty-Wylie, with no thought for his

**Lieutenant Colonel Charles Doughty-Wylie VC.**

**The grave of Doughty-Wylie VC on Hill 141. Little has changed since 1915.**

**Doughty-Wylie VC Grave.**

own safety, with initiative, skill and great gallantry, continued to direct the attack, and whilst climbing out of the moat was killed in the moment of victory. He was buried where he fell and, uniquely on the Peninsula, it is maintained as a solitary burial by the CWGC. Just behind the grave the remains of the moat are still evident, although little can be seen of the fort itself. It is believed that his wife, Lilian, visited his grave in November 1915, the only woman to have stepped upon these shores during the campaign.

Leave Doughty-Wylie's grave and take the track back to the main road. Follow this road for about 1.5 kilometres, past the Helles Memorial and Hill 138 on the left. Stop at **Lancashire Landing CWGC Cemetery (13) (40°03′12.6″N 26°10′24.5″E)**. The cemetery, which is set back from W Beach, was started immediately after the landings. It stands on a small ridge, Karaja Oghul Tepe, that leads up to Hill 114 (Tekke Burnu). There is a total of 1,171 graves from the United Kingdom, twenty-seven from Australia, fifteen from New Zealand, two from Canada (i.e. Newfoundland, which at that time was not part of Canada)), one man from the Zion Mule Corps, another from the local Mule Corps and seventeen Greek labourers. The unidentified graves number 135, with eleven special memorials to those who are known to be buried here. There are also graves moved here after the war from the islands of Imbros and Tenedos. The register contains details of 1,101 burials and commemorations. The larger part of the cemetery (Rows A to J and part of Row L) was made between the landing in April and the final

**Lancashire Landing CWGC Cemetery in 1920.**

**Lancashire Landing Cemetery.**

evacuation of the Peninsula. Row I contain the graves of over eighty men of the Lancashire Fusiliers who died in the first two days following the landing. The ninety-seven graves in Row K and graves 31 to 83 in Row L were brought in after the Armistice from the Aegean island cemeteries of Imbros (Imbroz) and Tenedos (Bozcaada).

Amongst those buried is the politician Captain Harold Cawley MP (*row A, grave 76*), 6/Manchesters, who was killed defending a mine crater (later named Cawley's Crater) near Gully Ravine. Cawley was the fourth MP to die in the war and was one of three sons that the long-serving Liberal MP Sir Frederick Cawley was to lose in the war. Before his death Cawley had written a letter home to his father that included a scathing criticism of the mishandling of the Dardanelles campaign. As a Member of Parliament, his correspondence was not subject to military censorship, enabling him to convey a frank assessment of the situation. He wrote, for example, of Major General Sir William Douglas, 42nd Division, that:

> 'He has a third-rate brain, no capacity to grasp the lie of the land, and no originality or ingenuity … He has been in the trenches three times since he landed, hurried visits in which he saw next to nothing … He is always thinking of himself, his food, his promotion, his health.'

Interestingly, in 1916, Cawley's father served on the Dardanelles Commission that inquired into the conduct of the campaign.

**X Beach today.**

Also buried here is a former Irish Rugby Union player, Lieutenant Vincent McNamara RE (*row L, grave 9*). McNamara was a tunnelling officer. On 29 November he detonated a charge under a Turkish tunnel. When he went down to investigate its effect he was asphyxiated by the resulting gas from the explosion that had not had time to disperse. Lance Sergeant John Keneally VC (*row C, grave 104*) won the Victoria Cross on W Beach on 25 April. He died of wounds received at Gully Ravine on 29 June.

Leave the cemetery and follow the road in a north-westerly direction for one kilometre until you see a narrow, sign-posted, track that leads down onto **X Beach (14) (40°03′43.7″N 26°10′35.2″E)**. X Beach was also known as 'Implacable Landing' because of the close co-operation of HMS *Implacable* in support of 2/RF. Retrace your steps back 750 metres to the rough track on the right of the road. This will lead you past Hill 114, where 2/RF and 1/LF joined up during the morning of the landings. After 400 metres the track will fork. Take the right-hand turn, which leads 250 metres down to **W Beach (Lancashire Landing) (15) (40°03′01.2″N 26°10′06.7″E)**.

The cove is also known as Tekke Koyu, whilst the high ground between the beach and Hill 114 is known as Tekke Burnu. There is little evidence that remains from the landing with the exception of Turkish trenches that still line the cliff tops on both sides of the beach. After the landing this cove became the main supply base for VIII Corps and evidence of this can still be found, such as the skeletal remains of stone

182

Lancashire Landing beach today. Inset: Wrecked lighters and piers still exist.

piers and jetties, wrecked lighters, concrete water troughs and remains of dugouts. On the eastern side of the beach there is a large area of rough ground that looks as if a large section of the cliff had fallen away. This was actually caused when the munitions and supply dumps were detonated during the early morning of 9 January 1916, the last day of the evacuation. A large field of rock and boulders still cover the area, clear evidence of the enormous force of this explosion.

It is possible to follow the field boundaries and walk from the eastern side of the beach, up onto the cliffs and over the fields to Hunter-Weston Hill and the Helles Memorial, thus walking in the footsteps of 4/ Worcesters. Alternatively, and an easier route, return to the foot track and follow this back two kilometres to the Helles Memorial.

### Optional Visit: French Gun Battery
North of the village of Sedd-el-Bahr, on the road that leads from the Doughty-Wylie Grave to Lancashire Landing Cemetery and close to the turning to the Helles Memorial, is a track, signposted with an information board, that leads into the fields to a **French Gun Battery (16) (40°02′58.8″N 26°11′06.0″E).** Following this track for 220 metres

**French guns in action.**

will lead you to the first pair of four 24cm French guns, which are positioned in their original gun emplacements, dug into the fields on the right of the track. Further along the track, no more than a hundred metres, are another two guns, together forming a four-piece gun battery. When the last French division evacuated Gallipoli in December 1915 they left behind this battery of guns to support the British. One of them was manned by Noel Sergent, *10e Régiment d'Artillerie*, amongst the last of the French to leave Gallipoli.

**One of the French guns today.**

'Our battery was the last French battery to go off. They fired up to 5 in the evening, then at 7 the Captain, Lieutenant, another, myself and seven men remained at the guns. We rammed earth sacks down the mouths of the guns, then put twenty-six dynamite cartridges in each and a Cordon Bickford and more sacks. Then we got our packs and banged about with a sledge-hammer, put the breeches of the guns on the trucks and started off. At the crossroads we met the 52nd Division coming down, quite noiselessly, in fours. This was the last division and that meant that if the Turks chose to attack they could simply come straight through, as our trenches were empty.'[71]

**The gun at the time of the evacuation.**

You will notice that the guns are facing towards the Asian shoreline, evidence that they were used for counter-battery fire. The guns could be rotated and thus could also fire towards Turkish positions on Achi Baba. You will notice all four have had their barrels 'spiked'. These were purposely destroyed by their French crews shortly before the final evacuation of Helles on 8/9 January 1916; these gunners were the last Frenchmen to leave Gallipoli.

# Tour 3

# Gully Ravine

This is a walking tour of three kilometres over road, rough track, beach and field boundaries. Its purpose is to give you a feel of Gully Ravine and the hive of activity that would have surrounded this area during the campaign.

Allow two hours for the tour, which starts and finishes at Pink Farm Cemetery, where there is ample parking for a vehicle. For additional walks in and around Gully Ravine, please refer to my Battleground Europe book *Gallipoli: Gully Ravine*.

To find your way to the mouth of Gully Ravine, leave the Helles Memorial, passing Lancashire Landing Cemetery and X Beach. When the road takes a sudden curve to the right, moving away from the sea, you will be above the entrance to Gully Ravine (approximately 4.3 kilometres from the Helles Memorial). Continue another 400 metres to **Pink Farm CWGC Cemetery (17) (40°04′21.9″N 26°11′26.3″E)**, where you can park your vehicle off the road, making use of the shade of the trees.

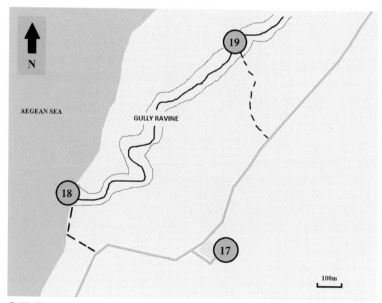

**Gully Ravine.**

During the campaign Pink Farm was a ruined stone building, originally called Sotiri Farm. It was close to a cart track, called West Krithia Road. In a letter from Noel Sergent, who served in *10er* Régiment *d'Artillerie*, he wrote that after he left Pink Farm he *came into the loveliest country. I could hardly believe my eyes; it was just like Valescure* [Côte d'Azure]. *Small tufts of pine trees, thyme, donkey-pepper and heather.** Today, little has changed.

Trenches in the woodland by Pink Farm.

Known to the troops as Pink Farm because of the local colour of the soil, the area was used as a forward supply dump, serving also as the headquarters of VIII Corps Mining Company. The farm also acted as a collection point for the wounded to be taken down from the front line; from here they were taken to the field hospitals, by mule-drawn ambulance if needed. In the surrounding woods there are also remains of trenches and dugouts.

The grave concentration at Pink Farm Cemetery, which was begun in late April 1915, brought together several smaller cemeteries after the Armistice. During the campaign there were originally three cemeteries here, Pink Farm No.1, No.2 and No.3. After the war these and six other smaller cemeteries – 29th Division Cemetery, 52nd Division Cemetery, Aerodrome Cemetery, Oak Tree Cemetery, Gully Beach Cemetery and Gully Farm Cemetery, were closed and the remains reinterred here. Pink Farm Cemetery now contains a total of 602 graves: 209 from United Kingdom forces, three from New Zealand, two from Australia, five from the Indian Army and 164 of whom are unidentified. The total number of burials in the cemetery is 383 and special memorial tablets amount to 219. The register contains details of 352 burials and commemorations.

Amongst those buried here are Captain Christopher Birdwood (*plot IV, row A, grave 6*), 6/Gurkhas, who was mortally wounded during the Third Battle of Krithia, dying of wounds on 7 June at 108/Indian Field Ambulance on Gully Beach. He was a distant relation to a fellow

---

* Sergent, JNB, 'With The French Artillery', *The Gallipolian*, No.67, Christmas 1991, p.20.

**Pink Farm CWGC Cemetery.**

Indian army officer, General Sir William Birdwood, the ANZAC commander. A senior officer buried here is Lieutenant Colonel George Stoney DSO (*Spec. Mem. 204*), commanding 1/KOSB. He had only just returned from Suvla with his battalion when he was killed by a shell. Stoney, one of four brothers who joined the army, was Military Landing Officer at V Beach on 25 April, where he had organised parties of the Dublin and Munster Fusiliers in preparation for the attack to clear Sedd-el-Bahr and Hill 141. Corporal John Ranken, (*Spec. Mem. 192*), 4/RS, died of wounds received during the Battle of Gully Ravine. Private Herbert Grant remembered Ranken being in the centre

**Corporal John Ranken, 4/ Royal Scots, who died of wounds 29 June 1915.**

of a bomb fight that was raging in a Turkish communication trench. *I grabbed the bag of bombs and went down to the place. Fortunately Corpl. Ranken (Grenade Corporal)* [his rank is erroneously recorded as a private on his memorial stone] *was there and we threw them at the Turks as fast as I could light them. There was an explosion that sent me flying.* Ranken, who received a Mention in Despatches for this action,

188

was mortally wounded, dying on 29 June; he was originally buried in Gully Beach Cemetery.

Leave Pink Farm on foot and walk in a westerly direction for 400 metres, back to the curve in the road, where you will find a couple of rough tracks that lead down to the beach. Follow the track to Gully Beach and the sea.

Gully Ravine was also known as Zigin Dere, Sighin Dere or even Lone Pine Creek. Along the length of the beach used to run the original beach road, constructed out of sight of the enemy during the early summer of 1915. It ran beneath the cliffs, from Lancashire Landing to Gully Beach, and thence up Gully Ravine to the front line. This beach road, remnants of which survive between Tekke Burnu and X Beach, also served as a route for the evacuation. The beach bustled with activity from May 1915 onwards and anything from Field Ambulances to canteens were soon taking up prime sea view locations. The headquarters of both the 29th and 42nd Divisions were once located here. Two men were 'shot at dawn' on this beach: Private Thomas Davis, 1/RMF, who was charged with quitting his post and was executed on 2 July; and Sergeant John Robins, 5/Wilts, who was charged with wilfully disobeying an order and was executed on 2 January 1916. Both received posthumous pardons in August 2006.

Close to **Gully Beach (18) (40°04′30.3″N 26°11′05.0″E)** is the wreck of General Maude's 'X' Lighter. It was accidentally run aground during the evacuation on 9 January 1916. Beside the lighter are the remains of Gully Pier, used during the campaign for smaller boats to dock in order to transfer supplies and take off the wounded. It was last used during the evacuation. The remains, now just piles of rock, reinforced with iron and concrete, can still be clearly seen emerging from the sea. In the mouth of the ravine itself is a Royal Engineers' water well, which was constructed in 1915. The well is referred to in *Gallipoli As I Saw It*, the work of veteran Joseph Murray of the Hood Battalion, RND. If you look closely, you can still make out the words '*RE 135 COMPANY*' etched into the

**Gully Beach HQ in 1915. Now scrub covered, its terraces can still be traced.**

**Gully Beach today.**

top of the concrete. There was a chronic water shortage at Helles, to the extent that additional water supplies had to be shipped to Gallipoli from Egypt.

Turn your back to the sea and look at the scrub covered ridges and plateau where sign can still be found of terraces and dugouts, at one time busy with the hustle and bustle of troops. Everywhere on the Peninsula you will find fragments of earthenware rum jars, which make a useful path for following the British in battle, particularly here at Gallipoli but also on parts of the Western Front. Some still bear the initials 'S.R.D',

**The Royal Engineers 135 Company Well.**

officially Supply Reserve Depot, although the troops referred to it as 'Seldom Reaches Destination', amongst many other names. Another legacy of war are the many bullets and bones that are found lying on the surface of the fields or in the nooks and crannies of the ravine, clear evidence of the once heavy fighting in this area, exposed and then buried again whenever there is heavy rainfall, which rushes down the gully to the sea.

*The Gully is a strange and disturbing place; if ghosts walk anywhere they walk in Gully Ravine.*** Entering Gully Ravine from the beach you will soon notice, once inside its mouth, that the sea breeze suddenly stops and that the heat and silence of the enclosed gully forcibly hits you. This part of the ravine is fairly wide, but soon the walls close in on you, tall and steep. This is the same route the troops would have taken during 1915. In dry weather it is perfectly walkable, although there are limited options to exit the ravine once committed. In this walk the first main exit will be taken, just over a kilometre into the ravine.

**Gully Pier and General Maude's 'X' Lighter as it appeared in 1919.**

---

** Sellers, Leonard, "Incident at Gully Ravine", *RND Magazine*, No.2, September 1997, p.139

The ravine was a hive of activity during the war, being the main communication link for the front line on the western part of Helles. Gully Ravine became a warren for the troops that lived, slept and died through those now distant months of 1915. In the surrounding scrub there are many remnants of the occupation, from broken rum jars, glass bottles and jam tins to the odd button, bullet and shrapnel piece. Many of the other small offshoot gullies sheltered everything from Indian and Zion Mule Corps mules to cookhouses, stores, ammunition dumps and field dressing posts. There even sprang up a small Divisional School, where they constructed a rifle range and held bombing classes, both giving useful experience to newly arrived reinforcements.

Continue into the ravine for just over a kilometre, keeping a look out for two rough tracks that will lead you out of the ravine. On the right hand, eastern, side, you can see a steep dirt track going up to Fir Tree Spur. This is **Artillery Road (19) (40°04′48.8″N 26°11′31.5″E)**, built by the British during the campaign, which leads to West Krithia Road and Pink Farm. Almost opposite this track, on the western side of the Ravine, another wartime track leads up onto Gully Spur, called Artillery Row, at the top of which British artillery used to be located. Follow Artillery Road out of the ravine and after about 200 metres you will reach the fields on Fir Tree Spur. Cross the field boundary and walk about a hundred metres to the road. Turn right, and walk in a southerly direction for about 300 metres, returning to Pink Farm Cemetery to complete your tour.

# Tour 4

# Krithia Nullah

This is a walking tour of five kilometres over road, track and field boundaries. Its purpose is to give you a feel of the central part of the Helles battlefield and the fighting of May, June and August 1915.

Allow two-three hours for this tour, which starts and finishes at Redoubt Cemetery, where there is parking for a vehicle.

**Redoubt Cemetery (20) (40°04′41.4″N 26°12′53.9″E)** is located on the Krithia road, which runs between Sedd-el-Bahr and the village of Alçitepe (Krithia). It takes its name from a line of Turkish entrenchments dug during the May fighting, later called the Redoubt

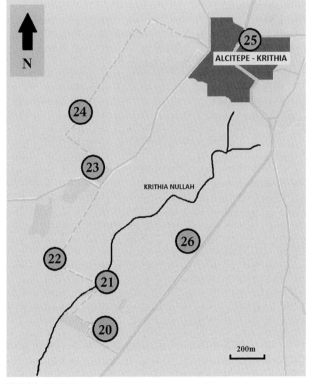

**Krithia Nullah.**

Line. It was here that the British and Australian advances were repulsed during the Second Battle of Krithia. Tommies' Trench, as associated with the Australian attack, was located about 200 metres south east of the cemetery, between the nullah and the road. To the north east of the cemetery is the infamous 'Vineyard', today an olive grove that bears no scars of the fighting that occurred here in August 1915.

The cemetery was started by 2 (Australian) Brigade in May and continued in use until the evacuation. After the Armistice, when the battlefields were cleared, graves were brought in from smaller cemeteries: Krithia Nullah No.1 and No.2, West Krithia Nullah, Brown House, White House and Clapham

Avenue of trees leading to Redoubt CWGC Cemetery.

Under the shade of the Duckworth Oak Tree. Inset: Second Lieutenant Eric Duckworth, 1/6 Lancashire Fusiliers.

**Gartside's grave.**

**Lieutenant Colonel Robert Gartside, commanding 7/AIF.**

Junction. There are now 2,027 servicemen buried or commemorated in this cemetery. Of those buried, 1,393 are unidentified and there are special memorials that commemorate 349 casualties known or believed to be buried here.

As with almost any CWGC cemetery, it is beautifully planted with small plants and shrubs, whilst mature trees grow majestically, providing valuable shade on a hot sunny day. There is one notable tree, an English oak, which was planted as a special memorial in 1922 by the father of Second Lieutenant Eric Duckworth. Duckworth was killed in action near this spot on 7 August during the fighting at The Vineyard. His body was never found. In a letter to his mother in June 1915 he wrote, *I have made a discovery – you never realise the full value of peace until you are deprived of it and living in hourly danger of being deprived of life itself.*

Lieutenant Colonel Robert Gartside *(I.B.21)*, commanding 7/AIF, was killed on 8 May. An orchardist of Castlemaine, Victoria, he is said to have been rising to lead one of the final rushes, saying, *Come on boys, I know it is deadly, but we must get on*, when he was hit in the abdomen by machine-gun bullets. Whilst Gartside's body was recovered and identified, for many others it was not possible. Private Herbert Lloyd, 5/AIF, recalled *a burial party went out and buried 86 in one grave.*[72] Among the notable graves in this cemetery is that of Sepoy Saudagar Singh, 14/Sikhs, who was killed at Gully Ravine on 4 June during the Third Battle of Krithia. It is Sikh custom for their dead to be cremated, so why he was buried is uncertain. His is one of only a few Sikh graves at Gallipoli.

Leave Redoubt Cemetery and walk around the western side of the cemetery wall, skirting the woodland for about a hundred metres towards Krithia Nullah. The woodland contains deep communication trenches, marked on period trench maps as 'Avenues', which would have once led up to the front line.

Sepoy Saudagar Singh's grave marker. Killed on 4 June 1915.

Follow the tree lined nullah for 250 metres, crossing the sites of what would have been the Redoubt Line and Burnley Road trenches, established here in May 1915. Near the site of **Wigan Road Trench (21) (40°04′52.8″N 26°12′53.3″E)**, the remains of which can still be seen nearby in the wooded thicket, cross the nullah to its western banks. The trench lines would have continued here, bearing more names inspired by the Manchester region, such as Oldham Road and Ardwick Green, all named by the regiments of the 42nd Division, a territorial division formed from units from East Lancashire and that fought in this area from May 1915.

Whilst noting the ford to cross the nullah, it is worthwhile venturing another 150 metres to the nullah's bifurcation. Bitter fighting involving the 42nd Division occurred here between May-August 1915. Whilst great advances were made well past this position in the attacks on 4 June and 6 August, the British could not establish their line on the tongue of ground between the branches of the nullah until December, when the 52nd Division held the area. It is interesting, if not surprising, to note the new trench names, such as Vincent Street, Argyle Street, Cathedral Street and Govan Road, all synonymous with Scotland and the Lowland Division.

Return to the ford and cross the nullah, following the field boundary in a westerly direction for about 200 metres, where you will come to a track which once marked the **Divisional Boundary (22) (40°04′57.6″N 26°12′44.2″E)** of the 29th and 42nd Division's in June 1915. Prior to that, during the fighting of 6–8 May, this marked the furthest advance of the Canterbury Battalion. Fir Tree Wood, although different in shape today, runs along the top of Fir Tree Spur, on the southern side of Twelve Tree Copse. In front of Fir Tree Wood was a large open field that was covered in white daisies and red poppies, becoming known as the Daisy Field. It was on this ground that the Auckland and Otago battalions met such withering fire from the Turks.

**The killing fields of 4 June 1915 where the 42nd Division attacked.**

This is also the approximate position of the British front line for the opening of the Third Battle of Krithia. It was just forward of this position that one of the most controversial Victoria Crosses of the campaign was won, that of 18 year old Lieutenant George Raymond Dallas Moor. In the words of the 29th Division's commander, Major General de Lisle, Moor shot 'the leading four men and the remainder came to their senses'.

Follow the track in a northerly direction for another 400 metres to **Twelve Tree Copse CWGC Cemetery (23) (40°05'15.1"N 26°12'54.6"E)**. Twelve Tree Copse was originally a small group of pine trees, situated just south of the present-day cemetery, named by the men of the 29th Division when they reached this area on 28 April. The copse is set a few metres north of Fir Tree Wood, to the right of the pre-war West Krithia Road. The contemporary road follows this very closely. The cemetery, which was built after the Armistice, contains a total of 3,360 graves, formed by the concentration of smaller cemeteries and isolated graves from the battlefield. These include Geoghegan's Bluff Cemetery, Fir Tree Wood Cemetery and Clunes Vennel Cemetery, all of which had their bodies exhumed by the Graves Registration Unit in 1919.

The cemetery contains the graves of 462 soldiers from the United Kingdom, thirteen from New Zealand, two from Australia, and 1,953 whose unit could not be ascertained. The unnamed graves number 2,226; and special memorials are erected to 644 soldiers from the UK, ten from New Zealand, one from Australia, and two from India known or believed to be buried among them. Of these, forty-seven are to men of

197

**Twelve Tree Copse CWGC Cemetery looking across the battlefield.**

the 7/Cameronians (Scottish Rifles) who fell on 28 June during the battle of Gully Ravine; and 142 to those of 1/Essex, who died on 6 August during the diversionary action at Helles for the Anzac breakout and Suvla landing. There is also a New Zealand Memorial to the Missing, one of four on the Peninsula, with 180 New Zealand names of those killed during the Second Battle of Krithia in May 1915.

Three senior officers of 156 Brigade are buried here: Brigadier General William Scott-Moncrieff (*Special Memorial C. 132*), commanding the brigade, Lieutenant Colonel John Boyd Wilson (*Special Memorial C. 406*), commanding 7/Cameronians and Lieutenant Colonel Henry

**Grave marker of Smith VC.**

**Second Lieutenant Alfred Victor Smith VC.**

198

Hannan (*plot VII, row A, grave 7*), commanding 8/Cameronians. Other notable burials include Second Lieutenant Alfred Victor Smith VC, *Croix de Guerre* (*Special Memorial C. 358*), 5/East Lancs, a pre-war police inspector who was posthumously decorated with the Victoria Cross for an action of self-sacrifice at Fusilier Bluff on 22 December. Smith, who was a highly-competent bombing officer, was originally buried in a battlefield grave above Y Beach, but his body was exhumed after the war. His citation in the London Gazette of 3 March 1916 reads:

He was in the act of throwing a grenade when it slipped from his hand and fell to the bottom of the trench close to several officers and men. He immediately shouted a warning and jumped clear to safety. He then saw that the officers and men were unable to find cover and, knowing that the grenade was due to explode at any moment, he returned and flung himself upon it. He was instantly killed by the explosion. His magnificent act of self-sacrifice undoubtedly saved many lives.'

Sergeant John Robins, 5/Wilts (*Special Memorial C. 259*), was one of three Gallipoli men executed during the campaign. Robins was 'shot at dawn' at Gully Beach on 2 January 1916, charged with *wilfully disobeying an order given by a superior officer in the execution of his duty*.

Leave Twelve Tree Copse Cemetery and follow the field track that begins on the northern side of the cemetery for about a hundred metres. This track marks the approximate position of a trench system named Worcester Flat, which straddled the road during the campaign. It was between here and Krithia Nullah where 88 Brigade (29th Division) failed to capture the 'H' trenches in their attack on 6 August. Follow the track to the right; after about fifty metres you will come to the site of **Sap 30 (24)** (**40°05′24.6″N 26°12′51.9″E**), where Brigadier General Scott-Moncrieff was killed on 28 June whilst watching 156 Brigade enduring heavy casualties in an attempt to capture the Turkish H.12 trench line. This position marks the furthest advance the British made towards Krithia. Stay on this track for a further one kilometre, making for the elusive village of Krithia.

**Alçitepe, Krithia (25)** (**40°05′41.4″N 26°13′30.6″E**) was an important objective that was never captured during the campaign; the closest British troops came to Krithia was on 25 April, when an officer patrol from Y Beach reached the outskirts of the village. Ottoman Greeks had been settled in the village before the war but were later moved to Anatolia during the military build-up on the Peninsula in 1915. To the east of the village

**Worcester Flat and the attack of 29th Division, 4 June 1915. Looking towards Krithia Nullah.**

there used to be a small cluster of windmills, used for extracting oil from olives, but all of these were destroyed during the war and never rebuilt. The village, also known as Kirte, was resettled in the 1930s, when it was renamed Alçitepe. The village today has a variety of Kofta restaurants, a few small shops and market stalls, public toilets and probably the oldest campaign museum on Gallipoli: the private collection of Salim Mutlu.

**Note**: If you are interested in visiting the top of Gully Ravine and Y Beach, you can leave Alçitepe on its western road. This will take you towards Fusilier Bluff via several Turkish memorials: the Son Ok ('Last Arrow') Memorial, which commemorates an action during the Third Battle of Krithia; the Ziğindere Field Dressing Station Memorial and Cemetery; and, at Fusilier Bluff, the Nuri Yamut Memorial and the nearby Ziğindere Military Cemetery. For further details see my Battleground Europe book *Gallipoli: Gully Ravine*.

Leave Krithia by its main, eastern, 'Krithia road'. After about one kilometre you will pass the site of **The Vineyard (26) (40°04′54.4″N 26°13′15.0″E)**, sign-posted to the west of the road. The area was the site of very heavy fighting in August 1915 and the place where Lieutenant William Thomas Forshaw, 9/Manchesters, won his VC. Forshaw led his company in a fiercely fought defence of a captured Turkish position for forty-one hours close to where you are now standing. His citation reads:

'For most conspicuous bravery and determination in the Gallipoli Peninsula from 7th to 9th August 1915. When holding the northwest corner of the 'Vineyard' he was attacked and heavily bombed by Turks, who advanced time after time by three trenches which converged at this point, but he held his own, not only directing his men and encouraging them by exposing himself with the utmost disregard to danger, but personally throwing bombs continuously for 41 hours. When his detachment was relieved after 24 hours he volunteered to continue the direction of operations. Three times during the night of 8th–9th August he was again heavily attacked, and once the Turks got over the barricade, but, after shooting three with his revolver, he led his men forward and recaptured it. When he re-joined his battalion he was choked and sickened by bomb fumes, badly bruised from a fragment of shrapnel, and could barely lift his arm from continuous bomb throwing. It was due to his personal example, magnificent courage and endurance that this very important corner was held.'

After the action Forshaw was reported to look yellow as a result of cordite and cigarette fumes and was visibly shaken. He survived the campaign and war, later serving in the Home Guard during the Second World War. He died of a heart attack in 1943, aged only 53.

Return the last 800 metres to Redoubt Cemetery.

The Vineyard, showing the approximate position of the British trench.

The Vineyard sign on the Krithia road.

# Tour 5

## The Royal Naval Division's Sector:
## Kanli Dere

This is a walking tour of four kilometres over road, track and field boundaries. Allow two to three hours for this tour, which starts and finishes at Skew Bridge Cemetery, where there is parking for a vehicle. Its purpose is to give you a feel of the central part of the Helles battlefield and the fighting of May, June and August 1915.

Begin this walk at **Skew Bridge Cemetery (27) (40°03′35.1″N 26°11′59.3″E)**, which lies just off the Sedd-el-Bahr to Alçitepe (Krithia) Road. The cemetery was begun in early May 1915 at about the time that engineers built a wooden 'skew' bridge across Kanli Dere, located behind the cemetery.

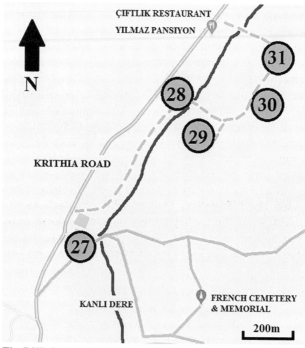

The RND Sector: Kanli Dere.

**Skew Bridge CWGC Cemetery.**

Skew Bridge Cemetery only held fifty-three graves at the end of the war, after which time it was greatly enlarged when bodies were brought in from smaller cemeteries (Orchard Gully, RND, Backhouse Post and Romano's Well) and battlefield burials. Today it contains 607 burials, of which 351 are unidentified; but special memorials commemorate a number of casualties known or believed to be buried among them. The early graves mostly date from May 1915 and the Second Battle of Krithia, when the RND were engaged in the fighting north of this cemetery. Observation Ridge, an important British observation position, still has the remains of trenches and dugouts, whilst locations like Backhouse Post, Romano's Well and the White House, all important in the RND's history, can still be located.

Amongst those buried here are Lieutenant Colonel John Quilter *(II.B.4)*, a Boer War veteran who served in the Grenadier Guards and commanded Hood Battalion. Quilter, while carrying an oversized walking stick, was killed leading his men on 6 May. Prior to the outbreak of the war he had served as the Military Secretary to the Governor General of Australia. The following verse was written in his memory:

> *All honour to Colonel Quilter,*
> *The Battalion mourns his loss.*
> *The only things we could give him*
> *Were a grave and a wooden cross.*

He is joined by three other RND colonels: Colonel Frank Luard (*II.B.3*), Portsmouth Battalion; Lieutenant Colonel Edmund Evelegh (*II.E.13*), Nelson Battalion; and Lieutenant Colonel William Maxwell (*Sp. Mem. B.19*), HQ 2 (Naval) Brigade. All three led by example, demonstrating courage to their men. Evelegh, for example, was last seen on the parapet *in advance of any of his men and, standing under a hail of shrapnel, he took off his cap and cheered the men out of the trenches as if he was cheering on a pack of hounds. He was a fine sight.*[73] Also in HQ 2 (Naval) Brigade was Assistant Paymaster Harry Biles (*II.E.12*), a

**Lieutenant Colonel John Arnold Cuthbert Quilter, commanding Hood Battalion.**

witness to the destruction of the Collingwood Battalion on 4 June. He was killed on 13 July whilst taking ammunition and bombs up the line. Mortally wounded near Backhouse Post, he died later that night.

Epitaphs are often quite moving and on occasion give information as to how a soldier died. 19-year-old Private Albert Prince (*II.F.4*),

Plymouth Battalion, was killed on 15 July, *Shot Rescuing a Comrade*; the line above this in his epitaph shows that he was Mentioned in Despatches (MID). The only posthumous awards available in 1915 were MID and the Victoria Cross. An Accrington lad, Drummer Joseph Townsend (*Sp. Mem. B.4*), 1/4 East Lancs, was killed on 18 June, aged just

**Harry Biles.**

**Grave of Assistant Paymaster Harry Biles.**

15 years. Joe was the youngest British soldier to die at Gallipoli; he was the son of Company Sergeant Major Townsend, the recruiting officer for his home town. Joe was one of three sons in the same battalion. One of them witnessed Joe's death. He wrote home with the sad news, saying that he saw his brother hit in the chest, causing a severe wound and from which he died within a few minutes.

Leave the cemetery and follow the Krithia Alçitepe Road onto Observation Ridge. The whole wood is full of trenches and dugouts and is well worth exploring if you have time. Most of the trenches can be found on the eastern side of the road, especially where the road kinks about 700 metres from the cemetery.

From Skew Bridge, continue along the road for 1.4 km, where you will find a track on the right of the road. Follow this track for 200 metres into the woods, bearing to the left as the track leads down into **Kanli Dere (28) (40°04′08.6″N 26°12′33.7″E)**. If you continued to follow this stream north it would lead into Achi Baba Nullah. Cross the ford and carry on for another 100 metres to the end of the track. To the right of the track you will see several wells, the site of **Romano's Well (29) (40°04′04.4″N 26°12′35.2″E)**. Romano's was an important watering hole in this sector, which allowed piped water to be taken up towards the front. It was thought that this watering hole was named after a salubrious restaurant-cum-club on The Strand in London; in Edwardian times it was frequented by a Bohemian set: authors, journalists, artists of all kinds, soldiers, sailors (only officers), lawyers, financiers and maybe the odd crook or two. At the track junction turn left.

**A large HQ style dugout, about 300m northeast of Skew Bridge.**

**British trenches.**

**Romano's Well.**

After another 150 metres you will come to area of the **Brown House (30)** (40°04'11.2"N 26°12'48.7"E) and the **White House (31)** (40°04'15.16"N 26°12'48.47"E). The White House was captured by Hood Battalion, RND on 6 May 1915, as described in great detail by Joe Murray in his book *Gallipoli As I Saw It*. It was in this area where Hood lost half its strength and its commander, Lieutenant Colonel Arnold Quilter, in the fighting. Whilst there is little evidence of the Brown House today, at the White House location there are the remains of a building's foundations, hedges, old vines and roses. Joe Murray mentions the building quite clearly (see Chapter 3) as he notes that only four men managed to get through a gap in the hedge unwounded.

The RND advance came to a standstill barely ten metres further on, thus marking the forward position of Hood Battalion at the end of Second Krithia, and not far from where Collingwood Battalion was destroyed as they came up to drive the 4 June advance forward.

After the Second Battle of Krithia open warfare came to an end and trenches were dug. Many in this area followed a London theme, such as Romano's of The Strand. Communication trenches, which had names such as Oxford Street, Piccadilly Circus and Regent Street, are all long

**The RND killing fields near the White House. In spring they are covered in poppies and wild flowers.**

gone, but would have once been dug in these fields, taking men to the front and back in relative safety.

You will note the Çiftlik Restaurant and the Yılmaz Pansiyon guest house to the left, on the Krithia Alçitepe Road. Follow the field boundaries in the direction of the Pansiyon, where you will find a track that crosses the Achi Baba Nullah, taking you to the road. There are refreshments that can be purchased here, a small pond and restaurant.

Return to Skew Bridge via the main road, a distance of 1.8 kilometres.

# Tour 6

## The French Sector: Kereves Spur

This is a walking tour of seven kilometres over road, track and field boundaries. Allow four hours for this tour, which starts and finishes at Morto Bay, where there is ample parking for a vehicle. Its purpose is to give you a feel of the French sector of Helles.

Because most people will have a vehicle, the starting place for this walking tour (although note that parts can be driven) is the Otopark on the shoreline by **S Beach (32) (40°03′04.1″N 26°12′56.4″E)** and below the

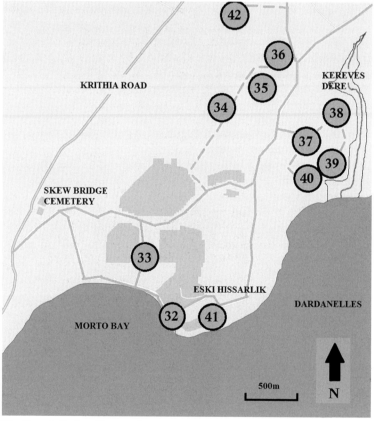

**The French Sector: Kereves Spur.**

**Turkish Çanakkale Martyrs Memorial on the Eski Hissarlik promontory.**

site of Turkish Çanakkale Martyrs Memorial, built on the promontory known as Eski Hissarlik. There is a cafe here for refreshments and there are toilets. Where there is now a car park was the site during the campaign of *Le Cimetière de la 1er Division*, the cemetery of the French 1st Division. The graves here were exhumed in the 1920s and moved to the main cemetery, up on the ridge.

S Beach was the most easterly of the British landings on 25 April 1915. Three companies of 2/SWB, under the command of Lieutenant Colonel Hugh Casson, were landed from HMS *Cornwallis*. The 2/SWB successfully captured the Turkish observation post and defences known as De Tott's, situated on a promontory known as Eski Hissarlik. The battalion maintained this position until 27 April, when the French *175e Régiment d'infanterie (175 RI)* relieved them. After this the whole area was passed to the French *CEO*. The stone jetty you can see stretching out into Morto Bay is believed to have been constructed by the French during the campaign.

Leave your vehicle and follow the shoreline for about 750 metres; on the right is a road that takes you to the French Military Cemetery, nestled up on the ridge to the right. Ascend the steps to reach the cemetery. From the top of the steps there is an impressive view of Morto Bay: to the left is the Asian coast and forts of Kum Kale; to the right is the village of Sedd-el-Bahr.

The beach here was commonly used by the French and British for swimming, but it was too exposed to be used as a main landing beach due to the enemy guns on the Asian side of the Dardanelles. Within this bay HMS *Goliath* was torpedoed and sunk by the Turkish torpedo boat *Muavanet i Milliye* during the night of 12–13 May. This was one of three capital ships that the British lost in a fortnight to torpedoes. The buoy marker for the wreck can be seen out in the middle of the bay.

**An old, abandoned French memorial that still stands within the nearby forestry.**

The French referred to the ridge you are now standing on as Falaise des Oliviers, or the Cliff of Olives. Enter the **French Cemetery and Memorial (33) (40°03′26.0″N 26°12′36.7″E)**. The cemetery contains 2,340 identified graves and four ossuaries containing the bones of 12,000 unidentifiable soldiers. There were other French cemeteries and memorials during and immediately after the war, the remains of some of which can still be found in the surrounding woodland; but all of these were concentrated after the war to this single, large cemetery and memorial. There were two main communication trenches in this area, *Boyau Nord* No.1 and No.2, both exiting near the French Military Cemetery. The remains of these communication trenches can still be traced in the area to the north of the cemetery.

At the southern entrance of the cemetery is an information plaque giving a brief history of the *CEO* and the cemetery. It lists six original French cemeteries on the battlefield; Le Cimetière Galinier, Le Cimetière de L'Ambulance, Le Cimetière de la 1er Division, Le Cimetière de la 2e Division, Le Cimetière Zimmermann and Le Cimetière de Kereves Dere. In 1919 the French began gathering in all their fallen into two newly built ossuaries, named after the French generals Masnou and Ganéval, both of whom died during the campaign. In 1923, after the signing of the Treaty of Lausanne, the French consolidated all the cemeteries and ossuaries into this cemetery. This also included those who were

**French Cemetery and Memorial.**

buried on Lemnos and some graves from the Allied occupation of the area. On 9 June 1930, General Gouraud, the original GOC of the *Corps Expéditionnaire d'Orient*, inaugurated the cemetery; at the end of June 1915 he was seriously injured and had to have an arm amputated. He ended his war as a successful commander of the French Fourth Army.

The *CEO*, made up of French *Métropolitaine* and French colonial African troops, came ashore at Helles on 27 April and fought alongside the British for the best part of eight months. The Corps was responsible for the right of the line at Kereves Dere, a deep gully about two kilometres northeast of this cemetery and the Turkish memorial (Çanakkale Martyrs Memorial). The battles for Kereves Dere failed with huge casualties, the consequence of a number of attempted advances to take the Turkish positions. Those fighting in places with infamous names such as *Ravin de la Mort, Le Fortin "Le Gouez", Haricot, le Quadrilatère* and *Le Rognon* Redoubts, included not only French born soldiers but also men from the French colonies, such as Algeria, Morocco, Guinea, Sudan and Senegal.

Despite several battles, which would account for 27,000 French casualties, of which up to 15,000 died, their endeavours achieved little. The French Military Cemetery is the largest on the Peninsula, containing the graves of some 3,236 men. Each grave is marked by a black iron stake that looks similar to a barbed wire picket, with its ends

An Ossuary that contains the bones of 3,000 unidentifiable French soldiers.

flared into a *fleur-de-lys* style design. The graves have a simple metallic plaque that bears the name and a common MORT POUR LA FRANCE (Died for France) epitaph. The graves are laid out according to rank; the officers at the top end of the cemetery and the soldiers in the remainder. (Perhaps remarkable for a republic that has *Liberté, Egalité, Fraternité* for a motto.) What is unusual are the number of officer marked graves that still contain their original stone markers, moved from their original cemetery locations before all the French burials on Gallipoli were consolidated here.

The French Memorial with its wall of plaques.

Close by the officers' graves is the Memorial Wall (*Mur des Souvenirs*). This wall, constructed in 1926, is the main monument upon which numerous marble plaques have been imbedded from the different monuments that used to stand on the battlefield itself. The memorial recalls the loss at the Dardanelles of French sailors from warships like *Bouvet* and the four French submarines that were lost: *Joule, Mariotte, Saphir* and *Turquoise*. Marble plaques to all the French infantry units involved are also shown. In Latin, across the front of the obelisk, is carved *Ave Gallia Immortalis* (Hail Immortal France) above a verse from Victor Hugo's *Anthem*.

There are several senior officers buried here, one of whom is General Marie François Ganéval (*Grave 36*), who was killed on 7 June, aged

61. A senior officer, he was criticised for his handling of the French *62e Division* on the Western Front during the fighting in August and September 1914 in which it suffered heavy casualties. He left this division at the end of September and sailed for Gallipoli in 1915, taking command of the *2e Brigade (2e Division)*. On 7 June, accompanied by an interpreter and liaison officer, he visited the British trenches in the Achi Baba Nullah sector. Ganéval was in a trench only a hundred metres from the Turks when he was sniped, falling mortally wounded and dying in a dressing station. He was buried the following day with full military honours and in the presence of General Sir Ian Hamilton, General Gouraud, General Bailloud (GOC *2e Division*), Brigadier General Simonin (*4e Brigade Mixte Coloniale*) and a number of other senior officers. The guard of honour comprised a detachment of Zouaves. Regardless of rank, nowhere and no-one was safe at Gallipoli.

Next to Ganéval is Commandant (Major) Jacques Romieux (*Grave 37*), who was killed on 12 July when a Turkish shell landed on the *ler Division's* staff dugout. Romieux was killed outright; General Masnou received a mortal wound to the head and several other officers were wounded. Moving from a general to a private, Private Kone Moussa (*Grave 1156*), *56 RI*, was killed in action at Kereves Dere on 29 July. Moussa was from Senegal, in West Africa, a notable recruiting ground for French colonial forces at the time. Captain Gabriel Leroux (*Grave 972*), *176 RI*, was a well-established pre-war writer; he was killed on 9 June. Another famous author and poet was Leon Gauthier-Ferriéres, who was killed on 17 July; he has no known grave but is believed to be interred in one of the ossuaries.

Military chaplains were also casualties. Buried here is Marie Lafont de Contagnet (*Grave 2225*), a chaplain to the *2e Division*. He was posthumously awarded the *Legion d'Honneur* and the *Croix de Guerre* with palm. It is said that he had *a quiet and smiling courage and never hesitated to visit the men in the front line, comforting the wounded and dying.* He was killed by shrapnel fire on 9 June whilst in the trenches close to the Turkish lines. He had only been in Gallipoli less than a month

**Grave of Captain Emmanuel Albert Laplanche, Régiment de Zouaves, who was killed 28 April 1915.**

213

before his death. Contagnet spent some of his early life in England, were he took his vows as a Jesuit in Canterbury in 1897. As a Jesuit, he would have spent thirteen years at least in preparing and training for ordination. He then moved to Jersey in 1899, and to Beirut in 1903, where he engaged in Biblical studies and teaching at the inter-ritual seminary and recently established Jesuit university there, before returning to France in 1907. He returned to work in Syria at an Armenian mission in Caesarea in Cappadocia until war broke

**Marie Lafont de Contagnet.**

out; he returned to his mobilisation centre in Briançon, was moved to Lyon and volunteered to go as a chaplain to Gallipoli.

Leave the French cemetery through its western exit and follow the track for a few metres to the asphalt road. This roughly marks the front line on 4 May 1915, before the Second Battle of Krithia, and the ground over which the Turks ferociously counter-attacked during 1–4 May. It is worth exploring these woods as they are full of trenches and dugouts, including the remains of some of the old French war memorials and the ruins of Zimmerman's Farm.

**One of the lost French memorials that can be found in the surrounding forestry.**

**Position of the Bouchet Redoubt today. The track leads onto the Haricot and Quadrilateral redoubts.**

As it is difficult to navigate the reader through the woods, the track we will follow is easier. At the road, turn right in an easterly direction and follow the asphalt road for a kilometre. As the road then bends to the right, take the paved track into the woods on the left of the road. Follow this for a hundred metres, where it joins an agricultural track, actually the old road from Sedd-el-Bahr to Kilid Bahr during the time of the campaign. Parallel to this road ran the long communication trenches known as *Avenue de Paris* and *Avenue de Constantinople*, both leading to the front. It was on this open ground, devoid of tree cover, that the French, in their bright blue and red uniforms with white cork helmets, became easy targets of the Turks entrenched on the high ground further along the track.

Follow the track in a north-easterly direction, noting how the ground rises gently onto Kereves Spur, also known as the 90-metre contour line. After a kilometre you will come to the site of the ***Bouchet* Redoubt (34) (40°04′06.0″N 26°13′28.7″E)**, a strongpoint that caused the French so many problems in the earlier attacks; it was finally captured on 8 May. No remains of this formidable position appear to remain today.

215

**Quadrilateral Redoubt trenches.**

Continue along the track for another 400 metres to the site of *l'Haricot* (35) (40°04'15.2"N 26°13'40.9"E), to the right of the track. So long a thorn in the side of the French, it was not captured until 21 June.

Continue along the old road for another 250 metres to *le Quadrilatère* (36) (40°04'21.6"N 26°13'47.7"E), the most infamous of the series of strong points. Perched on the top of Hill 83, this position was eventually captured on 30 June after bitter fighting. The Turks know Hill 83 as Kemal Bey Tepe, in honour of Staff Captain Kemal Bey who fell mortally wounded in this area on 21 June. His last order to his men was *Let's charge, fall as martyrs, so our homeland will be saved.* This site is quite well preserved, with trench lines still visible. Standing on the top of this position, it is easy to understand why it was so important as it overlooks the surrounding area, the approaches up Kereves Spur and is guardian to the top of Kereves Dere. Whilst further attacks took place during July, no further advances could be made at *le Quadrilatère*. This position marks the end of the French advances for the campaign. [See optional visit, p.219.]

Rejoin the asphalt road by the side of *le Quadrilatère*. Turn right and follow the road. It is difficult to imagine today, but alongside this road there was a maze of trenches, many named in memory of French commanders such as Masnou, Gouraud, Ganéval and Romieux.

Turkish Memorial to Major Hüseyin Hilmi Bey, commander of 17 Regiment, killed on 12 July 1915. Inset: Major Hüseyin Hilmi Bey, 17 Regiment.

After 700 metres you will reach a turning to the left. Follow this for 200 metres to the Turkish **'Hasan Bey' Memorial (37)**. There has been some recent research by Turkish scholars that has thrown doubt as to who the Hasan Bey Memorial commemorates. It is now believed that there was a mistake in the original translation of the Ottoman script that misidentified the officer as Lieutenant Colonel Hasan Bey; he actually survived the war. The memorial is now believed to be for Major Hüseyin Hilmi Bey, commander of 17 Regiment (6th Division), who was killed in this area on 12 July during the Kereves Dere fighting.

From the Memorial, it is possible to follow the field boundary to the edge of Kereves Dere. There are some excellent views to be had from this position. Although heavily wooded in places, the tree line and pine needles have preserved much of the French and Turkish trenches along the ravine. These are worth exploring. To the north-east of the Memorial is *Ravin de la Mort* **(38) (40°04′06.7″N 26°13′56.3″E)**, a Turkish position that was not captured until 21 June, but a position of immense importance, as it gave the French the ability to overlook Kereves Dere. To the south-east of the Memorial is the site of the strongpoint named *Le Rognon* **(39) (40°03′55.2″N 26°14′00.1″E)**, which resisted all French attacks until eventually falling on 12 July. Directly south of the memorial is the redoubt known as *Le Fortin Le Gouez* **(40)**

**(40°03′50.0″N 26°13′51.9″E)**, captured by a legionnaire battalion on 30 May. Positioned on the edge of Kereves Dere, these were formidable strongpoints that had thwarted many French attacks.

Return to the 'Hasan Bey' Memorial and the main asphalt road. Continue along this road in a southerly direction for 600 metres, where you come to a crossroads. In the wooden area in between this junction was a French dressing station, positioned to take advantage of a deep communication trench named *Boyau Central*, along which casualties could be evacuated. Turning right at this crossroads will take you to the French Military Cemetery and Sedd-el-Bahr. Turning left takes you in the direction of the Hasan Bey Memorial and *Le Fortin Le Gouez*. Whilst it is possible to descend into Kereves Dere from here, it is not recommended as the route is hazardous due to track erosion and scrub overgrowth.

**Turkish Martyrs Memorial.**

**Mustafa Kemal Atatürk Memorial and cemetery.**

218

Continue on for 1.5 km to the **Turkish Martyrs Memorial (41)** (Çanakkale Sehitleri Aniti) **(40°03′00.7″N 26°13′10.5″E)**. This huge memorial, forty metres high, the main Turkish memorial at Gallipoli, is signposted throughout the peninsula as Abide. The Memorial is built on the headland of Eski Hissarlik, which is also the site of an Athenian settlement called Elaius and the location of De Tott's Battery. The monument was opened in 1960 as a memorial to the 'Mehmets', the Ottoman soldiers who fought and died in the campaign, the story of which is told in friezes around the structure. Within the grounds is a military cemetery, with symbolic graves and various statues and other exhibits relating to the campaign. Souvenirs, refreshments and toilets are available.

Leave the Turkish memorial, taking the road that winds down 500 metres to S Beach and Morto Bay and from there to the car park and your vehicle.

### Optional Visit: Achi Baba Nullah and the Horseshoe
This is not the easiest site to locate on the battlefield today, but worthwhile, especially if you have an interest in the Lowland Division and RND.

The easiest way to find it is from the location of *le Quadrilatère* **(36) (40°04′21.6″N 26°13′47.7″E)** location. From here follow the road to Krithia in a northerly direction for 600 metres. Due west of this position, about 250 metres from the road, is the location of the **Horseshoe (42) (40°04′44.7″N 26°13′33.2″E)**, overlooking Achi Baba Nullah. The ground here takes on a distinctive horseshoe shape and was once a fortified Turkish earthwork. It, along with the trenches E.10 and E.11, was captured by 155 Brigade on 12 July. It was then integrated into the British front line, which remained here until the end of the campaign.

It was here that Alex Barclay, 1/1st Ayrshire Yeomanry, recorded being under a bombardment of hundreds of 10-inch howitzer shells during December 1915. In the fields to the south of this position, 157 Brigade attacked on 12 July and was partially successful, followed by a new attack by the RND on 13 July. There is little evidence of the trenches today, but pause and give a thought to the 3,000 British and over 5,000 Turkish casualties that fell in these fields during two days of July 1915.

# Advice to Tourers

GETTING THERE:
Turkey is very much on the tourist map and today Gallipoli and the nearby ancient city of Troy (Truva) are firmly part of that industry. If you are not already in Turkey, most people would fly to the major international airports in Istanbul or Izmir, although a small domestic airport in Çanakkale has recently opened. Before you travel you must check if you require a visa. See website http://www.evisa.gov.tr.

Çanakkale, the main city in the area, can be reached from Edirne and Istanbul by way of Tekirdağ and the Gelibolu highways. There is a reliable coach network and hiring cars is straightforward. From Çanakkale there are ferries to Kilitbahir and Eceabat. Because of the extent of the Gallipoli battlefields, car hire (recommended that it have air conditioning) is essential for the battlefield visitor, and can be arranged at the airport, hotel or locally in Çanakkale. If you have no vehicle, there are local tour companies in both Çanakkale and Eceabat that will take you to the battlefield, but for non-Anzac areas you may need to rent a taxi or bicycle.

TOURIST OFFICE:
For the latest information on visiting Turkey, explore the Turkish Tourism Office's website https://www.goturkeytourism.com or, once in Çanakkale, visit the Tourism Information Office that is located near the jetty square, where you can get detailed information, maps and tour ideas in the area.

Çanakkale Tourist Information Office (Çanakkale Turizm Burosu)
Iskele Meydani, 67
Çanakkale
Tel: + 90 (286) 217 11 87

ACCOMMODATION:
Most of the hotels in the area are not expensive and include breakfast and sometimes an evening meal. To find a hotel or pension of choice in Eceabat, Çanakkale and even Seddülbahir it is best to search on the

internet. There are also numerous camping sites in the area for those on a lower budget. Çanakkale, in particular, has a good selection of restaurants and cafes, which are all reasonably priced. If you stay in Çanakkale you will need to take the ferry every morning to cross the Narrows. The crossing takes approximately twenty minutes, is quite frequent and is an inexpensive and picturesque way of starting and ending your day.

EATING OUT:
During the day on the battlefield it is best to pre-prepare a packed lunch as there are few places to stop and eat. If you decide to eat in a restaurant or *al fresco*, several establishments are located in the villages and towns in the area. For lunch try traditional Turkish foods like gözleme, a flatbread and pastry dish or pide, a flat-bread of a similar style to pita, chapati, or western pizza. Of course, Turkish köfte, a delicious meatball dish, or a kabab are also worth sampling. In the evenings the seafront restaurants that border the Dardanelles in Çanakkale are a must, and there is a wide range of places that offer traditional Turkish food, some great seafood and a choice of western European foods if you prefer. Eceabat also offers a good choice, although on a smaller scale.

THE WALKS:
Even though most of these areas can be covered by car or similar vehicle in a day, this is not the purpose of this guide. To really see the battlefield, which is surprisingly small, it should be done on foot. When walking please be respectful of the area, much of which is private farmland. Be considerate of the crops to avoid doing them damage. Even in autumn, when there are fewer crops and the fields easier to walk, keep to the tracks and field boundaries and do not walk across the middle of the fields.

Since 2015, Helles, Anzac and Suvla fall under the control of the Gallipoli Historic Site Directorate (ÇATAB) which is responsible to the Ministry of Culture and Tourism. The site encompasses a total area of some 33,000 hectares. The entire region has been officially registered as a historical site of enormous cultural importance. Aside from those places of Great War interest, within the site there are also many archaeological sites and monuments, some of which date back to 4,000 BC. Troy is a mere stone's throw away just across the Dardanelles and reveals just a fraction of what remains buried in this entire area.

The Gallipoli battlefield is actually made up of three separate areas. There is Helles, the main British and French sector, situated on the southern tip of the Peninsula, and which includes the main villages of Seddülbahir (Sedd-el-Bahr) and Alçıtepe (Krithia). Further north is Anzac, the Australian and New Zealand sector, which contain few settlements, the closest being Kojadere. Adjoining Anzac is Suvla, the site of the August landing and again another predominantly British sector, which includes the local village of Anafarta.

EQUIPMENT:
When visiting the battlefields, preferably with at least one other person, always take a good supply of bottled water, a walking stick (also useful to fend off any shepherd's dogs), sun cream, a wide-brimmed hat, long trousers for any bush walking, camera, binoculars, pen, notepad, penknife and a pair of sturdy boots with ankle support, a small first-aid kit and a rain cape. If you are unfamiliar with the area and going off the beaten track, a map and compass are both recommended (useful in any case). Put all this in a small rucksack with this book, and you have a good recipe for an excellent tour. A mobile phone can also be useful in emergencies (with the number of hotel and, if applicable, the car hire or tour company). Be aware of the risks, especially in the more remote areas like Gully Ravine and Kereves Dere, as these areas are isolated and a long way from help. There is a general lack of toilets and refreshments for the visitor, indeed a lack of almost anything useful for sustenance and comfort, so travel well-prepared.

DANGERS:
Be aware that the whole of the Gallipoli Peninsula is a historical area, dedicated to the memory of those who fought and died on both sides.

**DANGER – Unexploded ordnance.**

222

Please respect this. A lot of the area is still farmland and private property. When walking. please be conscious of the crops and respect the privacy of the people who live here.

If you do find a wartime relic, such as a shell, grenade or bullet, leave it alone. Photograph it by all means, but do not touch it as these things are often in a highly dangerous condition and can still cause death and injury. If you see an unexploded shell or bomb, please note the exact location (GPS on your mobile phone) and report it to the Gallipoli Historic Site Directorate in Eceabat, telephone number: +90 286 814 11 28. They will contact the Jandarma for disposal.

It is strictly forbidden by the Turkish authorities to remove any artefact from the battlefield.

Lastly, the area has many goatherds and small farm settlements that keep dogs. These latter can be quite ferocious if you happen to go too close, so keep at a distance, keep together and always carry a stick. There have also been sightings of wild boar in some of the more remote areas of the battlefield, and snakes are occasionally seen basking in the sun, both potential dangers if you get too close and disturb them.

BATTLEFIELD NAVIGATION:
To help with their location, cemetery, memorials and the main locations of interest are identified in the tour section using Google Map/GPS coordinates shown in DMS format: Degrees, minutes, and seconds: 40°02'44.6"N 26°10'45.0"E.

The COMMONWEALTH WAR GRAVES COMMISSION (CWGC):
The Commission's registers, now computerised, hold the commemoration details of each casualty, along with information about all the cemeteries and memorials. These records are now accessible from the Commission's website, http://www.cwgc.org. If you are planning to visit a CWGC cemetery or memorial, please check the website for a plan/reference before travelling to Gallipoli. A full enquiries service is available from the Enquiries Section at Head Office, Maidenhead. Once in Turkey the local CWGC office in Çanakkale should be able to help you.

Commonwealth War Graves Commission (Turkey Office)
Tel +90 (286) 2171010
Web: https://www.cwgc.org/

THE GALLIPOLI HISTORIC SITE DIRECTORATE (ÇATAB):
The Gallipoli Peninsula was under the administrative control of the Ministry of Forestry and Water Affairs. From 1973, it was known as

the "Gallipoli Peninsula Historical National Park" and came under legal protection, which gave the area special status.

Gallipoli, one of the most well preserved battlefields, applied for listing in the "World Cultural Heritage List" with the support of the Ministry of Culture and Tourism and added to the UNESCO World Heritage Tentative List in 2014. A law promulgated in 2014 transferred responsibility and preservation to the Gallipoli Historic Site Directorate.

The Gallipoli Historic Site Directorate (Çanakkale Savaşlari Gelibolu Tarihi Alan Başkanliği) is responsible for protecting, sustaining, developing and transferring the historical, cultural and sentimental values of the Gallipoli Historic Site for the next generations. The Directorate also presents the site to national and international organisations and is responsible to the Ministry of Culture and Tourism in Ankara.

The Directorate has been founded to highlight the history, locate, protect and commemorate the fallen of all sides with a multidisciplinary concept and comprehensive approach, as well as promoting the area as a viable "commemorative tourism" destination to meet national and international demand, by providing the necessary structural, cultural and agrarian development.

You can visit the Directorate and obtain books, guidebooks and maps, which have been published by the Directorate in English.

Tel +90 (286) 8141128
Email: tarihialanbaskanligi@kultur.gov.tr
Web: https://catab.ktb.gov.tr/

THE GALLIPOLI ASSOCIATION:
Founded by Gallipoli veteran Major Edgar Banner in 1969, it is the foremost association for the Gallipoli campaign. The key focus is education; by raising public awareness of the campaign, the Association encourages and facilitates study, with the aim to keep the memory of the campaign alive, ensuring that all who served in it and those who gave their lives, on all sides, are not forgotten.

The Gallipoli Association.

The small annual subscription will give you access to notice of events, merchandise, an excellent website and their published journal, *The Gallipolian*, in which related articles of historical, academic and literary merit appear.

Email: secretary@gallipoli-association.org
Web: http://www.gallipoli-association.org

# The Gallipoli Legacy

The Gallipoli operation was the largest and most ambitious amphibious operation in history to that date. Although characterised by countless deeds of heroism and endurance, a campaign that was flawed from the very start had resulted in a costly and embarrassing defeat for the Entente powers, in particular the British.

At some stages of the campaign there was a glimmer of hope that this scheme could work but for great 'what-ifs': if only the fleet had continued the naval attack on 19 March; if only the landings at S and Y beaches were exploited; if only the Anzacs had landed in the right place; if only reinforcements were available to push home the Krithia attacks; if only IX Corps had pushed on sooner at Suvla. This list is not endless but undoubtedly British political and military prevarication and bungling prevented success, turning Gallipoli into one of the First World War's most disastrous and tragic campaigns. Even General Sir Ian Hamilton, referred to the campaign after the war as the 'Dardanelles Dustbin'. Although he, along with Churchill and Kitchener, must share the blame for its failure, the root cause can only be ascribed to the lack of political and military will in sanctioning a campaign with inadequate, to put it mildly, planning and resources: above all too few men, and an inadequate supply of artillery and munitions. That said, the British had seriously underestimated the fighting prowess and stamina of the Turks; this was never going to be an easy walkover as some might have hoped.

Although the operation was a dismal failure and every one of the principles of war compromised in the planning and execution of the enterprise, the evacuation ranks among the most impressive, imaginative, audacious and best-executed operational successes of the entire war. A withdrawal of an army in the face of the enemy, with its subsequent evacuation by sea, is a complex and dangerous military operation of the first magnitude. And it is this success that is an important legacy. Studying the evacuation reveals many of the essential ingredients of amphibious warfare: unity of command, close joint service coordination, detailed planning, clear objectives, tactical ingenuity, constant and flexible operational supervision, disciplined forces, operational security and, finally, good luck. There is much that can be learned from the Allied debacle at Gallipoli, as there is much to be learned from the brilliant success of its evacuation. Without its detailed military study the later amphibious landings at Salerno, Anzio, Normandy, Iwo Jima and San Carlos may not have been so successful had the lessons of Gallipoli not been learnt.

Some 559,000 Allied personnel were committed during the whole campaign, of whom 420,000 were British and Empire troops, from the Dominions 50,000 Australians, 9,000 New Zealanders and a battalion of Newfoundlanders; and 80,000 French. The Allies had over 250,000 casualties, of whom over 58,000 died; approximately 196,000 of these were wounded or sick. Casualties to the Ottoman forces, including some Germans, numbered in excess of 300,000 and over 87,000 died. It was a campaign where disease and sickness produced substantially more casualties than the fighting itself.

Mustafa Kemal, who rose to supreme power in the confusion of post war Turkey as Kemal Ataturk, 'Father of the Turks', acknowledged all who had died in the course of the Gallipoli Campaign:

*Those heroes that shed their blood in this country! You are in the soil of a friendly country. Rest in peace. You are lying side by side, bosom to bosom with Mehmets.*

# Notes

1. Diary of GMD Maltby, private collection (S. Chambers).
2. James, R. R., *Gallipoli*, p.144.
3. Chambers, S., *Gully Ravine*, p.28.
4. Kannengiesser, H., *Gallipoli*, p.131.
5. Wolf, K., *Victory At Gallipoli*, p.140.
6. Murray, J., *Gallipoli As I Saw It,* p.58.
7. Hamilton, Sir I., *Gallipoli Diary, Vol I,* pp.194–195.
8. Malthus, C., *Anzac: A Retrospect.*
9. AWM: AWM45/2/7: Kitchener to Hamilton, 4 May 1915.
10. Lorey, *Der Krieg in den türkischen Gewässern*, p.124.
11. Murray, J., *Gallipoli As I Saw It.*
12. Southland Times, Issue 17516, 20 May 1915.
13. Cecil, M., *Anzac: A Retrospect.*
14. Ibid.
15. Lancashire Fusiliers Annual 1915.
16. Aspinall-Oglander, *Military Operations*, Vol.1, p.347.
17. James, RR, *Gallipoli*, p.157.
18. Bruckshaw, H., *The Diaries of Private Horace Bruckshaw Royal Marine Light Infantry*, pp.46–47.
19. Noman Dewhurst MC, (H.J. Edmonds, Brussels 1968).
20. Ashmead-Bartlett, E., *Some of My Experiences in the Great War*, pp.130 & 131.
21. W. Ker quoted in, *The Hawke Battalion: Some Personal Records of Four Years, 1914–1918*, pp.55–56.
22. Marshall, W., *Memories of Four Fronts*, p.79.
23. Kannengiesser, H., *Gallipoli*, p.179. Peters was killed on 7 September 1915.
24. Creighton, O., *With the Twenty Ninth Division in Gallipoli: A Chaplain's Experience.*
25. Murray, J., *Gallipoli As I Saw It.*
26. Ibid.
27. Ibid.

28. A memorial to the battalion stands today at 'Collingwood Corner' on the Salisbury to Blandford Road.

29. Letter to his father. (Private collection of Clive Harris).

30. Weil, R., quoted in *Dardanelles Orient Levant, 1915–1921.*

31. Naci, I., *Farewell: A Turkish Officer's Diary of the Gallipoli Campaign.*

32. Brotherton Special Collections Library (Liddle Collection), C. Thierry, typescript translation diary.

33. Hamilton, Sir Ian, *Gallipoli Diary*, (1920), Vol.II, p.13.

34. JM Findlay, *With the Eighth Scottish Rifles, 1914–1919*, pp.34–37

35. My Gallipoli Story by Sgt. S. Evans, 1/Border Regiment, *The Gallipolian*, No.46, Christmas 1984, p.20.

36. Diary kept by the Officers of "C" Company, 4th Battalion The Royal Scots (Queen's Edinburgh Rifles) during their journey to and stay on the Gallipoli Peninsula May and June 1915. This was written by Captain RWG Rutherford, killed 28 June, and Second Lieutenant LR Grant.

37. Letters from Frank, European War, August 4th, 1914, *The Gallipolian*, No.57, Autumn 1988, p.18.

38. Letters from Frank, European War, August 4th, 1914, *The Gallipolian*, No.57, Autumn 1988, p.16.

39. Creighton, O., *With the Twenty Ninth Division in Gallipoli: A Chaplain's Experience*, p.146.

40. Diary kept by the Officers of "C" Company, 4th Battalion The Royal Scots (Queen's Edinburgh Rifles) during their journey to and stay on the Gallipoli Peninsula May and June 1915.

41. Thompson, R. R., *The Fifty-Second (Lowland) Division 1914–1918*, p.53.

42. Thompson, *Op.Cit.*, p.52.

43. Letters from Frank, *Op.Cit.*, No.57, Autumn 1988, p.18.

44. Patterson, JH, *With the Zionists in Gallipoli*, p.187.

45. Ryan, DG, *Historical Record of the 6th Gurkha Rifles*, p.111.

46. Patterson, *Op.Cit.*, p.188.

47. Ewing, W., *From Gallipoli to Baghdad*, p.90.

48. Hamilton, Sir Ian, *Gallipoli Diary*, Vol.II, p.9.

49. Yuille, D., 4th RSF, quoted in R. R. Thompson, *The Fifty Second (Lowland) Division 1914–1918*, p.90.

50. Nixon quoted in GF Scott Elliot, *War History of the 5th Battalion King's Own Scottish Borderers.*

51. IWM DOCS: GGA Egerton, Typescript account, pp.2–3.

52. Diriker, A., *42nd Regiment: Gallipoli 1915*, (Lindenbrooks 2018), p.22.
53. London Gazette, 15 September 1915.
54. Aspinall-Oglander, *Official History, Vol.2*, pp.168–169.
55. http://www.cradleylinks.com/cradleys_at_gallipoli.html – *The "Cradleys" at Gallipoli* by Terry Evans
56. The Gallipoli Oak, Martin Purdy and Ian Dawson, pp.131 & 132.
57. WT Forshaw quoted in *Ashton Reporter*, 16/10/1915 http://ashtonpals.webs.com/
58. H. Grantham quoted in *Ashton Reporter*, 16/10/1915 http://ashtonpals.webs.com/
59. T. Pickford quoted in *Ashton Reporter*, 18/3/1916 http://ashtonpals.webs.com/
60. S. Bayley quoted in *Ashton Reporter*, 11/9/1915 http://ashtonpals.webs.com/
61. Bean, James., Command, Battle Planning and August's 'Helles Diversionary Attack', *The Gallipolian*, Winter 2019, p.54.
62. Murray, J., *Gallipoli As I Saw It*.
63. Vassal, JMJ (1916). *Uncensored Letters from the Dardanelles*.
64. Churchill, *The World Crisis, Volume II*, p.908.
65. Gillam, J., *Gallipoli Diary*, (Stevenage, The Strong Oak Press, 1989), p.304.
66. Kannengiesser, H., *Gallipoli*, p.258.
67. Barclay, A., 'Proud Trooper Converted to 'PBI'', published in the *The Gallipolian*, the journal of the Gallipoli Association, No. 32 Spring 1980, p.13 and continued in No. 33 Autumn 1980, p.17.
68. Giguel, G., quoted in *Dardanelles Orient Levant, 1915–1921* (Paris: L'Harmattan, 2005), p.70.
69. Stack, H., *The Worcestershire Regiment in the Great War* (1928).
70. The fatality is nameless, although he is mentioned in the London Gazette, 11th April 1917 – Admiralty Despatch. Several soldiers were killed in action on 8 January 1916, but as part of the daily attrition and not directly related to the evacuation.
71. Noel Sergent, 10e Régiment d'Artillerie. (From a letter dated 23 January 1916, quoted in *The Gallipolian*, Christmas 1991, pp.23–25.)
72. Austin, R., *The White Gurkhas*, 1989, p.118.
73. Aspinall-Oglander, *Official History*, Vol. 11, p.301.

# Select Bibliography and Recommended Further Reading

Ashmead-Bartlett, E., *The Uncensored Dardanelles,* (Hutchinson, 1928).

Austin, R., *The White Gurkhas: Australians at the Second Battle of Krithia*, (Slouch Hat, 1989).

Bean, C.E.W., *The Story of Anzac,* (AWM, 1924).

Bell, C.M., *Churchill and the Dardanelles*, (OUP, 2017).

Cassar, G. H., *Reluctant Partner*, (Helion, 2019).

Chambers, S.J., *Gallipoli: Gully Ravine,* (Pen & Sword, 2002).

Chambers, S.J., *Anzac: The Landing,* (Pen & Sword, 2008).

Chambers, S.J., *Suvla: August Offensive,* (Pen & Sword, 2011).

Chambers, S.J., *Anzac: Sari Bair,* (Pen & Sword, 2014).

Chambers, S.J., *Walking Gallipoli,* (Pen & Sword, 2016).

Chambers, S.J. & Emden, van, R., *Gallipoli: The Dardanelles Disaster in Soldiers' Words and Photographs,* (Bloomsbury, 2015).

Crawley, R., LoCicero. M., *Gallipoli: New Perspectives on the MEF,* (Helion, 2018).

Creighton, O., *With the Twenty Ninth Division in Gallipoli* (Longmans, 1916).

Denham, H.M., *Dardanelles: A Midshipman's Diary*, (Murray, 1981).

Doyle, P., *Battle Story: Gallipoli 1915,* (The History Press, 2011).

Erickson, E.J., *Gallipoli: The Ottoman Campaign*, (Pen & Sword, 2010).

Erickson, E.J., *Gallipoli: Command Under Fire*, (Osprey, 2015).

Gillam, J.G., *Gallipoli Diary,* (Allen & Unwin, 1918).

Gőncű, G., Aldoğan, S., *Gallipoli Battlefield Guide*, (MB Books, 2008).

Hamilton, Sir. I., *Gallipoli Diary,* (Edward Arnold, 1920).

Hargrave, J, *The Suvla Bay Landing*, (Macdonald 1964).

Hart, P, *Gallipoli*, (Profile Books, 2011).

Hickey, M., *Gallipoli,* (John Murray, 1995).

Holts, T & V., *Major & Mrs Holt's Battlefield Guide: Gallipoli,* (Pen & Sword, 2000).

Malthus, C., *Anzac. A Retrospect*, (Whitcombe & Tombs, 1965).

Moorehead, A., *Gallipoli,* (Hamilton, 1956).

Murray, J., *Gallipoli As I Saw It*, (William Kimber, 1965).

North, J., *Gallipoli. The Fading Vision*, (Faber & Faber, 1936).

James, RR, *Gallipoli,* (Pan Books Ltd, 1984).

Newman, S., *Gallipoli: Then & Now* (After The Battle, 2000).

Oglander, Aspinall-, *Military Operations Gallipoli,* (Heinemann, 1929–32).

Oral, H, *Gallipoli 1915 – Through Turkish Eyes*, (Türkiye İş Bankasi, 2007).

Prior, R., *Gallipoli: The End of The Myth*, (Yales, 2009).

Pugsley, C., *Gallipoli: The New Zealand Story*, (Reed 1998).

Rodge, H and J, *Helles Landing: The Landings at Helles 25 April 1915,* (Pen & Sword, 2003).

Snelling, S., *VCs of the First World War – Gallipoli,* (Sutton Publishing, 1995).

Steel, N and Hart P., *Defeat at Gallipoli*, (Macmillan, 1994).

Steel, N., *Gallipoli,* (Leo Cooper, 1998).

Still, J., *A Prisoner in Turkey*, (John Lane, 1920).

Taylor, P., and Cupper P., *Gallipoli: A Battlefield Guide*, (Kangaroo Press, 1989).

Travers, T., *Gallipoli 1915*, (Tempus, 2001).

Wolf, K., *Victory at Gallipoli 1915*, (Pen & Sword, 2020).

# Index

Gouraud, Gen H, 62, 63, 88, 90, 91, 94, 120, 122, 147, 210, 213, 216
Grantham, Sht H, 139
Grant, Pte H, 188
Grant, 2/Lt L, 103, 106

Hamilton, Gen Sir I, 2, 12, 18, 22–4, 30, 40, 41, 44, 45, 50, 52, 57, 58, 61, 63, 66, 71, 90, 104, 120, 122, 128, 143, 148, 171, 213, 225
Hannan, Lt Col H, 198–9
Hare, Br Gen S, 11–12
Hersing, Lt Cdr O, 64
Heys, Lt Col G, 74
Heywood, Pte, 138
Hilmi Bey, Maj H, 217
Holbrook, Lt Cmdr N, 63
Horridge, Lt W, 72, 84
Howarth, Pte N, 138
Huguenin, Lt, 39
Hunter-Weston, Maj Gen Sir A, 2, 5, 9, 12, 18, 21, 23–6, 30, 41–2, 44, 62, 63, 66, 67, 96, 113, 120, 122, 124, 129, 171

Isherwood, Lt Col J, 49–50

Johnston, PO F, 103

Kadri, Maj, 1
Kane, Capt, 33
Kannengiesser, Col H, 35, 75, 88
Karasevdas, Maj P, 60
Kay, Lt G, 84
Kelly, Pte H, 53
Kemal, M (Atatürk), Col, 23, 226
Kemal Bey, Capt, 167, 216
Kesmi Bey, Maj, 36
Kitchener, Lord H, xiv, 22, 42, 44, 58, 90, 148, 150, 225
Koe, Lt Col A, 3–5

Lee, Brg Gen N, 67, 72, 74
Leplanche, Capt E, 213
Leroux, Capt G, 213
Lloyd, Pte H, 195
Lockwood, Lt E, 66
Lockyer, Capt H, 8
Love, Bdr, 33
Lowe, CSM D, 107–109
Luard, Col F, 29, 125
Lucas, Br Maj C, 8

Maltby, Mid, G, 29
Malthus, Pte C, 51
McCay, Lt Col J, 53–5

McLaren, Lt F, 70
McNamara, Lt V, 182
McNicoll, Lt Col W, 55–6
Marshall, Br Gen W, 8, 18, 27, 30, 67, 100
Martin, Pte R, 15
Masnou, Gen J, 36, 45, 126, 210, 213, 216
Matthews, Lt Col G, 3–5
Maude, Lt Gen Sir S, 161–2, 189, 191
Maxwell, Lt Gen, 22
Milward, Capt C, 10, 18
Monro, Lt Gen Sir C, 149–50
Morgan, Capt F, 34
Moriarty, Sgt D, 33
Moussa, Pte K, 213
Murdoch, K, 149
Muir, Capt A, 28
Muhlmann, Maj C, 36
Murray, AB J, 40–1, 47, 78–80, 145–7, 159, 189, 206

Naci, Lt I, 92, 169
Napier, Br Gen H, 18
Nasmith, Lt Cmdr M, 63
Newenham, Lt Col H, 8
Nixon, Pte, 123
Nogues, Col, 92

O'Dowda, Brg Gen J, 161
O'Hara, Lt, 112
Ogilvy, Maj G, 75–6

Paris, Gen A, 53
Parson, Lt Cmdr, 79
Pattison, 2/Lt R, 110
Pawley, Bdr, 33
Payne Gnr W, 34
Peters, LS, 75–6
Pickford, Cpl T, 140
Porter, Pte W, 138–9
Prince, Pte A, 204

Quilter, Lt Col A, 47, 203–204, 206

Rabenau, Sub Lt, G von, 75–6
Rafet Bey, Col, 96
Rankin, Cpl J, 188
Remsi Bey, Col, 39
Reuf, Col, 22, 57, 96
Rifaat, Col, 118–19